Luminos is the open access monograph publishing program from
UC Press. Luminos provides a framework for preserving and
reinvigorating monograph publishing for the future and increases
the reach and visibility of important scholarly work. Titles
published in the UC Press Luminos model are published with the
same high standards for selection, peer review, production, and
marketing as those in our traditional program. www.luminosoa.org

The Pitfalls of Protection

The Pitfalls of Protection

Gender, Violence, and Power in Afghanistan

Torunn Wimpelmann

UNIVERSITY OF CALIFORNIA PRESS

University of California Press, one of the most distinguished university presses in the United States, enriches lives around the world by advancing scholarship in the humanities, social sciences, and natural sciences. Its activities are supported by the UC Press Foundation and by philanthropic contributions from individuals and institutions. For more information, visit www.ucpress.edu.

University of California Press
Oakland, California

Suggested citation: Wimpelmann, Torunn. *The Pitfalls of Protection: Gender, Violence, and Power in Afghanistan*. Oakland: University of California Press, 2017. doi: http://doi.org/10.1525/luminos.32

Library of Congress Cataloging-in-Publication Data

Names: Wimpelmann, Torunn, author.
Title: The pitfalls of protection : gender, violence and power in Afghanistan / Torunn Wimpelmann.
Description: Oakland, California : University of California Press, [2017] | Includes bibliographical references and index.
Identifiers: LCCN 2017001096 (print) | LCCN 2017003969 (ebook) | ISBN 9780520293199 (pbk. : alk. paper) | ISBN 9780520966390 ()
Subjects: LCSH: Women—Afghanistan—Social conditions—21st century. | Women's rights—Afghanistan—21st century. | Women—Violence against—Afghanistan—21st century. | Sex crimes—Afghanistan—21st century. | Afghanistan—Politics and government—21st century.
Classification: LCC HQ1735.6 .W54 2017 (print) | LCC HQ1735.6 (ebook) | DDC 305.409581/0905—dc23
LC record available at https://lccn.loc.gov/2017001096

25   24   23   22   21   20   19   18   17
10   9   8   7   6   5   4   3   2   1

CONTENTS

Abbreviations   vii

Note on Language   ix

Acknowledgments   xi

Introduction: The Politics of Violence against Women   1

PART I. LEGAL REGIMES

1. Intrusions, Invasions, and Interventions: Histories of Gender,
   Justice, and Governance in Afghanistan   27

2. "Good Women Have No Need for This Law": The Battles over the
   Law on Elimination of Violence against Women   51

PART II. NEW PROTECTION MECHANISMS

3. Brokers of Justice: The Special Prosecution Unit for Crimes
   of Violence against Women in Kabul   85

4. With a Little Help from the War on Terror: The Women's Shelters   108

PART III. INDIVIDUAL CASES

5. Runaway Women   131

6. Upholding Citizen Honor? Rape in the Courts and Beyond   152

Conclusions: Protection at a Price?   169

Notes   *181*

References   *197*

Index   *207*

AIHRC	Afghan Independent Human Rights Commission
ALP	Afghan Local Police
AWN	Afghan Women's Network
CLRWG	Criminal Law Reform Working Group
DOWA	Department of Women's Affairs
EVAW	Elimination of Violence against Women
IDLO	International Development Law Organization
ISAF	International Security Assistance Force
MOWA	Ministry of Women's Affairs
PDPA	People's Democratic Party of Afghanistan
UNAMA	United Nations Assistance Mission in Afghanistan
UNIFEM	United Nations Development Fund for Women (merged into UNWOMEN in 2011)
UNODC	United Nations Office on Drugs and Crime
USAID	United States Agency for International Development
WAW	Women for Afghan Women

NOTE ON LANGUAGE

The official languages of Afghanistan—and those most widely spoken—are Dari (a dialect of Persian) and Pashto. Both contain a number of Arabic loanwords. For words that have become common in English, such as *sharia, ulema,* and *mullah,* I have used the established form. Words less common in English appear in italics throughout the text, with a brief explanation the first time they are used.

ACKNOWLEDGMENTS

When carrying out this research, I benefitted from the support, insight, and inspiration of numerous people. I am deeply grateful to the Research Council of Norway for financially supporting this work through the grants *Violence in the Post-Conflict State* (project number 190119), *Governance, Justice, and Gender in Afghanistan: Between Informal and Formal Dynamics* (project number 199437) and *Violence against Women and Criminal Justice in Afghanistan* (project number 230315).

Chr. Michelsen Institute, where I have been employed throughout this research, has been a great institutional home, and I wish to thank my colleagues there for their encouragement and help. My debt and sense of gratitude to Astri Suhrke for her advice, enthusiasm, mentoring, and great company are enormous. In more than one way, this project could never have been realized without her. Arne Strand first introduced me to Kabul and gave me the confidence to carry out fieldwork in Afghanistan again and again. Karin Ask provided invaluable suggestions at important junctures of this work.

Deniz Kandiyoti has been an immensely generous, inspiring, and thorough supervisor, and I cannot thank her enough for agreeing to take on this role, for her many pieces of crucial advice, and for her close reading of my drafts.

In Afghanistan, numerous people shared their time, knowledge and company. Above all, I want to thank Mohammad Jawad Shahabi. His research assistance during the first part of this work and our subsequent collaboration on what is now chapter 3 of this book have been invaluable. I remain immeasurably grateful for his insights, skills, and efforts over the years.

I am also very grateful to Farangis Elyassi for her committed and skillful data collection in the special prosecution unit for crimes of violence against women.

Orzala Ashraf Nemat introduced me to the world of women's activism in Kabul, provided friendship over many years, and has been instrumental to my initial understanding of the politics of law reform in Afghanistan.

The Cooperation for Peace and Unity (CPAU) and Peace Training and Research Organization (PTRO) were ideal places to be based and their staff great colleagues. I am grateful to Mirwais Wardak for his help in facilitating my stay at both places and for numerous stimulating conversations.

Wazhma Forough and her staff at the Research Institute for Women, Peace, and Security unfailingly supported the research on the prosecution of VAW crimes.

Of the many people in Afghanistan who in various ways generously offered their time, help, and knowledge, I would particularly like to thank Obaid Ali, Phyllis Cox, Sandy Feinzig, Alexandra Gilbert, Fawzia Koofi, Ismaeil Hakimi, Michael Hartmann, Zia Moballegh, Shinkhai Karokheil, Abdul Subhan Misbah, Soraya Sobhreng, and Royce Wiles.

A number of people read and offered thoughtful comments on parts of or entire drafts of this work; among them are Liv Tønnessen, Nefissa Naguib, Sippi Azarbaijani-Moghadam, Gilda Seddighi, Frode Løvlie, Hilde Granås Kjøstvedt, Elin Skaar, Jonathan Goodhand, Tania Kaiser, Nadje Al-Ali, and John Heathershaw. Naqeebullah Miakhel compiled helpful information on the implementation of *hadd* punishments.

Jennifer Eastman skillfully and carefully edited the manuscript, and Niels Hooper and Bradley Depew at the University of California Press were supportive and efficient throughout the process of publication. I am particularly appreciative for their efforts in facilitating my book's publication as Open Access with the generous support of the Luminos Member Library Program.

Finally, my deepest thanks to my family for their unfailing support and love. My Norwegian family has endured a lot during my long and frequent stays in Afghanistan, and I am forever grateful for their help and enthusiasm. Aziz Hakimi has been both a stimulating colleague and my most treasured companion.

As I write this, Afghanistan is in its fourth decade of war, with no end in sight. Its people, increasingly fenced in by the rest of world, face deepening hardships and uncertainty. I dedicate this book to them and to their ability to summon so much grace, perseverance, and generosity of spirit under very difficult circumstances.

Introduction

The Politics of Violence against Women

In the early summer of 2012, another case of sexual abuse reached Afghan television screens and the international press. Lal Bibi, an eighteen-year-old nomad woman from the province of Kunduz, came forward in Afghan media recounting how, on May 17, 2012, she was seized by men linked to a local armed group. She was held captive for five days and sexually assaulted as revenge for her cousin's elopement with a woman from the family of one of the kidnappers. Lal Bibi's family declared to journalists that unless justice was done, they would have no option but to kill her. However, Afghanistan's women's right activists quickly mobilized in support, and pressure mounted on the government to arrest the perpetrators.

But back in Kunduz, the man accused of the rape protested that no such thing had taken place. He argued that there had been an agreement of *baad*—a practice in which a woman or girl is given in marriage as a form of compensation for a crime or an affront. A mullah had married Lal Bibi to him just before intercourse, and "once the marriage contract is done, any sexual intercourse is not considered rape" (A. J. Rubin 2012). In present-day Afghanistan, this version of events did not necessarily exonerate him from having committed a crime. Women's rights activists pointed out that forced marriage was also an offense, according to Afghan law and particularly the new Elimination of Violence against Women law (EVAW law), which had become a cornerstone of gender activism in the country. Moreover, his attempt to justify his actions with reference to a framework of *baad* implicated others. A friend of mine, who happened to be in Kunduz on fieldwork at the time, told me upon his return that the elders who had sanctioned the kidnapping (as an appropriate redress for the affront to the honor of the eloped girl's father) now found themselves being investigated for crimes against the EVAW law on the grounds that they had facilitated a *baad*.

Lal Bibi was one of several Afghan women and girls who have appeared in national media in recent years with harrowing stories of sexual abuse, accompanied by relatives demanding justice from the Afghan government. Yet the role of the government, as well as other powers, in intervening in abuses against women was fiercely contested during the first fifteen years following the United States–led overthrow of the Taliban in 2001. The questions of whether, to what extent, and how central authorities should intervene in different forms of gender violence—and the very questions of what exactly constituted violations and who was the violated party—were matters that went to the core of Afghan society. How was rape to be understood—as a crime against the woman herself or primarily as an affront against her family? Was "forced marriage" a crime, or should parents (particularly fathers) be left in peace to arrange their daughters' marriages as they saw fit? Could adulterous women call upon the protection of the state? Was beating disobedient wives the prerogative of husbands or something that the government should jail men for? The answers to questions such as these had—and continue to have—great implications for women's lives in Afghanistan. But there were also other issues at stake—where to draw the boundaries between private and public domains; which and whose notions of justice, rights, and obligations should prevail; and, ultimately, how the answers to these questions affected competing claims to exercise supreme political power in the country.

The terrain on which these battles were fought out was extraordinarily fluid and fragmented. A beleaguered group of women's rights activists in the capital, many of them recently returned from exile, made tenuous alliances with parts of the international donor community, but this turned out to be a difficult balancing act between concessions to conservative adversaries and dependence on external actors. An alliance of women's rights activists, personnel from foreign embassies, and progressive justice officials succeeded in getting the new EVAW law promulgated. But the process revealed bitter divisions within women's groups and difficulty in gaining wider acceptance for their ideas. It also exposed their dependence on a friendly executive branch and a degree of isolation from broader political constituencies. In courts and prosecution offices, some officials refused to apply the EVAW law altogether, saying that its legal status was unclear—the law had been passed as a presidential decree and had not been approved in Parliament. At the same time, Western aid donors made the implementation of the EVAW law a central condition for aid disbursements, and a massive internationally supported apparatus was mobilized to disseminate and enforce the law.

The unpredictability produced by these competing legal regimes was acutely felt by numerous women and girls who fled unwanted marriages or family abuse and sought the assistance of the courts and the protection of shelters. These institutions were a testing ground for what kind of gender relations would be officially sanctioned. In some cases, they upheld women's claims. On many other occasions, however, they sided with the families' counterclaims, sending the women back to their families or even to jail, which signaled that public regulation in this domain would reinforce kinship and conjugal claims over women rather than support a transformation that granted women full legal personhood. Meanwhile, the shelters housing many of the "runaway" women faced a conservative backlash, stirred up by media campaigns that drew upon popular discontent with a prolonged and dysfunctional Western intervention and denounced the shelters as a foreign implant.

Even the outrage surrounding rape cases like Lal Bibi's contained ambiguous agendas. To many people, the popular demand for state intervention in cases of rape was a significant shift that signaled support for women's rights over family privacy. However, a closer look at the campaigns for justice suggested that they were driven by many different concerns, some of which had little to do with women's rights. In other words, whether this new "openness" surrounding rape would constitute progress for women was, like many aspects of gender violence in post-2001 Afghanistan, still an open question.

These contestations are at the center of this book. I explore the struggles over the meaning of violence against women during the first fifteen years of the post-Taliban order in Afghanistan and their implications for gender and power. The rest of the introduction lays out the analytical departure points of the book. I start by showing how definitions of violence against women in a given context serve as windows into gender relations and how the construction of certain abuses against women as private—and therefore beyond the law and political intervention—establishes a hierarchical gendered relationship in which women are placed under the *sovereign* power of male family members. I then argue that attempts to define and govern gender violence also illuminate broader fields of power, such as the regulatory power of the state. However, I suggest that the separate, discreet units of analysis in much of the literature on gender and governance—whether "the state," "the global," or "the tribal"—is misleading in the Afghan case. Instead, I present *transnational assemblages of rule* as a more useful concept to capture the forms of power at work in contemporary Afghanistan. The final sections of the introduction provide the reader with an account of methodological choices and fieldwork trajectories and finally a discussion of some of the ethical pitfalls of doing research in post-2001 Afghanistan.

VIOLENCE AGAINST WOMEN AS ANALYTICAL ENTRY POINTS

This book is filled with people who sought in various ways to have their ideas about gender violence accepted by others. For some it was a matter of immediacy.

Young women would stand before a judge hoping to avoid a jail sentence—or even execution—by asserting that what had happened to them was rape or that they had acted within the limits of the law when escaping with a man or from an unwanted marriage. Grandmothers would make anxious calls to the local police, trying to convince them that they should arrest a runaway granddaughter. Fathers would look into a television camera, demanding to know where the honor of the country's leaders had gone, since they were incapable of stopping the violation of schoolgirls. Other men would defend their right to conduct a marriage without the consent of the bride's family, and yet others their right to kill a rebellious niece or to be compensated for a runaway wife.

For some of the people in this book, the issue of gender violence was a question of principle rather than personal circumstance. In order to convince their colleagues that wife beating should be a punishable crime, some members of Parliament urged a less literalist interpretation of the Quran, while their opponents countered with warnings against the implications of straying away from the holy scriptures. As controversies over women's shelters peaked, a journalist convinced of the self-serving ways of the NGO women who ran the shelters would attempt to discredit shelter residents as dangerous seductresses. Some shelter managers, in order to ensure their institutions' independence from the government, appealed to Western fears of the Taliban, depicting a government takeover of the shelters as a first step toward conceding defeat to terrorism.

The structuring theme of this book is that whatever acts people consider or call *violence* (*khoshonat* in Dari, the Afghan dialect of Farsi) is always specific to and situated within a particular context. *Violence,* in English and in many other languages, connotes transgression and illegitimacy. Describing something as an *act of violence* suggests that it is a threat to the social, sexual, and political order and that it must be stopped, punished, or avenged. On the other hand, the nonrecognition of violent acts renders them unproblematic—or even, in some cases, necessary—thereby permitting or sanctioning their continuation. Naming violence is therefore invested with great political importance, and it follows that categorizations of violence are not fixed; they are sites of contestation (Merry 2009).

Applied specifically to gender, this perspective means that delineations or definitions of violence against women in a given historical context are entry points to the gender relations in that context. Feminist analysis has long pointed out how the construction of a private/public dichotomy in which certain abuses against women are considered private (and therefore beyond the law and political intervention) in effect establishes a hierarchical gendered relationship (Schneider 1991). I propose that the concept of *sovereignty* is useful for appreciating this relationship. As Comaroff and Comaroff write, "We take the word sovereignty to connote the more or less effective claims on the part of any agent, community, cadre or collectivity to exercise autonomous, exclusive control over the lives, deaths, and conditions of existence of those who fall within a given purview, and to extend over them the jurisdiction of some kind of law" (2006: 35).

When violence and even murder of women at the hands of their husband or family are considered permissible, women are effectively placed under their sovereignty, rather than under the sovereignty of public authorities, such as the state. In this sense, a form of what Humphrey calls a "localized sovereignty, nested within higher sovereignties" but "nevertheless retaining a domain within which control over life and death is operational" is granted to the household head (2004: 420). The feminist analysis and activism aimed at making violence against women a public issue have thereby been mounting a challenge to the sovereign claim of families over women. Indeed, the very act of naming an act as a violation against someone other than the family sovereign signifies a challenge to absolute sovereignty, as it names other people as holders, or partial holders, of rights. This is also the case with violations carried out by people outside the family. The framing of sexual violence as an offense against a woman, as opposed to an offense against her husband or father, constitutes women as legal persons to whom other sovereigns hold obligations, and it potentially signifies a radical transformation of gender relations. As we shall see, the contestations over gender violence taking place in Afghanistan embodied these competing claims of sovereignty at their heart. Families claimed sovereign rights over women—to preside over their marriage and sexuality and to sanction insubordination, sometimes through violent means. Counterclaims asserted women's autonomous status and their right to make independent decisions and to make claims of damage against their own families or against others.

At this point in the discussion, however, it seems necessary to deal with the fact that the term *violence against women* carries a historical baggage of its own. Since it moved to the center of transnational women's activism in the early 1990s, violence against women (VAW) has become an established term and a particular discursive frame underpinning a global apparatus of action, intervention, and regulation. The emergence of VAW as an established phrase happened after feminist activists around the world—who had set up shelters, counseling centers, and treatment programs for batterers (Merry 2009: 76) and launched antirape campaigns—formed an international campaign to have violence against women defined as a human rights violation. Their demand proved phenomenally successful. It resulted in a series of U.N. resolutions and declarations, the creation of a special rapporteur on violence against women, the enumeration of certain kinds of sexual violence as serious crimes in international law, and the articulation of the principle of due diligence, which went some way in making states accountable for human rights violations inflicted on women by non-state actors, such as family and community groups (Saghal 2006). As Merry points out, within this universe, the meaning of VAW has expanded from "male violence against their partners in the form of rape, assault and murder" to include "female genital mutilation/cutting/excisions, gender-based violence by police and military forces in armed conflict as well as everyday life, violence against refugee women and asylum seekers, trafficking in sex workers, sexual harassment, forced pregnancy, forced abortion, forced sterilization, female foeticide and infanticide, early and forced marriage, honour killings and widowhood violations" (Merry 2009: 82). And as we will see later, the Afghan EVAW law decreed in 2009 listed many of these acts as violence and added a number of other acts more particular to Afghanistan, which many Afghan women considered a violation of their rights, entitlements, or persons, such as the cursing of a woman or even the denial of an existing familial or marital relationship that would absolve obligations toward a woman.[1] In other words, the Afghan EVAW law was developed at the intersection of transnational and national registers.

As the global campaign against VAW moved to the center stage of international politics, it also, perhaps unsurprisingly, became entangled in existing global power structures. With the shift from national to global advocacy came a more professionalized, bureaucratic mode of operation, standardized programs and compliance mechanisms, and the arrival of international "VAW experts." In an influential article, Kapur (2002) scrutinizes the political effects of this global VAW discourse, noting that it rose to international prominence through the obfuscation of the power relations positioning Westerners, white women, and feminists differently from ethnic minorities and women in the Global South. It constructed women of the Global South and nonwhite women who are subjected to violence or abuse as victims of their culture and in need of (outside) protection. Kapur argues that this effectively amounts to a kind of gender and cultural essentialism that cannot accommodate the different positions that nonwhite women and women in the Global South inhabit, or take into account the historically specific forms that violence against them assume. It is difficult to think of an example of this more glaring than Afghanistan since 2001. Western claims to "liberate Afghan women" while entangled in the geopolitical interests driving the war on terror, exhibited many of the traits that Kapur warns against. Afghan women were frequently represented as victims in need of outside saving, trapped in a backward state, and suffering what the West knew to be violence and abuse—violence that occurred as part of Islam or Afghan culture.

Examining the employment and effects of such "victimisation rhetoric" (Kapur 2002) is integral to the analysis in this book, but a clarification nonetheless feels necessary. Stating that the book is about "violence against women" does not mean it places itself uncritically into the VAW discourse. I do not assume the existence of a fixed or absolute set of practices that await recognition as violence against women. This would suggest an endpoint of liberation and inevitably place countries along an axis of development or civilization, enabling the kind of global hierarchies Kapur draws to our attention. Instead, my aim is to examine competing claims made during a particular historical setting about the nature of certain practices and to examine whether they are regarded as violence or transgressions and, if so, against whom and with what consequences.

But while the book is not an attempt to uncritically reproduce the VAW discourse, it is also not a bid for relativism. I recognize the hierarchies generated by the VAW discourse and also believe that it is neither possible nor desirable to define, once and for all, out of context, and somehow prior to power relations, the exact register of actions that would constitute violence against women. I nevertheless maintain that this insight should not make us blind to the fact that, in a given context, the nonrecognition of certain practices as violence can become a blueprint for impunity and can be a symptom of unequal gender relations. Thus, it is the struggle over the meanings of violence against women in a specific period and context—and their implications for gender and power—that this book explores.

A final clarification. Throughout the book, I use the terms *violence against women* and *gender violence* interchangeably when referring to the empirical focus of my research—abuses committed against women. However, I recognize that each term is imprecise. As I have argued, *violence against women* is a categorization of an event or practice connoting transgression or violation, but it is also an established activist and policy discourse with particular political logics and effects. *Gender violence,* on the other hand, has come to delimit a field that comprises violence against women plus sexual violence against men. This is problematic in so far as it suggests that only certain forms of violence are gendered, when, in reality, all social practices have gendered dimensions (although some acts and events might have starker gender dimensions than others). In this book I use *gender violence* to refer to injuries inflicted only on women, but this usage is merely a practical matter—I do not wish to suggest that men cannot be on the receiving end of violence enabled by, or in response to violations of, gender orders.

VIOLENCE AGAINST WOMEN AND BROADER
FIELDS OF POWER

As the discussion has already hinted at, definitions of and negotiations over violence against women are not just entry points to looking at gender relations. They also illuminate other fields of power. As Hajjar points out, struggles over women's rights are also contestations over jurisdiction and authority (2004). Attempts to make gender violence a public issue could signify an important shift in the demarcation between the private domain of family and kinship on one hand and public authorities on the other. For instance, if a rape case is adjudicated in a state court rather than settled between the families involved or by a local leader or kinship group that traditionally settles disputes, this expands (or attempts to expand) the domain of the state—whether by conscious political strategy or as an unintended by-product. A large body of literature on the Middle East has, in fact, emphasized how rulers and states have attempted to break up kinship structures and assert state power by, for instance, promulgating family laws (Noelle-Karimi 2002; Joseph 2000; Kandiyoti 1991; Charrad 2001) or by taking over the policing of female sexuality from relatives and communities (Baron 2006). The attempts by successive Afghan rulers to curtail bride-price[2] and forbid child marriage espoused similar agendas (see chapter 1).

Yet, what exactly does it mean to say that gender violence is transferred from a private or non-state realm to a "state domain"? As legal anthropologists, in particular, have reminded us, state power or "the state" is a tricky concept. Claims to act on behalf of the state should not lead us to assume the actual existence of a monolithic, unitary state (T. Mitchell 1999). And in sites of global intervention like Afghanistan, stark transnational aspects to statehood mean that the notion of the "state" as a unitary actor wielding ultimate sovereign power over a territory makes even less sense. As is clear to even a casual observer of post-2001 Afghanistan, Western powers played a fundamental role in structuring Afghan statehood—to the extent that international actors explicitly tasked themselves with the wholesale *building* of the Afghan state. With this in mind, it is far from certain that the power exercised in a government court—for instance, if an Afghan man is prosecuted for rape or wife beating—is that of the Afghan state. As I will discuss in some detail in the chapters that follow, the ways in which the Afghan state intervened in cases of gender violence was often underwritten, funded, and even designed by global, mostly Western actors, suggesting that the sovereign power exercised in Afghan courts was partly global. At the same time, the economic and political resources flowing from the international interventions often constituted opportunities for local actors to exercise and consolidate power in ways unintended by the international "state builders."

It makes sense, then, to understand sites of international peace-building interventions as "fields of power where sovereignty is constantly contested and negotiated among global, elite and local actors" (Heathershaw and Lambach 2008: 269). In this vein, challenges to and negations of the nation-state (the sovereign) in (post-)conflict settings are best conceived not as from below or above (that is, from local or global sources), but as parallel or alternative alignments that often are transnationally woven. In order to make sense of the ways the global, the national, and what might be termed *the tribal* are entangled in Afghanistan, I draw upon Saskia Sassen's concept of assemblages (Sassen 2008: 67; Heathershaw 2011). She argues that thinking in terms of assemblages allows us to appreciate that the global can be "dressed in the clothes of the national" (Sassen 2011). In other words, Sassen underlines how national institutional capabilities are *reassembled* to serve global projects. Rather than an image of national versus supranational sovereignty as a zero-sum game in which *globalization* means the "withdrawal of the state at the hands of the global system" (Sassen 2008: 65), Sassen advocates thinking in terms of specialized orderings—assemblages that produce a standardized, but partial, global domain *through* national institutions. As I try to show in this book, this "partialness" of global influence was both a resource for and a constraint to local women's rights activists.

Claims about gender violence can do more than reveal gender relations and sovereign domains. They also constitute maps to broader ideological and political fields. The actors who made the claims and counterclaims about gender violence in Afghanistan articulated rights, entitlements, and obligations with reference to larger political narratives and ideological resources in ways that they thought would resonate with their audiences.

I suggest that these discursive strategies—and to what extent they gained traction—reveal broader fields of power—constituted by established social practices and repertoires of meaning, as well as more temporal political alignments. When, for instance, women in Parliament made careful attempts to boost their defense of the EVAW law by referring to sharia, their strategy revealed not only the enduring prominence of Islamic jurisprudence in the legal landscape of Afghanistan but also the current political dominance of the mujahedin,[3] whose credentials were closely linked to Afghanistan's foremost identity being an Islamic one. Similarly, the ability of a local journalist to discredit women's shelters by conjuring up images of corrupt and self-serving female activists who invoked the plight of poor women for their own financial benefit reflected an overall disillusion with the international aid industry and a skepticism toward "Westernized" women and their foreign allies, all of it given political force by the experience of a prolonged but ineffective external aid and military presence.

Often, however, the strategy in matters of gender violence was not one pursued by making daring public claims, but by calling in favors, discreet lobbying, and personal connections. Officials at the Afghan Independent Human Rights Commission (AIHRC), having failed to build up domestic human rights constituency that could have been mobilized in individual cases, often chose to develop close relationships with government officials so that they could at least extract certain favors.[4] Its international ally, the United Nations, often chose similarly discreet tactics. When a high-ranking government official seemed destined to be acquitted of the rape of a young girl who had fled her family and had been under his protection, UN staff chose to make a quiet phone call to the local governor rather than a public appeal for justice. These discursive and tactical maneuvers, and the level of their success, chart the political and ideological landscapes in Afghanistan and show the space that various actors perceived was at their disposal.

STUDYING POWER THROUGH THE
"AFGHAN WOMAN"

One of the chief aims of the book is to make a contribution to the field of Afghan gender studies by demonstrating that the study of gender in Afghanistan illuminates central questions pertaining to governance, sovereignty, and power. Perhaps one of the most politicized figures of global affairs in the last two decades, the "Afghan woman" is saturated with connotations. In a series of homogenizing representations, she has been invoked both as a victim whose circumstances necessitated bombing raids and military operations and as a haunting symbol of Western imperialism.[5] Her circumstances and appearance are constantly noted and made to serve as an indicator of diverse political assertions—the hypocritical hollowness of Western rhetoric, the backwardness of Afghan culture, or Afghanistan's foreign contamination. Funds are raised in her name, and numerous reports are devoted to give her a voice and uncover her true views. Those who can claim this identity have also learned to utilize its potential for mobilizing power. Claiming to speak as an "Afghan woman" to international media outlets can be a shortcut to influence in a setting where most other political channels have been closed off by violence and militarization.

Yet despite the many ways in which the "Afghan woman" has become a purveyor of broader political claims, the scholarly literature on the intersections of gender, power, and politics in Afghanistan is scarce. More recent literature tends to be based on textual examination of Western discourses in which the situation of Afghan women serves to legitimate domination or invasion (Schueller 2011; Stabile 2005; Ayotte and Husain 2005; Abu-Lughod 2002). On the other hand, contributions that elaborate on more localized relations of gender and power typically do so only as a side pursuit and often subscribe to a conceptualization of Afghan society as consisting of separate orders locked into a perpetual struggle over the control of women. For instance: "Rural Afghanistan is the root of tribally powers that have frequently doomed Kabul-based modernization efforts. Social traditionalism and economic underdevelopment of rural Afghanistan have repeatedly contested the center (Kabul), thus a better understanding of tribal controlled areas is essential to empower women in these regions. For women in rural Afghanistan, control over their lives and gender roles is determined by patriarchal kinship arrangements" (Ahmed-Ghosh 2003).

Quotes like this conjure up a spatial map of gender and power in Afghanistan. The central state resides in the capital and urban centers—enclaves of female emancipation—whereas the majority of women are hidden away in the deepest corners of tribalism in faraway villages and forts, kept out of reach by their menfolk and shielded from the grasp of government, modern law, and individualism. There is also an evolutionary dimension to this spatial optic; the gender order of the tribe is expected to gradually wither away as it comes into contact with the more modern state. Such notions reflect a tendency in studies of Afghanistan to infer from separate realms (in the sense of boundaries *made*, and thus in need of constant, active maintenance) the existence of separate, discreet "logics," or in the terminology of Edwards, different "moral systems" (Edwards 1996).[6] More recent work has slowly started to discard this framework (Coburn 2011; Green 2008; Sharan and Heathershaw 2011; Edwards 2002), instead approaching power and governance as hybrid and contingent on context. However, as the Ahmed-Ghosh quote above shows, notions of self-contained and insulated governance and political orders continue to hold sway in the limited scholarship on gender and politics in Afghanistan (for exceptions, see Kandiyoti 2007; and Billaud 2015).

This book attempts to address this gap by carrying out a study of women and power in Afghanistan that applies an open-ended, practice-oriented perspective through ethnographic examinations on statehood and authority—an approach that has especially been seen in studies on sub-Saharan Africa (Lund 2006; Bertelsen 2009; Comaroff and Comaroff 2006; Comaroff and Comaroff 2009; Hansen and Stepputat 2006; Hagmann and Péclard 2010). This open-ended approach enables me to make *transnationally* constituted assemblages of rule visible and available for analysis, and it allows me to accommodate complex governance orders that transcend dichotomies of tradition and modernity, or of the global and the local. For instance, the need to go beyond the binary of tradition and modernity is illustrated by the many incidences in this book where ideas of personal or family honor are seen to have affected government processes *within* the state apparatus— as opposed to honor being a tribal value incongruent with modern state governance. Similarly, I go beyond dichotomies of the global versus the local by showing how global templates and agendas did not simply displace local ones but instead created unique and new dynamics in which, for instance, international diplomatic pressure and Afghan personalized politics reinforced each other.

The book also aims to add to the comparative feminist scholarship on women, law, and power, a field in which Afghanistan has received little, if any, systematic consideration.[7] Rather than taking the field of family law as the starting point, the book centers on criminal law by making definitions of gender violence the topic of inquiry. In this sense, this book is also a contribution to feminist analysis of criminal law, which has been relatively sparse in the area of countries with Islamic legal traditions (Zuhur 2005).[8] More generally, I have sought to bring the issue of gender in Afghanistan into closer dialogue with the rich literature on gender in the Middle East, which, over the last three decades, has illuminated the great varieties of gender relations and government practices across time and space in Muslim-majority countries, and which has made important points about the imperative of seeing gender relations as historically specific, rather than as derivatives of religion or culture (Abu-Lughod 1998; Meriwether and Tucker 1999; Kandiyoti

1996; Tucker 2008; Kandiyoti 1991; Keddie and Baron 1991). In addition, a vibrant scholarship on gender justice and the limits of law as a tool of empowerment has emerged from South Asia in recent years (Basu 2015; Agnes and Ghosh 2012; Roychowdhury 2016; Roychowdhury 2015; Vatuk 2013). I apply the insights of this literature to place the efforts against gender violence in Afghanistan in a comparative perspective, again seeking to counter the exceptional status often bestowed on the country in academic discourse.

Finally, this book has also, in many ways, heeded Abu-Lughod's call to explore "the social life of Muslim women's rights" in order to "track carefully, across multiple terrains, the way both practices and talk of rights organize social and political fields, producing organizations, projects, and forms of governing as much as being produced by them" (2010: 32–33).

Given the enormous attention they have been afforded over the last decade, it is not at all surprising that Afghan women's rights have been pressed into the service of international and local agendas of various kinds: war, careers, and the accumulation of aid money, to mention a few. But the relationship between the "Afghan woman" question and practices of power need not always be so obvious or instrumental. In attempts to secure women in Afghanistan protection against gender violence, ambiguous victories, curious alliances, and novel hierarchies often materialized. These more subtle and mostly unspoken dynamics, which Abu-Lughod (2010) calls attention to, form part of the discussion in the book.

RESEARCH TRAJECTORIES

Afghanistan during the first decade and a half after the fall of Taliban in 2001 was a place of sharp fault lines and cleavages; of constant contest over the criteria through which power, authority, and the control over resources could be claimed; and of much anxiety about carving out a place in the new order. Moral universes, political repertoires, and hierarchies of knowledge and skills were of uncertain validity as old elites and newly assertive groups vied for position. Many Afghans returned from exile, including members of the former ruling classes, royalists, and old business and landowning families who had fled to neighboring countries, as well as Western-based diasporas armed with academic qualifications and bilingual fluency that suddenly were hugely marketable. The returnees were faced with newly powerful military commanders backed up with Western cash and arms and their self-assured young followers—and with an Islamic clergy who had seen their unprecedented influence and prestige under the Taliban government turn to dust with the new post-2001 order (Giustozzi 2008). By the middle of the decade, war was regaining pace. Explosions, assassinations, and raids fractured everyday life, throwing up uncertainty about the daring official declarations of a new beginning and the future shape and direction of the country. As NATO countries gradually realized that the country they had invaded in 2001 was sliding off the course they had staked out, their response was basically to accelerate everything. Money, troops, diplomats, and military operations flowed into Afghanistan in spiraling numbers, typically intensifying conflict lines, incentivizing the pillaging of resources, and increasing the devastation of war.

The research for this book started out as a PhD project. I arrived in Afghanistan for my initial fourteen months of fieldwork in the summer of 2009, in what promised to be a turbulent context for research. Like many of my informants, I would often get the feeling that at any moment, the rug could be pulled from underneath the universe we were inhabiting. It was clear that the country would not be an appropriate setting for bounded ethnography, in which much time is spent developing intimate relationships with a limited group of people in a small locality. Instead, my research would take the form of "mobile ethnography" (Marcus 1995). In pursuit of answers to how gender violence were defined, contested, and regulated in Afghanistan, I intended to trace a range of different cases and processes as they moved from one site to the next: court rooms, Parliament, official meetings and conferences, local councils, shelters, media forums, and a host of other settings.

My decision to draw upon the extended case method as a framework for data collection was partly influenced by my intention to follow processes from site to site. The extended case method, developed by the so-called Manchester school of anthropology, uses a case (a *case* being defined as an event or a process) as a way of casting light upon a particular society—or, more accurately, upon the social relations that are actualized in a particular context (Gluckman 1965; Velsen 1964; J. C. Mitchell 1956; Handelman 2005; Burawoy 2000). A case is a departure point from which one can "extend out"—bring social relations into view and available for analysis. This method, whose script was to follow events over time from one setting to another, resonated with my approach to use contestations over violence against women as windows into relations of gender, governance, and politics. Moreover, the extended case method provides a lens suitable for capturing the transnational dimensions of local practices. At a time when ethnography was often preoccupied with unearthing the underlying structure of what was assumed to be self-contained local communities, the 1950s anthropologists who pioneered the extended case method distinguished themselves from their contemporaries by looking at events as both locally and globally constituted. As Burawoy proclaims when explaining how the Manchester school would make global class relations and colonial history integral to their analysis of the practices of Zulu chiefs: "There never was any isolated tribe here!" (Burawoy 2000: 16). The importance of exploring both local and transnational aspects of the events and processes I was studying—whether debates over a new law, controversies over women "running away" from home, or the trajectory of an individual episode of gender violence— became one of my guiding principles.

As I began fieldwork in 2009, I started by establishing how cases of gender violence typically encountered the legal system and how they traveled through it. Little in-depth literature on the practices of the Afghan legal system existed, and developments over the previous two decades were particularly hazy.[9] Through these efforts, I also hoped to be able to eventually identify the cases of gender violence that would serve as the cornerstone of my material. I had thought that U.N. organizations in the human rights field might serve as a useful entry to cases that I could study, but they proved reluctant to discuss concrete episodes. At the time, there were good reasons for this. Much of the human rights community was shaken by the recent murder of Dilawar, the husband of the victim in a high-profile rape case. In a horrifying ordeal, his wife, Sarah, had been sexually abused and made to walk half-naked through her village after questioning a local commander and government ally about the disappearance of her son. Although the perpetrators of the abuse had been convicted, two of them were quickly freed through a presidential pardon. Sarah and Dilawar went to Kabul to pursue the case, and the local office of the U.N. human rights section played an important role in the public outcry that had followed, which had forced President Karzai to review the pardon. But the case took another sinister turn when Dilawar was murdered. The local U.N. human rights section realized they were becoming increasingly marginalized in a political climate where—both internally in the U.N. mission and externally in the country—realpolitik increasingly overrode accountability and legal procedures. In such a situation, it was not surprising that they were reluctant to share information with me.

However, in the summer of 2009, women's rights activists in Kabul and their international colleagues were preoccupied with two new pieces of legislation: the Shia Personal Status Law and the EVAW law. The Shia law, as it was widely called, had created an uproar among many women activists and politicians, as well as among Western embassies and public opinion, when it was ratified by the president in March 2009. Presented as a recognition of the Shia minority's right to adjudicate according to the sect's jurisprudence, the law contained what was widely felt to be an excessive codification of personal life, in many ways representing a rolling back of the rights in the existing Civil Code and certainly reversing the momentum in women's rights since the 2001 invasion. Despite protests both in Afghanistan and abroad, a revised version of the law (with many of its problematic provisions remaining) was signed into force by the president on July 19, 2009. A few days later, this setback was the subject of heated debate at a meeting of Kabul-based women's activists, both Afghan and foreign, that was called in response to the new law, and which I observed.

The discussions and atmosphere at the meeting appeared to reveal a women's movement fractured by diverging discursive reference points, by multiple modes of organizing and ideas about advocacy or lobbying, and by parallel reporting lines and constituencies. Most striking was the confusion and uncertainty regarding the legal framework. The participants at the meeting were trying to establish which law took precedence: the Constitution, the existing Civil Code, the newly decreed Shia law, or the EVAW law, which had been signed by the president on the same day. These laws contained contradictory implications for, among other things, restrictions on polygamy and the legal age of marriage. It took me some time to realize that the confusion I witnessed was not due to lack of preparation for the meeting, due to how hastily it had been organized, but it reflected two important aspects of the post-2001 legal reform process: a great opaqueness in the legislative process and contradictions within the rapidly expanding body of law itself.

The EVAW law, which many of the activists pinned their hopes on, enumerated twenty-two crimes as violence against women, stipulated their punishments, and outlined government responsibility (see chapter 2). It was to be introduced for ratification in Parliament that autumn. With my Afghan colleague Orzala Ashraf Nemat, with whom I was working on another project, I attended the initial debates in the Joint Commission meetings in Parliament, where the law was being discussed before being introduced in the plenary. This required considerable effort, and the help and goodwill of many members of Parliament (MPs). Parliamentary debates were generally not transcribed, not even plenary debates, and the proceedings of the Joint Commission were certainly not. In order to be present in Joint Commission discussions, we were dependent on MPs to sign us in as visitors and—equally crucial—to inform us of when and where the meetings would be scheduled. Often, meetings were called at the last minute, as a deliberate strategy to ensure that certain people were there (and that certain others were not). There was always a chance that we could be told to leave the room. MPs had the opportunity to invite guests, and many of them did, but this sometimes led to controversies, when the guests intervened in discussions. Although the parliamentary process for the EVAW law was eventually abandoned, I continued to follow the law by attending various conferences in which it was debated and by tracing how it entered the agenda of the numerous workshops and training courses that made up the extensive network of donor-driven gender activism (Kandiyoti 2009), which was by then fairly institutionalized in the country.

Meanwhile, I found a very useful source of information in a handful of legal aid organizations, whose staff generously shared information about how they worked on incidents of violence against women and the typical trajectories of such cases—from police investigations through to the courts. They also alerted me to cases they themselves thought were significant or interesting, and I started to follow these up. At this point, I was fortunate to have a research assistant, Mohammad Jawad Shahabi, who was then a student in the Faculty of Law at Kabul University and who would later become a long-term research partner. In pursuit of these individual cases, Jawad and I traveled, certainly not across the country, but to a good portion of the provinces that were considered stable enough for us to visit. Two of the cases I eventually decided to include in this book were from Taliban-controlled districts out of reach for the Afghan government as well as for me. Here I sought the help of two local researchers, who carried out some of the interviews. The material they gathered was then crosschecked and supplemented by other interviews, largely by phone, to local government officials, journalists, and others.

Few of the women at the center of the individual cases discussed in chapters 5 and 6 were interviewed. Some of them were dead, and others were imprisoned or had male family members who insisted on speaking on their behalf. It is the stories narrated by those around them, a web of information often contradictory and certainly disputed, that constitutes the material for my analysis in this section of the book. The focus of the interviews was to try to reconstruct particular events retrospectively, to establish what had taken place and what had been said. These accounts of what had happened were narrated by various informants and were therefore shaped by their particular views, but because data was triangulated through the interviewing of multiple informants, it was possible to establish some kind of chronology of events (the sequence of what had happened and what was said when) and to sort out the multiple readings of what had taken place (what was contested and what was generally or universally agreed upon).

From one perspective, the exclusion of the women themselves as informants can be seen as a weakness in the analysis of these cases. On the other hand, it would have been problematic to ask about—and reveal—intimate material from the women themselves in episodes that had already gained widespread publicity. It was also this publicity that generated so many divergent claims and narratives, and which made for a richer material to draw upon for analysis. After a while, I also developed some skepticism about the way in which certain women were *offered* to me as interview objects. Some shelter staff, for instance, would, on their own initiative, offer visitors, including me, free access to their residents, accompanied by the encouragement: "ask her whatever you want." While making use of some of these "opportunities" might make for captivating stories (A. J. Rubin 2015), it would also raise some questions about consent and voyeuristic writing.

It was a stay in the city of Herat, after some months of fieldwork in Kabul, that alerted me to the maneuverings by women's shelters, a new institution in Afghanistan. The shelters provided temporary accommodation for women who, for various reasons, could not or did not want to live with their families. These shelters were under constant scrutiny for allegedly undermining family and morality by encouraging women to leave their families and husbands. For women to live in a nonfamilial setting—except for arrangements like university dormitories—was generally unheard-of in Afghanistan. The shelters were a radical development. However, because adultery—and, according to some legal interpretations, "running away from home"—was criminalized in Afghanistan, the shelters were not only facing the outrage of conservative groups. They were also accused of housing criminals. In Herat, I was informed that, on this basis, women who could *not* prove that they had *not* committed adultery (i.e., women who had not come directly from their family homes to the shelters or government authorities—perhaps because they spent one or more nights with more distant relatives or in a hotel) would not be admitted to the shelter in the city. Attempts on my part to find out whether this was a universal policy among the dozen or so shelters across the country led me to probe them further as institutions, which revealed how they operated in a curious transnational space, navigating between international support and local skepticism.

Some months after my initial departure from Afghanistan, a controversy erupted that brought these tensions into sharp relief. The minister of women's affairs declared her intention to put all shelters, currently run by NGOs, under government control and to establish committees at the provincial level to decide whether individual women were qualified to enter the shelters. The NGOs and women's rights activists who ran the shelters protested, outraged by what they saw as government encroachment on their territory, with severe consequences for women's protection. During another visit to Kabul, in the spring of 2011, I retraced this chapter in the ongoing controversy around the shelters. By then, a well-organized campaign carried out by Afghan activists and international supporters had succeeded in reversing the minister's decision, and it appeared as if the shelters would be able to continue their tenuous existence for the time being.

Doing research in "official" Afghanistan was not straightforward. My efforts to contact the Supreme Court in order to obtain statistics on convictions and similar documentation bore little fruit. Sometimes even setting up interviews with judges was a challenge. Then, in 2013, after a research project commissioned by the World Bank had revealed systemic corruption in the courts, the Supreme Court proceeded to ban all Afghan judges from talking to researchers without a written permission from its top officials. Legal documents and rulings were generally not made available to the public and were frequently little more than loose notes in an official's drawer, if they existed at all. It often appeared as if information was a resource to be carefully guarded and to be given away only in a transaction of mutual benefit, whether in the form of other information or promises of future favors. As I sought to speak to specific individuals connected to a particular case or process— whether these individuals were family members, journalists, legal and government officials, aid workers, or politicians, many of whom were very busy—it sometimes took weeks, even months, and long chains of introductions to set up a particular interview. Appointments could be repeatedly cancelled, especially when explosions, attacks, or other security threats temporarily closed down government buildings, led to road closures, or resulted in staff in international organizations being ordered into several days of lock down. A few people declined to meet me altogether, such as certain high-ranking government officials like the speaker of Parliament and the chief justice. On the other hand, many people were extremely generous with their time and often agreed to multiple interviews.

Upon completing my PhD, I returned to Afghanistan with regular intervals. Then, in 2014, I embarked upon a two-year stay in Kabul to work on a project funded by the Norwegian Research Council on the prosecution of violence against women. The project was a collaboration between my home institution, the Chr. Michelsen Institute, and the Kabul-based Research Institute for Women, Peace, and Security. Two Afghan researchers and I formed a core team of three. Our task was to produce more precise data on the numbers and types of cases of violence against women exiting the criminal justice system, which we hoped would lead to a better understanding of why so few cases resulted in a criminal conviction. Although my two Afghan colleagues, Mohammad Jawad Shahabi and Farangis Elyassi, did much of the day-to-day data collection, upon which our joint publications are based (Shahabi and Wimpelmann 2015; Shahabi, Wimpelmann, and Elyassi 2016), they have generously allowed me to use some of the material for chapter 3 of this book.

That chapter details the everyday workings of the specialized unit for prosecution of violence against women in Kabul, based on long-term observation in the unit over seven months in 2015. The unit had been set up through donor funds and with the intention of strengthening the implementation of the EVAW law, although its achievement in this regard would prove quite ambiguous. Farangis Elyassi, a recent law graduate, sat for months in the special prosecution units for violence against women in Kabul, among the constant comings and goings of complainants and their families. Most of the time she would be in one of the two investigators' offices, where several groups of complainants, suspects, and witnesses would be interviewed by the prosecutors at any one time. Together we would review her field notes on a weekly and sometimes daily basis, producing a gradual understanding of the workings of the prosecution unit and whether it could be said to be functioning according to its official purpose.

In this period, I also undertook some additional research on the gendered workings of the justice system during two periods about which there is very little documentation: the years of Soviet and Taliban rule. Covering these periods comprehensively would be worthy of several separate book projects. The material I collected by interviewing former judges, prosecutors, and scholars forms part of chapter 1 in the book and amounts to a very modest contribution.

ETHICAL PITFALLS OF RESEARCH IN AFGHANISTAN

When I started my fieldwork in the summer of 2009, NATO's warfare in Afghanistan was about to reach its most intensive period, and the country occupied a prime place in the foreign policy agenda of most Western countries. The Obama administration was coming to terms with the fact that it had inherited a costly and deteriorating war, and it reinvigorated its efforts to "understand" Afghanistan and the conflict. Western media interest in the country was intense, and research reports and commentary were produced in abundance. As a foreign researcher in the midst of—and, to a certain extent, operating on the back of—the Western military operation in Afghanistan, I was also implicated in this knowledge-intervention nexus.

Research in a setting like contemporary Afghanistan, where so many careers have emerged out of a sudden imperial rush to understand, map, and transform the country, can quickly appear exploitative. An obvious aspect of this is that much, if not most, of the scholarly work has been produced by foreign researchers, often with limited linguistic skills and during brief fieldwork. I myself only speak and read Dari with some level of fluency, and I still prefer to use an interpreter for more abstract or technical conversations. Like many of my non-Afghan colleagues, I have relied extensively on Afghan colleagues for translation and for company when traveling outside of Kabul. As more Afghans obtain PhDs—like several of my close colleagues over the years—the relationship between Afghan and non-Afghan researchers might become somewhat more balanced. Yet the disparities of global knowledge production, at the heart of which is unequal access to higher education and funds, look to remain in place for the foreseeable future.

At the same time, like Julie Billaud (2015), I do not see my research as an attempt at representing or giving voice to Afghan women or to provide a definite account of "Afghan reality." That would, indeed, put questions of positionality and the right to speak for "the other" into even sharper relief. Rather, this book is a study of the particular dynamics and contradictions that emerged at the intersections of local and transnational attempts to define and address gender violence, which were situated within a larger context of highly conflictual politics. But as I proceeded with my data collection, a dilemma nonetheless made itself felt. It was between, on the one hand, a position of solidarity to the victims of violence and those working to support them and on the other hand, a more problematizing stance toward the power relations that they were enmeshed in. For instance, when researching and writing about the controversies around the shelters (chapter 4)—and exploring the hierarchies that their constitution as "transnational entities" dependent on Western support entailed—I sometimes felt uneasy about the way I was subjecting them to such critical examination. These were, after all, organizations providing an important service. As this book describes, shelters were often the only place where women fleeing abuse or an unwanted marriage could go. At times, it seemed petty to question their mobilization of Western funds and support when this obviously enabled them to offer shelter to women who had very few options. The uncompromising stand of some of the shelters—enabled by the relative autonomy from the government and Afghan society that their external support afforded them—also allowed them to accommodate a wider range of women, including women who might be excluded (as they were considered unworthy of protection) from shelters that were more in line with government policy. Refusing to compromise and pushing the boundaries of female propriety is an act of feminism, at least at face value. Should I not place myself squarely in solidarity with such a position?

Pointing out the trade-offs and shortcuts involved in the EVAW law accentuated similar ethical dilemmas. The EVAW law, as chapter 2 details, was promulgated and implemented in ways that were largely dependent on Western pressure and funds and that undermined the parliamentary process. The law was also technically flawed; in places it contradicted the rest of the legal framework, and it contained unclear legal terminology that would make it difficult for judges to implement it. Yet, as some women passionately argued, the EVAW law was a big achievement in many ways. Indeed, one high-level official in the Ministry of Women's Affairs told me directly to "leave the EVAW law alone" and avoid drawing attention to the questions around its legal status—or even to the law's existence. (The law had not been ratified by Parliament, and some of the law's supporters felt that conservative MPs would never approve it anyway, so the best strategy would be to discretely withdraw the law from Parliament in order to avoid its explicit repeal.)

Both cases brought to the forefront the tension between examining gender violence and scrutinizing the broader power relations that activists, shelter managers, and others operated within. I did not want to belittle the gender violence in Afghanistan—or the sense of urgency and outrage that activists were trying to generate around it. But at the same time, I thought it important to problematize the choices and compromises made by the women's rights advocates and the local and global power relations produced and maintained as a result. Of course, the latter can be a productive exercise also for activists—in the sense of engaging in reflective praxis. But I was not a fellow activist. I did not have a background as a feminist activist anywhere, certainly not in Afghanistan. I was a foreign researcher. In fact, I arrived to the field unprepared for the politics of feminism; I had not engaged much in conscious thinking about the different coalitions, imaginaries, and tactics that feminists employ—and disagree over—in the pursuit of women's rights. Instead, the main fault line that I expected to encounter was between feminists and their adversaries—those who sought to define gender violence in ways that reinforced patriarchal privileges or to explain it as a regrettable part of Afghan "culture." I had not given much thought to the more internal dilemmas of feminist political praxis: the tensions between the immediate and the long run, between making broader coalitions or seizing the moment, even if it meant forming uncomfortable alliances. But it was these questions around political *strategy* that increasingly would come to occupy my thoughts.

I found myself agonizing over an emerging conviction that real feminist gains could only be anchored in democratic political relations, but, at the same time, I could not see much possibility of this happening in Afghanistan. And at times I saw little interest among women in broader political mobilization or gaining independence from external support. For many of my female informants, the important thing was to get the infrastructure in place that could ensure women a measure of protection from violence—and to do it immediately—even if this meant relying on Western pressure and funds. They sometimes pointed to the difficulties of more directly confronting the conservatives in their country, who commanded significant power of intimidation. Although political violence against women was not all that widespread compared to settings such as U.S.-occupied Iraq, outspoken women always risked being labeled immoral or worse, which could cost them the support of their families and make them feel insecure.

To me—a citizen of a country where weighing your physical security against outspokenness and assertiveness was fairly inconceivable—taking a more critical approach to the strategies that the activists were using to further their goals sometimes felt like an exercise in academic indulgence. Up to a point, I have sought to resolve the dilemma I experienced between apolitical-ethical commitment and critical analysis by striving to be empathetic in my critique. As I elaborate in the conclusion, I cannot see any easy choices or infallible positions in the struggles that I write about. I have experienced for myself in Afghanistan how quickly and easily fear can make you conform. I recall how—especially during the first months of my research—my own anxiety was sometimes set in motion just by walking by myself for short stretches in Kabul, and how my main strategy for overcoming this was to dress modestly and sometimes (often quite subconsciously) to adopt a posture of feminine deference when walking around, so as to signal respectability and conformance.

My own feelings of insecurity were, of course, rooted in a different kind of positionality than that of my Afghan informants. It was generated by my formal identity as a war-waging Westerner, a kind of occupiers' or colonial paranoia, fuelled by rumors of kidnappings and attack plots. My endeavors to make myself as inconspicuous as possible by dressing modestly and acting discreetly was, in fact, mostly an attempt to set myself aside from the bad Westerners rather than from bad women. My point here is that the courage I sometimes needed to sum up to overcome such everyday apprehensions was miniscule compared to the fearlessness that many Afghans displayed when engaging in politics, travel, or just daily life. Therefore, if this book is to engage in critical analysis of Afghan feminist politics, then it must do so with the acknowledgment that in contemporary Afghanistan, the actors involved (and perhaps the author as well) were faced with a number of difficult dilemmas. No infallible choice was available—all options contained flaws of one kind or another.

ORGANIZATION OF THE BOOK

The main body of the book is divided into three parts, each consisting of two chapters. The first part, "Legal Regimes," examines the historical and contemporary struggles over laws and legal regimes governing gender violence. It analyzes contestations over the substance and processes through which laws regulating gender violence were promoted, and the political projects in which these efforts were entangled.

Chapter 1 traces past attempts to achieve closer public regulation of sexuality and of abuses committed within the family and how these attempts were shaped by larger political agendas. It briefly introduces the reader to the first reforms, made by Afghan kings in the late nineteenth and early twentieth centuries. The chapter then draws upon interviews with former leaders, judges, and other officials to provide an account of how the issue of gender has been addressed in Afghanistan's more recent history, especially during the communist (1978–92) and Taliban (1996–2001) eras. In the final part of the chapter, I dissect the contemporary legal landscape. I show how its fragmentary nature can be traced back to the multiple intersections of politics, justice, and gender of the past, while at the same time being a product of the political settlement of the post-2001 order.

Chapter 2 focuses on the law that would take center stage in gender politics in contemporary Afghanistan: the Elimination of Violence against Women law (EVAW law), decreed in the summer of 2009. The chapter explores the origins of the law, the tactics used to promote it, and the opposition it encountered in Parliament. Drawing upon several hundred interviews, observations of parliamentary sessions, activists' meetings, and other fora, as well as unpublished legal drafts and written correspondence, it shows how the EVAW law was promoted through a transnational coalition in which global gender expertise and institutions intersected with personalized and patrimonial local politics. The chapter shows how the partial status the law achieved—signed as presidential decree but never approved in Parliament—reflected the constant tension between three key aspects of the post-2001 order: foreign military operations, the rehabilitation of the mujahedin, and external attempts to promote Afghan women's rights. Supporters of the law nonetheless mobilized a massive apparatus to see it implemented. As the next chapter of the book shows, however, the impact was limited.

The second part of the book, "New Protection Mechanisms," examines how the novel protection infrastructure operated in practice, with a focus on the specialized prosecution units for violence against women and the women's shelters. The analysis explores the type of alliances their supporters entered into, what kind of protection they could offer as a result, and to what extent these institutions challenged predominant gender relations.

Chapter 3 describes how the specialized prosecution units were initially set up, with donor support, in the hope that they would prioritize cases of violence against women. Drawing upon a wealth of observational data, the chapter documents the everyday working of the prosecution unit in Kabul. It argues that, by and large, the unit did not function as donors intended. Many cases were closed prior to trial, sometimes because prosecutors were reluctant to pursue them, but sometimes because the victims or their families had other agendas altogether. Prosecutors, women, and their families bargained within a paradigm of gender norms in which women's rehabilitation into the family unit and restoring sexual transgressions into the framework of marriage transactions were key reference points. In these cases, the special unit served to reaffirm the notion that acts of gender violence were family problems—not criminal cases belonging in the formal justice system. I suggest that this was a predictable outcome, given how the special prosecution units operated at the intersection of donor pressure, government indifference, and a lack of attention to (or disinterest in destabilizing) broader social relations that cast women's existence outside of the family setting as deeply subversive.

Chapter 4 investigates a series of public controversies over women's shelters. The shelters, by opening up a space where conventional forms of social regulation of women's conduct could not reach, were seen as undermining family control over female sexuality. They encountered and sometimes collided with government practices that upheld family claims over women, such as the practice of detaining women who had "escaped from the house." Eventually, amid a growing populist backlash that depicted the NGO-run shelters as part of a Western plot against family, religion, and morality, the Afghan government made a bid to nationalize them. I argue that the shelters provide a stark example of how women served, on the one hand, as a marker for national sovereignty and religious purity and, on the other, as a litmus test of Western commitments to Afghan women. As Western acquiescence to the proposed nationalization of the shelters was equated with capitulating to the Taliban, the shelter issue was made into a question of military resolve, mobilizing an international outcry that eventually led the Afghan government to back down. Yet international support was a double-edged sword; it exposed the vulnerability of shelters as transnational entities. Western support gave the shelters considerable room to maneuver but, at the same time, left them with limited local anchorage and vulnerable to shifts in Western priorities.

The final part of the book, "Individual Cases," explores the complex avenues of intervention and protection in Afghanistan through the trajectories of individual cases of gender violence. I probe the fault lines revealed in these episodes by asking: What exactly was acknowledged as violations or transgressions? Just as importantly, what was not? How did public institutions of various kinds become involved in dealing with these incidents? The answers to these questions reveal whether gender violence has increasingly become a public issue in Afghanistan—and, if so, in what ways and with what consequences.

Chapter 5 details the stories of three women inhabiting the contested position that had implicated the shelters in so much controversy—that of the "runaway" woman. All the women discussed in this chapter had fled their families and the abuse inflicted on them. Based on more than hundred interviews with family and community members, local officials, journalists, and aid workers, the chapter traces the women's fates and the many actors seeking to intervene in their cases. The chapter documents how justice institutions often became mechanisms for reinforcing kinship control over female sexuality but in tenuous ways, forged out of contingent struggles and alliances. The stories of the three runaways show how difficult it was for individual women to escape family abuse in a setting where female subversion of family control featured as a principal transgression. Even if it was possible for some women to receive a sympathetic hearing in a government court, the paths they had to take to escape from abusive situations typically involved difficult choices that left them irrevocably tainted in the eyes of their communities and the law itself.

Chapter 6 examines how the justice system dealt with cases of rape. Specifically, it looks at what appeared to be an unprecedented willingness by families to take rape cases to court, inquiring whether this meant a redrawing of relations of gender and governance in Afghanistan, a redrawing brought upon a reluctant government by mobilization from "below." By examining a handful of highly publicized cases of rape—which were widely regarded as momentous in the way that they generated public demands for government action—I ask whether the new "openness" surrounding rape in Afghanistan signaled a changed position for women. Would rape mean a violation of women's bodily integrity—as opposed to an affront to their male relatives' honor? I further ask whether we can gauge from these cases the contours of a stronger Afghan state. My answer to both questions is a qualified no. The chapter argues that the public claims in these cases were articulated within "stable categories of gender" and sometimes directly as infringements of male honor. Moreover, through a detailed discussion of the aftermath of a rape case from northern Afghanistan, I show that the demands that the state punish the rapists were not necessarily a call for a stronger government role in regulating sexual violence. By situating the case in local and national power struggles, I demonstrate how discourses of affronted honor can instead function as a vocabulary in struggles over access to state power, and in this case, in fact, they were implicated in an attempt to alter the distribution of political power at the local level.

PART I

Legal Regimes

Intrusions, Invasions, and Interventions

*Histories of Gender, Justice, and Governance
in Afghanistan*

Afghanistan during the Karzai presidency (2001–14)—the setting of the greater part of the events in this book—evolved into a fairly extreme example of legal pluralism, with a number of legal systems functioning side by side. This pluralism was by design as well as by default and, in part, reflected the country's turbulent history of "state building." The official legal framework was a patchwork of codified laws derived from sharia, secular laws, and uncodified Islamic jurisprudence. Often, judges, prosecutors, and lawyers were uncertain about which laws took precedence, and at other times, they simply applied whatever applicable law they preferred. Naturally, this had great bearings on how gender violence was regulated. The meeting referred to in the introduction, at which local women's rights activists and international aid workers attempted to get clarity on which laws trumped which after the president had signed the controversial Shia Personal Status Law, is a case in point. Not only did the meeting reveal an acute confusion about which of the statutory laws—the 1970s Civil Code, the Shia law, or the EVAW law—overrode the others, but participants in the meeting also disagreed on the reference points for their arguments. Was it possible to counter the problematic provisions of the Shia law by reference to the human rights commitments in the new Constitution? Or would only arguments based on sharia suffice? The disagreement among expatriates was as strong as that between Afghans and internationals. When a Canadian advisor to the Ministry of Justice and advocate of feminist reinterpretations of sharia gave a lengthy explanation on why it was possible to make the case that the Shia law represented a regressive understanding of Islamic law, she was eventually interrupted by a senior U.N. official. This official, with more than a hint of impatience and frustration, stated, "But it's human rights that must be foundational. Human rights are sufficient [to make an argument], and they're inalienable. And that's there in the Constitution, in article 22."[1] Few in the audience seemed convinced by her intervention, and the conversation returned to a hither-and-thither discussion about which channel would be most effective for getting their views on the Shia law heard and making sure that the EVAW law would neutralize it. One woman, an Afghan activist working for an international NGO, offered to approach President Karzai personally, claiming that she currently had the ear of the president. Others argued that Parliament would be the most appropriate target of lobbying, although everyone agreed that this had to be done in an inconspicuous way, without any overt involvement of foreigners.

The multiplicity of legal frameworks and channels for influencing them was, in many ways, a mirror image of the fragmented politics of the Karzai era. The sharp ideological shifts of the preceding decades—from the authoritarian, secular socialism of the Soviet period to the (at least) equally intrusive reign of the Islamists—had left behind traces in the country's judiciary and laws that were constantly pulling in very different directions. Upon the installment of the Karzai administration, female judges who had started their professional life during the socialist period (only to be cast out by the Islamists) were reinstated and found themselves working side by side with Taliban-era judges who felt that referring to the country' statutory laws was optional and less important than their knowledge of uncodified *fiqh*—traditional Islamic jurisprudence.[2] Combined with the strong international interference in the justice sector during the post-2001 period, this made for a legal landscape that—much like the politics of the country itself—was extremely heterogeneous.

Even within the Western community, there were strong dividing lines. One, as shown above, was over whether the promotion of women's rights had to be anchored in Islamic law. Another disagreement was perhaps more fundamental. Around the same time that part of the international community in Kabul— primarily U.N. human rights staff, NGOs in the gender field, and sections of the NATO embassies—were working to support the EVAW law and the infrastructure of formal courts to implement it, another part of the expatriate community was promoting the country's informal legal practices based on customs. This initiative, which I have discussed in some detail elsewhere (Wimpelmann 2013), generated strong reactions among local women's rights advocates. They felt it was an attempt to return Afghanistan to the unequal and unaccountable rule of patriarchs and tribal strongmen, with problematic consequences for women. Although those who favored giving formal recognition to the informal justice processes argued that safeguards for women would be incorporated, in making their argument they certainly drew upon political symbols and ideas that differed starkly from those employed by the international supporters of the EVAW law. Whereas the latter advocated formal "state building," the supporters of a larger role for informal justice invoked notions of Afghanistan as a stateless, traditional society where reconciliation between parties, rather than the imposition of standardized laws, was true to local culture and therefore appropriate policy. These arguments did not come from nowhere; they drew upon established historical and political notions of Afghanistan's presumed unique statelessness and tribal nature that had roots going back to colonial times. The image gained prominence at a time during the NATO operation when military leaders, frustrated with the slow progress of the formal state-building process, turned to what they saw as traditional leaders for political allies. The result alienated a large part of the women's rights community.

This chapter provides crucial context to the contestations over gender violence analyzed in the rest of the book by dissecting the contemporary legal system in Afghanistan. It shows how its fragmentary nature can be traced back to the multiple intersections of politics, justice, and gender of the past while, at the same time, being a product of the political settlement of the post-2001 order. It also shows that the post-2001 era was not in any way unique in the way that particular political agendas were reflected in, and sometimes fought through, the regulation of gender relations. Since Afghanistan's inception as a modern state, the country's gender policies have mirrored—and have often been at the heart of—broader political fault lines.

MODERNIZING KINGS

In the historical chronicle *Siraj al Tawarikh* (Torch of Histories), Qazi (Judge) Abd al Shakur in Kandahar receives a royal reprimand for having "impulsively sentenced to death by stoning" an adulterous couple. The issue at hand is the failure of the *qazi* to have asked witnesses to testify twice, once on account of the act of adultery by the man, Qamar al-Din, and once on account of his unnamed female accomplice. Instead, the *qazi* had ordered both Qamar al-Din and the woman to be stoned on the basis of testimony by witnesses of the adultery of Qamar al-Din alone. This made the stoning of the woman illegal, and, "since from the current authoritative books of jurisprudence it is abundantly clear and understood that the act of adultery is a singular act as far as men and women are concerned," the stoning sentence of Qamar al-Din was also "completely irregular and totally unacceptable" (Kātib 2013: 1427–28). In other words, if there was to be a stoning, both parties must be stoned, and since the stoning of the woman was not just, the stoning of the man was not just either. Moreover, the letter continues, the *qazi* had failed in other requirements promulgated by royal decree, such as giving an account of a proper investigation of the witnesses' integrity. Unless the *qazi* could present "reasonable and citable evidence and proof" that his actions had been within the commands of the Lord and the Prophet, he was liable to pay blood money to the relatives of the executed Qamar al-Din.

The year of the execution of Qamar al-Din and the unnamed woman was 1895, when Amir Abdul Rahman Khan, ruler of Afghanistan since 1880, was fifteen years into an unprecedented and often brutal project to consolidate the power in the country into a central state. Pivotal to his centralization efforts was the development of a unified justice system (Tarzi 2003; Ghani 1983). The ulema—the Muslim clergy—who previously had adjudicated in a semiautonomous fashion, were turned into salaried bureaucrats subject to standardized rules and royal oversight. As the story of Qazi Abd al Shakur shows, they could no longer rely on their own knowledge of Islamic jurisprudence *(fiqh)* to arrive at judicial decisions. Instead, they were instructed to apply government manuals in which preestablished and government-authorized rulings of law and procedures were set out (Ahmed 2015: 286). This was, in effect, a first attempt at "codifying Islamic jurisprudence of the Hanafi school as the official law of the state," quite possibly modeled on similar modernist efforts by Ottoman rulers (287). At the same time, a network of courts was set up throughout the country for the purpose of establishing a government monopoly on the dispensation of justice.

Olesen points out that enlisting religious clerics in the administration of justice had less to do with a desire to foster closer adherence to religious doctrine and more to do with the amir's drive to consolidate power (1995: 66), which he did by claiming divine right to rule—and through the application of considerable coercive force. Abdul Rahman Khan's appointments of the ulema as state-employed justice officials were also part of his agenda to curb their influence. Having played an important political role by inciting the population to jihad against British invasions during the nineteenth century (Kamali 1985), the religious leaders had become powerful political actors. This had further increased their role in legitimizing the ruler (Nawid 1999).

As other Afghan rulers had attempted before him, Abdul Rahman Khan assumed jurisdiction over serious criminal cases—offenses against the state and whatever other cases he felt it pertinent to preside over—thus asserting the monarch's supremacy in the dispensation of justice (Olesen 1995: 65). He operated as an absolute ruler. Unencumbered by a constitution, the amir could proclaim laws and issue verdicts as he deemed necessary. Numerous laws were promulgated, some of which attempted to bring women and family under closer government regulation (Ghani 1983; M. M. S. M. Khan 1980). All marriages were to be registered with the authorities, a ceiling was placed on bride-price, and underage (prepuberty) marriage (when against the will of the girl) and levirate (marrying a widow to her deceased husband's brother) were prohibited. It is difficult to assess to what extent these laws were implemented, although the work of Ghani (1983) suggests that they were systematically enforced in courts in at least some provinces. Abdul Rahman Khan's attempt at judicial centralization also had a sectarian dimension. Mobilization for his conquest of Hazarajat, the central highlands where the Shia

Hazaras lived largely autonomously, took place through a call for jihad to force-fully convert the Hazaras to Sunni Islam. As part of this campaign, he appointed Sunni judges to all Hazara areas and instructed them to apply Sunni Hanafi juris-prudence (Ibrahami 2009).

Unlike Abdul Rahman Khan, the next great reformer, his grandson Amanul-lah (reigned 1919–29) had neither the backing and subsidies of the British nor a strong army to enforce his visions. Revered as national hero by some and ridi-culed as pompous dreamer by others, Amanullah's failed attempt to modernize Afghanistan—particularly its women—continues to figure as a key moment in Afghan historiography. At first, Amanullah gained great popularity among both nationalist and religious groups when he could claim to have defeated the British in 1919 during the Third Anglo-Afghan War. The brief confrontation, which had started when Amanullah proclaimed a war of independence in a bid to rid Afghanistan of its status as a British protectorate, ended with a treaty between the two countries that recognized Afghanistan as a sovereign state (Barfield 2010). Emboldened by his newly attained status as a defender of nation and religion against imperial forces, Amanullah embarked upon a series of ambitious legal and social reforms. At that point, splits between the modernizing monarch, inspired by Ataturk's Turkey and anti-imperial nationalism and an ulema concerned with defending Islam against infidel rule and Westernization became apparent.[3]

During his reign, Amanullah promulgated 140 regulations known as *nizam-namas,* as well as Afghanistan's first Constitution.[4] Among the *nizam-namas* were several versions of a new marriage code, first published in 1920. A more exhaus-tive version was published in 1923, requiring the registration of all marriages. Po-lygamous marriage was made subject to the court's permission, and marriages in which the bride had not yet reached puberty were banned outright (Nawid 1999; Gregorian 1969). Compared to subsequent legislation in the decades that followed, these were radical steps.

The Constitution of 1923 placed few limits on the power of the king, although it had some modest provisions for consultative government. It named Islam as the official religion but made no mention of the Sunni Hanafi school—an omis-sion designed to appeal to the Shia minority, which Amanullah had also released from slavery by decree. The Constitution recognized both secular and religious law and made no specification as to the authority of one versus the other (Olesen 1995: 122). It also bestowed equal rights on all citizens, a significant breach of ear-lier practices. The Pashtun Durrani elite would no longer be granted privileges, and non-Muslim minorities would no longer be treated differently (Olesen 1995; Nawid 1999). Amanullah also set out to codify Islamic criminal law and prescribe set punishments, resulting in the first Afghan criminal code (1924–25). The code classified crimes based on the four categories of classic Islamic criminal law: *hadd, diat, qisas,* and *tazir.*[5] The crimes covered by *hadd* prescriptions[6] and major crimes such as murder and bodily harm were to receive set punishments, whereas for lesser crimes, the judges were to give discretionary punishments *(tazir)* (Gregorian 1969; Kamali 1985). The ulema were deeply unhappy with Amanullah's reforms in the field of criminal law, as they reduced the number of crimes for which the Islamic judges could impose their own discretionary *(tazir)* punishments based on their knowledge of Hanafi *fiqh*. Moreover, the very specification of set punishments beyond those set by God (in crimes of *hadd*) was seen as contrary to sharia (Kamali 1985).

Many of Amanullah's female family members, including his wife, Queen Soraya, were instrumental to his reform program, which went beyond legal changes to the transformation of women's public and private roles. Queen Soraya gave speeches calling upon Afghan women to educate themselves so they could serve their newly independent nation, and she oversaw the establishment of girls' schools, a government-published women's magazine, and a new association through which women could petition for lawful treatment by their husbands (Majrooh 1989). Arbabzadah (2011) emphasizes that the queen's efforts were rooted in anticolonial and pan-Islamic ideology prominent throughout the Muslim world at the time and should not be understand merely as an attempt at Westernization. Nonetheless, photographs of the queen appearing unveiled and in sleeveless Western dresses, particularly in the company of male European leaders, became a central rallying point for the growing opposition against Amanullah among the country's religious leaders.

With the government facing a rebellion instigated, in part, by the conservative rural mullahs, who perceived Amanullah as an adversary to their values and positions,[7] the urban ulema seized the opportunity to assert themselves. A 1924 Loya Jirga (grand assembly) confirmed them as important power brokers. Upon the ulema's insistence, Amanullah was forced to retract many of his legal reforms. The Constitution was revised to reintroduce the discriminatory tax for religious minorities and to reestablish Hanafi *fiqh* as the official and sole religious law. A new criminal code in Arabic and based exclusively on Hanafi *fiqh* was to be compiled, and the right to determine *tazir* punishments was returned to the judges (Nawid 1999).

But upon successfully defeating the rebellion, Amanullah turned to face down the ulema with another attempt at legal reform. This time, he tried to sideline the ulema completely, perceiving them as an obstacle to the progress of the nation. In the end, however, Amanullah's confrontational stance toward the ulema—combined with the announcement a new series of reforms, his increasingly authoritarian style, and his lack of coercive resources to back it all up—led to his overthrow (Nawid 1999).

The next king, Nadir Shah, who rose to power following a brief interregnum, was beholden to eastern tribes and showed less personal disposition toward radical reforms. He made significant concessions to the ulema and tribal powers. The

Constitution of 1931 reinstated the Hanafi *fiqh* as the official religious doctrine and, in general, gave precedence to sharia over statutory law (Moschtaghi 2006). In addition, the clergy was given influence through the governmental Jamiat-al Ulema (literally, the society of religious scholars, the ulema council), who were entrusted with reviewing laws and government policies for adherence with Islam (Olesen 1995: 184). Not only were religious scholars now partly co-opted by the state, but Sufi networks also moved closer to state power with *pir* (spiritual leaders) taking up government positions such as minister of justice.

Nadir Shah was assassinated in 1933. His only son, Zahir Shah, ascended to the throne, but executive power was largely in the hands of his paternal uncles in the first three decades that followed. In this period of "limited guided modernization" (Sharani 1986), wide-ranging developments in education took place. Secular education was expanded, and a number of the government madrassas was established in order to formalize higher religious education and train judges in sharia. "The new modus vivendi which was established between the state and the traditional groups whose economic and political interests were being observed while the gradual reform measures (educational, administrative etc.) catered for the interests of the new elite of bureaucrats and educated middle class. A gradual transformation of Afghan society hereby took place which above all was characterized by its outward form of continuity but laid the basis of power political and ideological confrontations among the state supporting groups" (Olesen 1995: 172).

The legal system became increasingly bifurcated. Civil and criminal cases were adjudicated in sharia courts, whereas a number of statutory courts in each province had special jurisdiction over fields such as administration and business (Weinbaum 1980). This division also manifested itself in legal education. Two faculties at the newly established Kabul University taught law: the secular Law and Politics Faculty and the Faculty of Sharia. The Faculty of Law was based on the French model and supplied many of the civil servants. The Faculty of Sharia was influenced by Egypt's Al-Azhar University, where many of its lecturers had been educated. Then, as now, a degree from either faculty was not a requirement for appointment as a judge, who could also be appointed if he held a license from a government madrassa (Moschtaghi 2006). From the late 1960s onward, however, the government actively recruited graduates from the Faculty of Law for the judiciary, and, in line with the expansion of secular education more generally, the religious establishment gradually lost its monopoly on the state judiciary (Kamali 1985: 207).

In the 1960s Zahir Shah assumed full power for himself, resulting in the 1964 Constitution. A comprehensive and relatively liberal document (which was to serve as the model for the 2004 Constitution), the 1964 Constitution confirmed the dual court system that had been evolving since Amanullah's time.[8] The primary courts *(mahkama-ye ibtidaya)* continued to be staffed by scholars trained in Islamic law and had general jurisdiction over civil and criminal cases. In addition, there was a number of statutory courts in each province with special jurisdiction over fields such as administration and business (Weinbaum 1980). Provincial courts *(mahkama-ye murafia)* had original jurisdiction and also functioned as appellate courts for the primary courts. What was new in the 1964 Constitution was the establishment of an independent Supreme Court *(Stera Mahkama)* in Kabul, with authority to review all lower-level decisions as well as administrative power over the courts. The move toward an independent judiciary reflected the relatively liberal period in Afghan history under Zahir Shah.

The 1964 Constitution introduced another new institution, that of the attorney general *(Loy Saranwol)* to investigate and prosecute crimes. The attorney general's office was to be independent of the executive power of the government, reporting only to the executive. The judicial branch was not to interfere in its activities (Yassari and Saboory 2010). Compared to previous legal provisions, the 1964 Constitution also favored statutory law over Hanafi sharia. Only when no provisions in the Constitution or law existed for a case under consideration could the courts apply Hanafi jurisprudence, and then only within the limitations set forth in the Constitution. In the view of some, this effectively made Afghanistan a secular state, even while paying lip service to Islam (Dupree, quoted in Saikal 2004: 148).

The 1964 Constitution also made the cabinet accountable to an elected parliament. Two parliamentary elections were held, in 1965 and 1969. Voter participation was low and the intelligentsia could not compete with the traditional power holders, who formed the majority of those elected. As a result, Parliament and the elections functioned mostly according to patronage politics. There were no formal political parties (the King had refused to ratify a bill that would have permitted them), and this hampered the emergence of a political opposition, which continued to operate clandestinely, setting the stage for political developments in the years to come. Rather than the Parliament, it was Kabul University that emerged as the arena for oppositional politics (Dorronsoro 2005). Here, leftist student groups clashed with Islamic radicals over the path to modernization most appropriate to their society.

AUTHORITARIAN EMANCIPATORS

In 1973, political liberalization came to a halt when Zahir Shah was overthrown by his cousin (and former prime minister), Mohammad Daoud, in a military coup. Daoud, who had come to power with the backing of pro-Soviet communists, proclaimed Afghanistan a republic, dismantled the nascent gains in representative government, and took the country in an authoritarian direction. Despite its authoritarianism, the Daoud period nonetheless left some enduring footprints when it came to women's legal status and protection.

Prior to the Daoud period, urban women had been entering the workforce and higher education in increasing numbers for more than three decades. Initially working as teachers, nurses, and secretaries, by the mid-1970s, women were employed in public administration, at the universities, in Parliament, and in the courts, though they were few in numbers and rarely held high positions. Largely, the changes that had come about—such as the right of women to vote, in the 1964 Constitution—were the result of top-down initiatives led by men, as opposed to being the result of an organized women's rights movement (Dupree 1984). However, toward the end Zahir Shah's reign, a few events foreshadowed the more substantial mobilization of women that was to follow during the years of socialist rule. For instance, in 1968 hundreds of women took to the streets to protest a proposal by conservative members of Parliament to prohibit unmarried women from pursuing studies abroad (Zulfacar 2006). Two years later, several thousand women demonstrated in front of government ministries after a series of assaults on schoolgirls by a man opposed to the nascent changes to women's position in urban areas (Ehmadi 2002).

Reforms in the legal field went some way in supporting this change. In the Afghan year of 1354 (1975), separate family courts were established in Kabul, Kunduz, and Kandahar to deal with issues related to family law. They were intended to give women and female judges (most of whom worked in the field of family law) easier physical access to the courts. It appears that the main objective of this change was to uphold propriety rather than to radically alter gender relations. The regular courts were located within the governors' compounds, together with pretrial detention centers and security staff, and were considered masculine places where women would be uncomfortable.[9] Then, in 1976 and 1977, respectively, Daoud enacted new criminal and civil codes by decree. These remain in force today. The codes had been in the making for some time. The Civil Code included a section on family law, based mainly on Hanafi *fiqh* (Etling 2004). In some respects, the 1977 Civil Code was Afghanistan's most modernist legislation in this field since the time of Amanullah. It abolished child marriage of girls under the age of fifteen, introduced some restrictions on polygamy, and specified provisions for divorce, which had previously been regulated by reference to uncodified Hanafi *fiqh*.[10]

The Penal Code also proceeded from Islamic law. Its enactment, in 1976, followed decades of vacillation over whether *hadd* punishments (the set punishments such as amputation, lashing, and stoning for specific crimes, including adultery) should be included in the penal law. According to Kamali (1985), a 1971 version of the law had been discarded by the cabinet because it detailed such punishments. By contrast, the 1976 version merely referred to *hadd* without spelling them out. In its introduction, the Penal Code says, "This law regulates the Tazir crimes and penalties. Those committing crimes of Hudood, Qassas and Diat[11] shall be punished in accordance with the provisions of Islamic religious law [Hanafi religious jurisprudence]."

The criminal code thus recognized *hadd* punishments, but also provided set *tazir* punishments for crimes that are included under *hadd,* such as adultery and theft.[12] This conformed with legal practice at the time—during the decades leading up to the 1976 code, adultery had not been punished by stoning or lashing, but by imprisonment (Kamali 1985). The code did not, however, distinguish clearly between adultery and rape, but used one word, *zina,* to apply to both. Nevertheless, in some ways, the law introduced new protections for women; it made forced marriage a punishable offense (for men and women of majority age—eighteen and sixteen, respectively), with an increased punishment if the marriage was an arrangement of *baad* (a woman or girl given in marriage as a compensation for an infringement).

A new 1977 Constitution consolidated power in the hands of the executive and effectively made Afghanistan a one-party state. It was a prelude to Daoud's purge of his erstwhile allies, members of the People's Democratic Party of Afghanistan (PDPA), but the competing factions in the PDPA then united in a bloody military coup against Daoud in April 1978. The junior officers who had carried out the coup handed power to a revolutionary council and Afghanistan was proclaimed a democratic people's republic. Intending to transform the country socially and economically along socialist lines, the revolutionary council enacted a number of decrees, most notably regarding land reform, compulsory education, and women's emancipation. Decree number 7, "Dowry and Marriage Expenses," banned under-age and forced marriage, as well as excessive wedding celebrations and dowries, and it specified a punishment of six months to three years in prison for violators. The decree gained notoriety as a particular provocation to religious and tribal groups and as the cause of large-scale public outcry and the galvanization of support for the mujahedin insurgency (Malikyar 1997).

The PDPA's revolutionary zeal proved short-lived, and the Western-backed insurgency led by the mujahedin mounted. Fearing chaos on its southern border, the Soviet Union invaded the country in December 1979. By that time, at least twelve thousand people had been killed in political purges. The Soviets installed a more moderate government and another Constitution was promulgated in 1980. The new Constitution upheld the Supreme Court and provided for a Parliament, but its formation was to be decided by subsequent laws. "Less and less was said about Decree number 7" (Dupree 1984: 325), which faded into the background. In fact, women's legal rights came to be of relatively low priority for the PDPA government and party cadres. Women's emancipation was a central goal both to the leadership of the party and to its many female members, but the focus was on women's labor participation and education. The strategy appeared to have emerged out of a combination of the bitter experience of decree number 7 and a socialist inclination toward material empowerment. A former female PDPA member spoke with me, drawing comparisons between the PDPA era and the present period of American dominance.

Taraki [a PDPA leader deposed and killed in 1979] introduced some progressive legislation, but it was imposed too quickly. It was done in a rush, without preparing the ground, [and] imposed on a traditionalist society. So decree number 7 backfired. . . . It would have been better to do it slowly and prepare society for it.

Today there is a free market economy. There is no focus on poverty or economic opportunities. The talk about "women's rights." . . . It's formal; it's about violence against women, about legislation. But what about removing constraints [on women]: income, access to jobs, access to education? . . . The PDPA had an ideological commitment to change. Women were to have equal status. We focused on the work environment, on women's salaries and on childcare so that women could stay in the workforce. Children would be fed in the kindergartens, and a teacher would be provided for them. We even had subsidies on diapers and on clothing for children up to five years old. There were special shops for this. We focused on the foundational issues; we had five-year plans and so on. Compare the time of the Soviets with that of the United States. The Russians built factories, but the Americans are leaving nothing behind; there is nothing visible from them. Even their military bases they are taking back with them![13]

Women party members and government officials were reluctant to attempt to reform the 1977 Civil Code, which was based on Hanafi *fiqh* and therefore seen as unassailable. They did, however, begin a systematic campaign to strip party membership from polygamous husbands and women who had married as second wives.

On the whole, the PDPA era saw limited progress in terms of how the justice system treated women. The family courts founded in 1975 were in operation until 1987, when they were merged with the district city courts under a new court system based on the Soviet model. There are few indications that the family courts took particularly revolutionary or even reformist positions during the PDPA. Cases reported in the weekly column "Women, Society and Life" in the *Kabul Times* suggests that most of the caseload was made up of women seeking a divorce. Interestingly, the women who approached the courts for divorce generally had independent means of income, and many were already living separate from their husbands. Nevertheless, unless the husband agreed to the divorce, the courts tended to turn down the woman's request, even if beating and violence were alleged. Despite that lingering conservatism, women who worked as justice officials at the time recall a justice system much less interested in pursuing moral crimes than was the case under subsequent regimes. No women were prosecuted for running away from home, as they would be during the mujahedin, Taliban, and Karzai governments. There was also a cautious approach to prosecuting adultery. In the large cities, at least, adultery would be prosecuted only if a couple was caught red-handed or if one party had been deceived—typically a woman entering a relationship upon a promise of marriage that did not eventuate. In cases like that, the courts would normally use an adultery charge to pressure the man to uphold his promise.[14]

As the Soviet leadership lost faith in the possibility of defeating the mujahedin militarily, they engineered a transfer of power to Dr. Najibullah, who was tasked with overseeing a process of national reconciliation under which the Soviets could withdraw. Najibullah set out to downplay the party's Marxist ideology, reverting to more conventional frameworks of nationalism and Islam. Another Constitution, one that made no reference to Marxism and made Islam the official religion, was ratified in 1987. The Soviet military completed their withdrawal in 1989. Najibullah's government managed to stay afloat until 1992, when a sudden cut off of funds led to fatal defections and the takeover of the capital by mujahedin factions. It would mean a radically different gender regime. As one woman recalled, "Our generation was free and open. We went to the office in miniskirts. But in the last days of Najib [Najibullah], we heard that the mujahedin would punish those without [long] pants, so we kept a pair with us in our bags whenever [we were] going out. The day when the mujahedin came to Kabul, a woman called out, "Ladies, put on your trousers! The mujahedin are coming."[15]

ISLAMIST RULE

Seizing control over Kabul in April 1992, a loose coalition of mujahedin leaders formed a government and declared Afghanistan an Islamic republic for the first time in its history. The new government, under Burhanuddin Rabbani, issued an edict: "Now that . . . our Islamic country is free from the bondage of atheist rule, we urge that God's ordinances be carried out immediately, particularly those pertaining to the veiling of women. Women should be banned from working in offices and radio and television stations, and schools for women, which are in effect the hub of debauchery and adulterous practices, must be closed down."[16] This was followed by a decree by the Supreme Court in 1994, which stated that women should not leave their houses unless absolutely necessary and should not wear attractive or revealing clothing.[17] It was during the mujahedin government that the practice of incarcerating "runaway" women first started. As the capital collapsed into infighting, however, there were few possibilities to implement judicial administration of any kind.

By contrast, the Taliban—who rapidly established control over much of the country, which was fractured by rival mujahedin fighters and banditry—made Islamic justice and order the cornerstone of their claim to legitimacy to rule (1996–2001). The exact composition and workings of the Taliban government remains opaque. At its core were Pashtun rural mullahs and men—former refugee boys—educated in conservative madrassas in Pakistan. Although unevenly applied, their restrictions on women's movements and visibility were so extreme as to impose a virtual state of curfew on women (Kandiyoti 2007: 175). Apart from health workers, who were allowed to treat only female patients, women were banned from working, and girls were largely excluded from school. Women were only permitted to venture outside dressed in the all-enveloping *chadari* (known as *burka* in the West) and escorted by a male relative.

The restrictions were intended to prevent immorality and adultery and revealed an obsession with female sexuality as a danger to be contained at all costs.[18] In the 1996 *Ordinance Concerning Women's Rights and Duties,* issued by the Supreme Court in Kabul, the government concluded that "in brief, it is obscene and unlawful for women to go to school." Even if women were fully veiled and their teachers were Muslim, the edict continued, "experience has proved that such deeds have had evil effects on women and have resulted in corrupted morality." The edict stated that women were even forbidden from learning to write, "for writing is a tool for sedition and corruption. Literate women write about their unlawful wishes and desires to strangers." It was concluded that while there were some benefits to women becoming literate, the seditious effects far outweighed them. The edict also prescribed, in great detail, the manner in which women should appear in public. They were to be veiled in a manner that made the contours of their bodies undetectable, and they were to refrain from using perfume, makeup, or any kind of adornment; from speaking loudly or to strange men and from a number of other actions presented as offensive or even threatening to public order. In any case, women were not to go out at all, unless they were obliged by religion to do so.

While the Taliban's gender policies bore similarities with those of the rural Pashtun milieu many of them hailed from, they also differed in important respects. As Cole argues, the Taliban's policy constituted a counter-modernity vision rather than a return to the past (2008). Their Islamic Emirate of Afghanistan envisioned itself as instituting an Islamic order, novel in Afghanistan's history, taking inspiration from the Taliban's notions of an Islamic golden age rather than a reinstatement of Afghan traditions. Their use of state technologies to violently enforce infractions against this order was similarly a novel thing. Another rupture was the ban on *baad* and levirate (Cole 2008), which signaled that the Taliban, like Afghan rulers before them, attempted to subordinate tribal power to central control to some degree.

The Taliban never promulgated a new Constitution but declared their commitment to sharia and decreed a number of laws, particularly in the later phase of their rule. They established a notorious "vice and virtue" religious police modeled on and reportedly funded by Saudi Arabia (HRW 2001), who enforced, often violently and arbitrarily, the government's prescriptions for religious observance and the complete seclusion of women. The preexisting three-tier court system remained in place, but the Taliban eliminated the independent function of the Attorney General and ignored many aspects of the Penal Code (Tondini 2009; Hartmann and Klonowiecka-Milart 2011). Often, cases would be decided on the basis of testimony only, without the use of any other evidence. Sentences were typically meted out on the basis of the judge's knowledge of sharia, without reference to statutory law. The arbitrariness of the application of justice was shocking to many—and not just those who had supported the PDPA government. In Herat, members of the ulema council repeatedly tried to get the Taliban government to enforce due process,[19] according to which executions and corporal punishment such as amputations and lashing were to be approved by the primary court and two higher courts, as well as the supreme leader of the country, Mullah Omar (United Nations Commission on Human Rights 1998). This pressure had no effect, and implementations of those punishments continued to be carried out upon the orders of local judges, some of whom were military commanders with no judicial background. These punishments generally took place on Fridays as a public spectacle and included the flogging and execution of women, unprecedented in recent Afghan history (Coomaraswamy 2000).[20] In addition, the Taliban accelerated the practice of detaining women for running away, a practice that was to be upheld during the next government, with severe consequences for women's relationship with the law.

Despite all this, in some aspects, the Taliban did uphold women's legal rights. Compared to the mujahedin period, rape was severely punished, and public safety increased. Moreover, one judge reported that the Taliban would sometimes enforce women's inheritance rights. Her mother had obtained her inheritance from her father through the support of a Talib justice official, who stated it was in accordance with sharia.[21] Nonetheless, to a great number of Afghan women, the segregation imposed by the Taliban was unprecedented. Overt resistance was unfeasible, but many circumvented the new gender regime as best they could, most prominently by attending the substantial number of home schools set up in response to the ban on female education. Outside the country, members of the Afghan diaspora in France, the United States and beyond mobilized against Taliban's gender policies, thus contributing to the government's increasing international isolation during the final years of its rule.

GENDER AND JUSTICE IN THE NEW ORDER

In 2001, once again, a novel order ushered in a new set of conditions under which negotiations over women's positions and their protection against abuses took place. In the following, I sketch out the political alignments and fault lines of the post-Taliban period, and how they came to shape legal frameworks and infrastructure. This account forms the backdrop to the more detailed discussions of contemporary public regulation of gender violence discussed in the rest of the book.

When the collection of material for this book commenced, in the summer of 2009, Afghanistan was almost ten years into a radical disjuncture set in motion by the attacks in the United States on September 11, 2001. The U.S.-led military invasion that followed produced a drastic realignment of political forces in the country, which until then had been almost completely under the control of the Taliban. To remove the Taliban, the U.S.-led military coalition relied on a bombing campaign plus Afghan militia forces grouped in the so-called Northern Alliance. As the name suggest, this alliance was a collection of military factions from the northern parts of Afghanistan, who had their constituencies among the northern ethnic groups that had formed a temporary alliance against the Taliban when the latter first emerged in the mid-1990s (Pohly 2002). Members of these factions, particularly the Shura-ye Nazar (supervisory council), dominated by Tajiks from the Panjshir Valley, came to feature prominently in the political settlement that emerged after the invasion (Giustozzi 2009). This was a reversal of the historical dominance of the Pashtuns. The Pashtun aristocracy had ruled Afghanistan almost continually until the outbreak of war in 1978, and Pashtuns had also formed the backbone of the Taliban, though they were not from the traditional Pashtun ruling class.

The blueprint for Afghanistan's new political landscape was drawn up at the Bonn conference in December 2001, where a power-sharing agreement set out a political framework for the transition that was to follow. In an attempt to broaden the base of the settlement beyond the Northern Alliance, the chief intervening power, the United States, wanted to install a Pashtun head of state, and the choice fell on Hamid Karzai, who belonged to the Pashtun aristocracy and diaspora. Absent in the new coalition were members of the Taliban (Dorronsoro 2012).

In significant ways, the new order was shaped by the expanding international presence in the country, on which the Karzai government was militarily and financially dependent. Initially, Western military operations were focused on capturing and killing members of Al Qaida and the Taliban, who had melted away or fled. The United States mobilized a number of its allies, who gradually deployed troops across the country, some aiding the U.S. hunt for Taliban and Al Qaida members and others forming part of an U.N.-mandated stabilization force, the International Security Assistance Force (ISAF). Alongside the military engagement, a broad state-building agenda was pursued in line with an evolving international state- and peace-building blueprint overseen by the United Nations (Chesterman 2004). This blueprint entailed ambitious transformation of politics, the economy, and society more generally. In Afghanistan, the transformative agenda would famously include the liberation of the country's women. Yet the international "project" in Afghanistan contained within it tensions and contradictions from the outset (Suhrke 2011). The focus on capturing military adversaries led to alliances with armed commanders and so-called strongmen, alliances that ran counter to attempts to monopolize the use of violence and build a unified state. Pledges to end corruption and to support human rights and good governance often had to cede ground to the demands of short-term political stability and intelligence gathering.

These tensions also affected the reform of the legal framework and the justice sector, which formed a central part of the international state-building exercise. A number of legislative changes were undertaken, starting with a new Constitution in 2004. In the more optimistic climate of those early years, the Constitution was acclaimed as a momentous achievement and decisive step forward in the Western-led reconstruction of post-Taliban Afghanistan, even though the process surrounding its drafting and promulgation was not as democratic and inclusive as was claimed at the time.[22] The Constitution declared Afghanistan, once again, an Islamic republic. Article 3 stated that no law could be passed that contradicts "the beliefs and provisions of the sacred religion of Islam," and article 130 stated that Hanafi (Sunni) *fiqh* should be used in cases where there are no provisions in the law, within the limits set in the Constitution.[23] As detailed in chapter 4 below, article 130 would frequently be invoked by judges who claimed that as long as their verdicts were in accordance with Hanafi jurisprudence, they were free to impose punishments beyond those prescribed in the penal laws.[24] Significantly, for the first time in Afghan history, the Constitution recognized Shia jurisprudence, stating that members of the Shia sect could use Jafari (Shia) jurisprudence in personal law (article 131).

At the same time, noteworthy provisions were made to safeguard women's rights. Article 22 stated that "the citizens of Afghanistan—whether man or woman—have equal rights and duties before the law." In addition, quotas were set for female representation in the government—women would be guaranteed roughly 25 percent of the seats in the lower house of Parliament and 17 percent of the seats in the upper house, as well as two seats in each provincial council.[25] The Constitution also made frequent references to human rights. The preamble declared respect for the Universal Declaration of Human Rights and the Charter of the United Nations, article 7 stated that "the state shall abide by the U.N. charter, international treaties, international conventions that Afghanistan has signed, and the Universal Declaration of Human Rights," and article 58 obliged the government to establish an independent human rights commission, although with no independent powers.

The 2004 Constitution thus contained components from across the broad spectrum of Afghanistan's past legal traditions: the Islamist orientations of the mujahedin and Taliban period, the emancipatory goals of the communist government, and the strong executive that had been a consistent feature of the country's institutional design. Like many constitutions, it was open to contradictory interpretations. It was especially ambiguous on whether Islamic jurisprudence or the principles of human rights—including gender equality and principles of legality—took precedence.[26] Similar questions had been a matter of debate through much of the nineteenth century. Then as now, the resolution of these questions had important ramifications for whether punishments such as stoning would be permitted and for whether acts not defined as crimes in the statutory laws could nonetheless be prosecuted and punished with reference to sharia (Kamali 1985).

The constitutional clauses providing for strong presidential powers were a victory for President Karzai. The president, who had been seen as an isolated leader dependent on foreign support, gradually built a substantial power base. The issue of a presidential versus a parliamentary system had been bitterly contested, with representatives of non-Pashtun groups—the Uzbeks, Hazaras, and Tajiks—wanting a parliamentary system with stronger checks on executive power and central state power more generally, which historically were both Pashtun domains (B. R. Rubin 2004). With support from the U.S. administration, which wanted to see a strong executive (Suhrke 2011: 163), the presidential system prevailed. Equipped with significant means to expand and consolidate his power, Karzai set out to gradually displace the dominance of northerners in the central state apparatus, many of whom gravitated toward the opposition.

In 2005 the first parliamentary elections produced a legislature with almost 30 percent female members—a percentage higher than in many Western countries, though this was due to the quotas established by the 2004 Constitution. As detailed in the next chapter, women MPs were largely unable to establish alliances that could pursue gender issues—or, in some cases, they were not interested in doing so (Azarbaijani-Moghaddam 2006; Larson 2016). Many were beholden to powerful male patrons or were seeking to position themselves as the go-to champion of women's rights for Western embassies.

Two partly overlapping groups became particularly visible in the new National Assembly—a northern-dominated opposition group and a group made up of former mujahedin commanders. The first group was centered around the Tajik speaker of Parliament, Yusus Qanooni, and Dr. Abdullah—who would be Karzai's chief challengers in the 2004 and 2009 presidential elections, respectively. The former mujahedin commanders had originally risen to power as a result of the Cold War rivalry that played out in Afghanistan after the Soviet invasion of 1979. Western countries, Saudi Arabia, and Pakistan had quickly stepped up their support to the anti-Soviet resistance, which coalesced under the banner of jihad, with its fighters calling themselves *mujahedin* (Dorronsoro 2005: 105). The mujahedin groups were subsequently discredited in the eyes of much of the Afghan population, however, after their failure to establish order after the collapse of the Soviet-backed government, descending instead into infighting, chaos, and banditry—a development that paved the way for the Taliban government. But their fate was not sealed by that failure. When the United States chose them as allies to overthrow the Taliban government, the mujahedin received an opportunity to restore their credentials and positions. The Bonn agreement in December 2001 reflected the mujahedin's restored power and was an early indicator that participation in the jihad against the Soviets would once again constitute a key mark of legitimacy. The preface of the agreement stated, "*Expressing* their appreciation to the Afghan mujahidin who, over the years, have defended the independence, territorial integrity and national unity of the country and have played a major role in the struggle against terror-ism and oppression, and whose sacrifice has now made them both heroes of jihad and champions of peace, stability and reconstruction of their beloved homeland, Afghanistan."

Their rehabilitation contributed to an ideological field where the defense of the nation was equated with the defense of religion, and where the mujahedin could stake out a claim to superiority by virtue of their status as national liberators, whereas an openly secular orientation was tantamount to treason. But already in 2001, protests had been voiced against the Bonn agreement's rehabilitation of the mujahedin, who had committed serious crimes, especially during the civil war of 1992–95. At the 2003 Constitutional Loya Jirga, one of the female delegates, Malalai Joya, strongly denounced the proceedings for giving a platform to warlords and war criminals, upon which her microphone was silenced and she was temporarily made to leave the Loya Jirga tent (Kuovo 2011). Nonetheless, human rights actors, including the Afghan Independent Human Right Commission (AIHRC), invested much of their efforts in a campaign to investigate and prosecute war crimes. Giv-en the dominance of war criminals in the post-2001 order, this amounted to an attempt to fundamentally change the political status quo. These efforts received a serious blow in 2007, when a number of MPs—former military commanders, most of them with mujahedin backgrounds, put forward a law that would grant themselves amnesty from prosecution of war crimes. Those who had embraced the vision of a new order based on human rights saw the law as a definite proof of the government's real power base—and the muted protests from Western embas-sies as evidence of the hollowness of Western pledges toward supporting a human rights agenda in the country (Suhrke 2011: 174). The episode also illustrated in stark terms that the mujahedin had solidified as a powerful political bloc. This was clearly expressed in a warning uttered by Abdul Rasool Sayyaf, a former com-mander of one of the mujahedin parties, during a rally against the amnesty law: "Whoever is against the mujahedin is against Islam, and they are the enemies of this country."

The efficiency displayed in passing the amnesty law was not representative of the overall workings of Parliament. Seldom did it exercise its authority to pro-pose legislation (Ahmadi 2016). This did not mean, however, that legislation was not produced; over two hundred laws were promulgated between 2001 and 2010 alone.[27] Most of these laws were presented to Parliament by government agencies or as presidential decrees, typically drafted by small groups of actors outside the government, who then used their connections to get the law tabled. This led to an extraordinary fragmentation of the legal framework, with a number of stand-alone pieces of criminal legislation on issues such as money laundering, terrorism, corruption, and violence against women. The law about violence against women (the EVAW law), which is the subject of the next chapter, embodied many of the contradictions that this kind of fragmentary lawmaking produced, such as inconsistency in the legal corpus as a whole. It also illustrated an opaque legislative process in which informal political connections took precedence over open debate.

Legal reform also entailed programs to rebuild and reform the administration of justice. At first, the justice sector had been somewhat neglected by the donor community, who instead focused their efforts on health, education, and strengthening the security forces. But donors soon came to believe that the justice sector had been overlooked and constituted a weak link in the international attempts to restructure the country—partly due to the pathetic efforts of the Italians who had been in charge in the early years after the U.S.-led invasion. A period of more extensive aid and a proliferation of activities intended to strengthen the rule of law followed, but it quickly led to Western disillusionment, as rapid results failed to materialize.

The 2004 Constitution had largely confirmed the three-tier court structure and the historical positions of the three justice institutions, the Supreme Court, the Attorney General, and the Ministry of Justice. The Supreme Court proved an assertive counterpart to the often chaotic international attempts to reform the justice system. As an institution, it wielded considerable power. It nominated judges for presidential appointment, oversaw court administration, ran the professional training course (the *stage* course[28]) for judges, served as the final court of appeal, and had the right to interpret the Constitution. A high percentage of criminal cases was appealed to the Supreme Court. As a result, the head of its criminal division presided over the outcome of almost all serious criminal cases in the country, making the division a powerful actor and potentially a target of attempts of bribery and other undue influence. During my fieldwork, I often heard about cases that had proceeded through due process at the lower courts, only to be obviously influenced at the Supreme Court level, resulting in acquittal or reduced sentencing.[29] This was particularly obvious when a government official stood accused of a crime.

The Supreme Court was generally considered a bastion of conservatism, at least by Western reformers, and especially during the tenure of Fazal Hadi Shinwari, the chief justice from 2001 to 2006. As testimony to the fact that the close relationship between the justice system and the religious establishment was still in place, Shinwari was also the leader of the national ulema council. The council was generally supportive of the president, and Shinwari had close ties to Abdul Rasool Sayyaf, a jihadi commander and Wahabist-inspired religious scholar with considerable power in the post-2001 settlement, and an important ally of Karzai. During his tenure, Shinwari—who had no formal qualifications beyond a madrassa education—established a religious council within the Supreme Court. The council issued a number of fatwas (binding religious opinions) that horrified liberal Westerners and Afghan human rights advocates.[30] In 2006, the donor community and some of its Afghan allies succeeded in placing a more moderate person, Abdul Salam Azimi, in the position as the chief justice. Azimi nevertheless proved disappointing to many of his backers. He spent a lot of his time abroad and was unable to carry out the substantive reforms his supporters had hoped for, including countering cronyism in judicial appointments and reorienting training and staff appointments in a more secular direction. It was evident that the Supreme Court exhibited a certain degree of esprit de corps. It was able to guard its autonomy against outside attempts to redesign criteria for professional requirements for its cadres, and it resisted encroachments on its jurisdiction. It proved less inclined to resist influence from the executive and proved a reliable ally to President Karzai, particularly in his attempts to sideline and influence Parliament. The profession as a whole was heavily dominated by men. In 2008, it was estimated that around 7 percent of sitting judges were female, a number that had increased to almost 8.5 percent by 2013 (IDLO 2014). Most female judges were presiding over family and juvenile courts (O'Hanlon and Sherjan 2010).

The attorney general's office (AGO) was also a powerful institution, appointing and overseeing prosecutors at all levels. Under the executive arm of the government, the office was responsible for investigating crimes, preparing them for trial, and prosecuting in court. The office had not undergone "restructuring" (as civil service reform was called)—as had the judges—and, as a consequence, had much lower salary levels. (An exception was the prosecutors working for the specialized units for crimes of violence against women (see chapter 3), some of whom received top-up salaries from their international supporters.)[31] Of the three justice institutions, the Ministry of Justice was the minor actor, tasked with overseeing the administration of the justice system and with drafting and reviewing laws through its *Taqnin* (legislation) department. But that role of the Ministry of Justice makes it central to many of the processes analyzed in this book, as will be explored in chapter 2.

After 2001, defense lawyers and legal aid featured as relatively new elements of the justice system. A national bar association was reestablished in 2008, and an Advocates Law promulgated, with the support of the International Bar Association. Numerous national and international organizations provided representation in court or legal advice for defenders, funded by international aid money. Although lawyers often complained that they received little respect—and sometimes faced outright hostility—from judges and prosecutors, the idea of legal representation appeared to gain traction over time. In general, lawyers had a noticeably different background than the other legal professions. Most were graduates from the secular law faculties, and many spoke English and held positions in foreign-funded NGOs. Some had gained reputations as fearless defenders of human rights, although a few of the legal aid organizations were perceived as mostly motivated by financial gains.

Expatriate advisors frequently lamented the lack of coordination that characterized the justice sector reform, but this state of affairs was, in large part, a product of the proliferation of aid. As Tamanaha points out, justice sector aid is not a field with an internal logic; it is better understood "as an agglomeration of projects perpetuated by motivated actors supported by funding" (Tamanaha, cited in Mason 2011b). More often than not, external support to the justice sector in Afghanistan took the form of what aid organizations and private contractors were able to secure funding for, rather than what national strategies or needs dictated. By 2010, Kabul was swamped with a number of short legal-training courses provided by various donors and organizations—many of which were criticized for being superficial, supply-driven, uncoordinated, and overly focused on criminal law. This kind of training was rarely evaluated and was typically conducted without a baseline, making it difficult to assess its impact. Generous per diems (daily allowances, ostensibly to cover travel, but in reality serving as a monetary incentive for staff to attend) made many institutions keen to secure training places for their staff, and this reinforced the appearance of a training *industry*. The three justice institutions often competed for funds and influence and, to a certain extent, succeeded in playing donors against each other. Most assertive was the Supreme Court, which blocked an attempt to establish a joint *stage* course for all legal professionals and, instead, negotiated a bilateral agreement with one of the donor agencies.

At the same time, the entire justice system was eroded from within by the proliferation of organized crime and the profitable narcotics trade—and, more generally, by a political system characterized by informality and patronage. As Giustozzi writes, Karzai, in expanding his power, was "not so much interested in institution building, as in the centralization of patronage" (Giustozzi 2009: 96). He and his family largely followed a kingly recipe of equating the expansion of state power with that of increased influence of the ruler and his inner circle (Forsberg 2010: 21). No group was permitted to become too strong or too independent from the government. The government's (or Karzai's) tenuous control over the countryside was achieved through a series of deals and accommodations with local power holders, many of whom had initially established their position as military strongmen in the immediate post-2001 period, often with the backing of international military forces.

Karzai repeatedly clashed with Western embassies and officials over appointments and policies as he worked to strengthen his own powerbase. The technocrats favored by Western donors, and who had often professed an ambitious reform agenda targeting nepotism and corruption, lost ground to more political actors, particularly members of *Hizb-e Islami*[32] and northern power brokers. The expansion of ISAF forces to the south of Afghanistan also brought tensions to the relationship between the Afghan president and his foreign allies. Karzai strongly condemned the civilian casualties caused by NATO military operations and resented what he saw as NATO countries' tendency to override his wishes and infringe upon the country's sovereignty.

When the Obama administration took office in 2009, it was evident that the NATO-led military coalition was in trouble. Attacks, primarily against coalition and Afghan forces and government officials, had risen yearly, and by the summer of 2009, more than half the country—including three of the four main roads out of the capital—was considered unsafe. The U.S. Defense Department was arguing for an expanded military operation (referred to as a "surge"), accompanied by higher levels of development aid to underwrite the military campaign. Others in Washington argued for a smaller U.S. military presence and a reduction of stated aims in Afghanistan—the abandonment of broader goals of development and state building. The outcome was a compromise, which gave the military much of its troop expansion, but on a limited time scale, with the U.S. president declaring that he wanted to start troop withdrawals after two years, in July 2011.

The military escalation took place under a particular counterinsurgency doctrine calling for all aspects of the international activities to support military efforts. As a result, international—and, in particular, United States—assistance was increasingly put in the service of a security agenda of stabilization and political outreach. The justice sector became conceptualized as a cornerstone of the war effort, with the U.S. military claiming that government shortcomings in this area were an important driver of the insurgency. The insurgents, for their part, were targeting justice officials as part of an overall campaign against the government. In many districts, posts went unfilled, and in many provincial capitals, judges and prosecutors were working under siege, holed up in fortified compounds and in fear for their lives. Paradoxically, it was in these areas that much of the aid agencies funded by the United States were told to focus their effort. One USAID official complained that they were instructed only to work in the south and east of the county, where it was impossible to get anything done because of insecurity. Judges were so afraid that they never left their compounds, and they spent their nights in the courthouse. Yet aid agencies had to continue to focus on these areas: "It's the military. They say, 'We want you there.'" Frustrated, the official said that he was hoping to be do something in north, but "low profile, so we don't upset the military guys."[33]

But the security situation continued to worsen, and the "state building" that was now considered integral to the war effort was bringing few results, at least not according to the military schedule. A considerable blow came with the Kabul Bank scandal in the autumn of 2010, when it emerged that supporters and officials in the Karzai administration had received close to a billion U.S. dollars in fraudulent loans from one of Afghanistan's main commercial banks. As Western frustrations grew, there were calls for the abandonment of professed goals of institution building, democratization, and development. It was claimed that Afghan culture and society were inherently unsuitable to "Western" institutions of governance, an argument that also absolved the West of any responsibility. The military, in particular, experimented with "traditional" institutions such as tribal councils. The urgency invested in reforming the legal system led to reinforced calls for international support to informal justice processes, amid claims that there was simply no time to wait for the formal system to develop. This saw the proliferation of international, ad hoc attempts to cultivate justice provisions through traditional councils and to formalize their status through a national framework. Overall, however, the objective of military victory was gradually replaced by one focused on enabling Afghan security forces to take over responsibility.

CONCLUSIONS

In late 2014, a considerably more pro-Western government, less inclined to publically question NATO's warfare, was inaugurated in Kabul—the so-called national unity government headed by Ashraf Ghani. The new government had been formed after a long and unusually disputed election process, characterized by high levels of fraud and uncertainty. Rather than arriving at a final result, the two contenders, Ashraf Ghani and Abdullah Abdullah, agreed to a power-sharing government brokered by the United States. Despite the unconstitutional nature of the arrangement, initial expectations of the new government were high. The new president, in particular, had run a campaign promising reform, economic development and to address corruption. Women activists found much hope in his rhetoric on gender issues and in the fact that his wife immediately took up a public role as the First Lady, whereas Karzai's wife had been secluded from public life. In the justice sector, some attempts at change were made. New appointments to the positions of chief justice and attorney general generally found favor with reformists. Ghani also made an attempt to uphold his election promise to appoint a female Supreme Court judge, but this pledge was left unfulfilled when Parliament refused to approve his nominee, Anisa Rasouli. In general, however, much of the first year of the new administration was spent wrangling over appointments, while the economy and the security situation deteriorated drastically. As I was writing this book, it remained to be seen to what extent Ghani presidency would be substantially different from the Karzai era when it came to gender politics and the legal sector. Karzai's presidency had been characterized by attempts to appease both conservative power bases and the demands of women's rights advocates and international donors in a highly personalized and unpredictable way. The starkest example was President Karzai's approach to the EVAW law, which is the subject of the next chapter.

One of the structuring assumptions of this book is that the ways in which gender relations are publically regulated are not determined by religion, culture, or other fixed societal attributes but are contingent on situational politics. Indeed, the historical sketch provided in this chapter shows close relations between attempts at sanctioning specific gender relations and broader political projects, whether it was the state centralization of Abdul Rahman Khan, the modernization of Amanullah, the socialist transformation of the PDPA, or the Islamist agenda of the Taliban. The infrastructure that the more routine regulation of gender relations depends on—the legal system—has similarly been shaped by specific historical trajectories. It is only by looking back at the tumultuous state-building history of Afghanistan that we can comprehend the origins of the unusual heterodoxy of the contemporary legal system, a heterodoxy that would prove to have important bearings on individual fates. By keeping a historical perspective, we can also more easily appreciate what was novel about the post-2001 order—an unprecedented international or external interest and intervention into the detailed working of the legal system, including its treatment of women. That such an interest did not translate into absolute power and often produced paradoxical outcomes will be detailed in the chapters that follow.

"Good Women Have No Need for This Law"

The Battles over the Law on Elimination of Violence against Women

On July 19, 2009, President Karzai signed two laws. One was a revised version of the Shia Personal Status Law, which had created an uproar both in Afghanistan and abroad for its conservative articles on gender relations.[1] Despite having undergone a review triggered by the protests of women's rights activists and international donors, the Shia law, as it was usually called, still contained a number of articles that these groups considered problematic. This final version appeared to sanction underage marriage, made women's right to marry dependent on their fathers' or grandfathers' permission, and constructed a marital relation in which wives were supposed to submit to sexual relations on demand—or risk forfeiting claims of maintenance from their husbands.[2] The other law signed that day, however, was considered a triumph by many women's rights activists. It was the Law on the Elimination of Violence against Women, *(Qanon-e maneh khoshonat alie zan)*, normally referred to as the EVAW law in English. Four years had been spent drafting it. It was unprecedented in Afghan history, listing twenty-two acts as violence against women and mandating punishments for them. It also obliged the government to take specific actions to prevent violence and to support victims.

The EVAW law was regarded as important because, unlike the existing Penal Code, it designated rape *(tajavoz-e jinsi)* as a crime distinct from consensual adultery, provided considerably stricter punishments for forced and underage marriage, and criminalized a number of violations of women's civil rights, such as the deprivation of inheritance or preventing a woman from pursuing work or an education. In general, the law was regarded by many as an important tool of advocacy, signaling that women were independent holders of rights and that the

Afghan state had an obligation to protect them from abuses at the hands of their families. Although the existing Penal Code covered crimes such as beating and murder, those who supported the new law argued that there was a tendency in legal practice and more broadly in Afghan society to view such acts as crimes only when they were committed by people outside the family. For its advocates, the new law was important because it explicitly stated that these acts were also punishable crimes when they took place within the family.[3]

In this chapter, I explore the significance of the EVAW law. I ask whether and to what extent the law challenged prevailing gender relations by making the state responsible for enforcing a new set of standards for women's rights. Did the EVAW law signal a transformation whereby women were constituted as legal persons in their own right, under state protection, and where family sovereignty over women was replaced—or at least modified—by that of the state? As my analysis will make clear, these questions cannot be answered unequivocally, and this ambiguity is an essential part of the story of the EVAW law.

After explaining the complicated history of the EVAW law, the chapter explores the substantive debates about the law, its actual text, and its proposed and accepted revisions. However the key to understanding the significance of the law is in the *processes* through which it was promoted and implemented. These processes demonstrate how meaningless it is to talk about a singular state authority in contemporary Afghanistan. In turn, this point carries important implications for the impact of both local and donor-driven women's rights activism in the country. The fact that the EVAW law was contradicted on several points by the Shia law, and yet President Karzai signed them both on the same day and at the same gathering was an indication of this. That the president should almost simultaneously sign two laws in direct contradiction with each other was remarkable. It was one sign that, even if ratified, the EVAW law would only serve as a partial and ambiguous framework for the public regulation of gender violence in Afghanistan.

I show why and how this was the case by tracing how the EVAW law was conceived, promoted, contested, revised, and implemented. Important aspects of women's rights activism, the logics of legal reform, and the political landscape in Afghanistan are revealed by chronicling and disentangling these processes. I find that the particular dynamics of these fields and their contingent interactions gave form to a partial "EVAW law assemblage". In the context of a polarized political climate, the intimidating ascendancy of jihadi leaders who were able to dominate broader public debate (empowered, to a great extent, by the international intervention *and* the resentment against it), external dependence, the precedent of getting laws passed through informal political pressure instead of consensus and debate, the importance of claiming personal credit, and the need to produce "output," the law's supporters eventually chose a discreet and top-down strategy. The supporters of the law abandoned their earlier attempts to get parliamentary approval and to rectify technical limitations in the text. Instead, the EVAW law was kept as a presidential decree and its technical weaknesses ignored for the moment. The mechanisms that were involved in the push for implementation of the law similarly revealed a top-down, discreet mode of action in which external support to some degree compensated for the lack of broader national anchoring.

THE TRAJECTORY OF THE EVAW LAW

At the time that the EVAW law was drafted, Afghanistan still had the civil and criminal codes dating from the late 1970s in place. The 1976 Penal Code included general provisions for murder, beating, and injury. These provisions did not differentiate between men and women, although in practice, intra-familial violence was normally regarded as less serious, if considered a crime at all. However, the 1976 Penal Code did include some provisions explicitly related to gender violence. Among these were an article significantly reducing punishment for "honor killings," some rather unclear provisions on the punishments for rape and adultery, and articles criminalizing the forced marriage of an adult woman. Article 398, for example, stipulated a significant reduction of the punishment in cases of murder if the victim was a relative or spouse caught in the act of adultery: "A person, defending his[4] honor *(namus)*, who sees his spouse, or another of his close relations, in the act of committing adultery or being in the same bed as another and immediately kills or injures one or both of them, shall be exempted from punishment for laceration and murder but shall be imprisoned or punished for a period not exceeding two years, as a *Taziri* punishment."

Section 2, chapter 8: "Adultery, Sodomy, and Violation of Honor"[5] contained provisions regarding rape and adultery. First of all, article 426 provided for *hadd* punishments (stoning or lashing) of adultery, stating that if in the crime of adultery "the conditions for *hadd* are not fulfilled[6] or the charge of *hadd* is dropped, . . . the offender shall be punished according to the provisions of this article." Articles 427–28 went on to set out the *tazir* punishments for "adultery and sodomy" (long-term imprisonment, i.e., no less than five years and no more than fifteen)[7] and various aggravating conditions. The use of the term *zina* (adultery) to seemingly include both rape and consensual sex outside of marriage (both premarital and extramarital sex), means that there was effectively no legal distinction between consensual adultery and rape in the code. In addition, article 429, perhaps referring to attempted rape or sexual assault, stated that a person who, "through violence, threat or deceit, violates the chastity *(namus)* of another or initiates the act" shall be sentenced to long-term imprisonment, not exceeding seven years. Finally, article 517 criminalized forced marriage (but only when the woman involved was of majority age). It also provided for stricter punishments if forced marriage happened under the pretext of *baad*.

Rather than amending this existing legal framework, a group of women's rights advocates, Afghan bureaucrats, and U.N. officials came to the conclusion that the most effective way to address the issue of violence against women would be to create a new law altogether, one that would directly criminalize a number of forms of violence and abuse. Most of my informants traced the first conceptions of the law to meetings in a commission established in 2005 by the Ministry of Women's Affairs (MOWA) and UNIFEM to coordinate government responses to violence against women. The EVAW Commission, as it was called, was modeled on U.N.-directed efforts to combat violence against women elsewhere, which was, in turn, part of a broader global campaign against gender violence. Along with members from MOWA and UNIFEM, the commission also included members from other government officials, including female judges and prosecutors, representatives of different U.N. agencies, and various staff working at NGOs that focused on women's rights and the justice system. The commission often discussed reprehensible individual cases, and soon a consensus emerged that a new law that explicitly criminalized violence and abuses against women was needed.

Subsequently, and rather swiftly, the first version of the EVAW law was drafted by the legal department of MOWA. MOWA then officially submitted the draft to the *Taqnin* ("legislation"[8]) department in the Ministry of Justice on the International Women's Day in 2006. UNIFEM (who had a large program on gender-based violence and also worked closely with MOWA on various issues) and many of the civil society organizations in Kabul had not been included in the drafting process, something that they viewed as an attempt by MOWA to retain control over the law as its own initiative. This was to be one of several incidents where MOWA's complicated relationship with NGOs and women's rights activists, often one of mistrust and sometimes competition, manifested itself.

Mandated in the 2001 Bonn peace agreement, MOWA was charged with mainstreaming gender into the policies and programs of other government ministries and quickly became a focal point for gender targeted donor assistance. The ministry, which had no core budget, was filled with a number of foreign advisors and Afghan "embeds" (Afghan staff from international organizations who were on assignment at the ministry), and its achievements would prove modest. It suffered from what was probably a deliberate strategy of ministerial appointments from President Karzai, who did not want a strong minister in a controversial field, and it was completely dependent on donor funding.[9]

The bulk of the implementation of the gender interventions was subcontracted to a myriad of international and national NGOs and private contracting companies. Some of these were staffed or led by Afghanistan's fragmented local women's rights activists, many of whom had recently returned to the country after living as refugees in neighboring countries, especially Pakistan. Staff at MOWA accused foreign-funded NGOs of resisting government coordination and operating according to their own whims. The latter contended that MOWA attempted to monopolize the gender field and did little to solicit the opinions and skills of civil society. The tensions between MOWA and the NGOs would culminate in a 2011 standoff over the status of the women's shelters (detailed in chapter 4), but they also played a role in the development of the EVAW law. The fact that MOWA had drafted and submitted the EVAW law without including NGO staff, many of whom worked with shelters or provided legal aid to abused women, had upset members of this community. One of the Afghan activists later told me, "In 2005, MOWA started to draft a law. They invited the Supreme Court, Kabul University, people from the Ministry of Justice. This law was more like a code of ethics, very vague, a very weak law. They were hiding it from civil society. Actually civil society only got a copy of it around [International] Women's Day, when the draft was presented to the media."[10]

In a bid to create a stronger law, a group of civil society activists—the Afghan Women's Network, the Afghan Independent Human Rights Commission, Rights and Democracy, Humanitarian Assistance for the Women and Children of Afghanistan—together with UNIFEM, started to work on a revised draft, reluctantly presented by MOWA to the *Taqnin* in late 2007.[11] Shortly thereafter, however, yet another draft was submitted, this one by the Women's Affairs Commission of Parliament. This draft, no more than four pages long, was perceived by other participants in the process as a blatant attempt by the female MP chairing the commission, Qadria Yazanpardast, to counter criticism that she could point to no tangible achievements so far in her role as chair. She denied this, stating that she had been unaware of the drafts others had produced and merely had wanted to give Afghan women "a gift on Women's Day."[12]

The *Taqnin* set out to create a single version from the three competing drafts, effectively discarding the third, short draft from the Women's Affairs Commission. In early 2009, as the *Taqnin* was nearing the completion of its work on the EVAW law, concern over the Shia Personal Status Law was deepening and women's rights activists and donors started to look to the EVAW law as a possible counterbalance. The Shia law had created a storm in Afghanistan and abroad when details about it leaked to the international press. The law had its origin in the Constitution's article 131, which recognized the right of Shias to apply their own jurisprudence in matters of family law. This was a breakup of the monopoly that Sunni jurisprudence had hitherto maintained in official Afghanistan, and to many Shias, it represented a historic recognition of their existence. Predictably, when an initiative to codify a personal status law based on Shia (Jafari) jurisprudence got underway, it quickly became entangled in identity politics (Oates 2009; Chaudhary, Nemat, and Suhrke 2011). Drafted under the supervision of prominent Shia cleric Asif Mohseni, seemingly on his own initiative, the law was an excessively detailed and conservative codification of Jafari *fiqh*. Among its contentious articles were provisions compelling wives to sleep with their husbands every fourth night and to apply makeup on their husbands' request, articles stating that women could not leave the house without their husbands' permission and that obedience and sexual submission were obligatory in order to receive maintenance, and a number of articles permitting marriage with underage girls.

The Shia law passed through Parliament in obscure circumstances, prevented from proper distribution and discussion. Many Shia MPs were told that the important thing was to get a separate family law for Shias and that questioning the content of the law should be avoided, because it would risk derailing the entire process. Conservative Sunni MPs argued that, as Sunnis, it was not right for them to debate the law, and MPs with a more secular outlook struggled to obtain copies of the draft and to find out when and where debates about it were taking place (Chaudhary, Nemat, and Suhrke 2011). As the law was quickly passed in both houses of Parliament and was signed into force by the president, details about it eventually appeared in the international press, creating outrage in Western countries (Boone 2009; Gall and Rahimi 2009). At this point, human rights networks in Kabul, who had been trying to mobilize attention to the Shia law, received a sudden explosion of international support. However, by then, these networks had experienced much difficulty in accessing the process around the Shia law—obtaining the current version of it, finding out where in the parliamentary system it was, and even engaging with the text, which was complicated and full of Arabic legal terminology. Given the difficulties they had faced in attempting to revise the Shia law, the networks had started to think of the EVAW law as a counterpoise to the Shia law. This line of reasoning was made possible by the fact that the EVAW law, like many laws promulgated at the time, contained an article stating, "The provisions of this law, if contradicted with provisions of other laws, shall prevail" (article 43).

That the EVAW law could prevail over the Shia law was evidently also an idea that President Karzai and the minister of justice found convenient. They were keen to placate the constituencies who had promoted the Shia law, but at the same time, they needed to address the anger of women's rights activists and the donor community. Signing the EVAW law instead of revising the Shia law meant that they would stay clear of accusations of giving in to Western pressure. Thus the logic presented at the gathering on July 19, when the president had assembled a handful of female politicians and officials, was that the Shia law would be invalidated by the EVAW law. One of those present, a female MP, later told me that when she pointed out that the Shia law still contained problematic articles, they tried to "bribe" her with the EVAW law. Finding little support from the others present, she eventually endorsed the signing of both laws.

> When I was in the office of the president, he asked me if I was happy with the [Shia] law. I said, "We are very happy, Mr. President, but there are some articles that we

would still like to change." The Shia law had an article about orphans that seemed to permit child marriage, and I had suggested that to avoid this, there should be a minimum age of marriage at sixteen, or at least fifteen. I also raised the article that linked maintenance with obedience, the right of the husband to not give food if the woman is not obedient. [I said,] "In Iran, this article has proved difficult, because what exactly does it mean to be disobedient, and who can prove it? So, in the end, they removed the article. We should do the same in Afghanistan. Also, polygamy should not be unconditional, but by permission of the court."

I spoke about these things, and the president said, Okay, I will send it back one more time to the [Shia] ulema. [Another woman present] then said, "No, it's okay. Don't send it back; Mosheni will be upset." The minister of justice was saying, "Look, you have the EVAW law." They were trying to bribe me with the EVAW law. All of them were saying that the Shia law is okay. What could I do? And [the minister in charge of] MOWA was there, but she did not say anything."[13]

The Shia Personal Status Law had already been ratified by Parliament, but the signing of the EVAW law was based on article 79 of the Constitution, which allowed room for the president to adopt legislation during parliamentary recess in "emergency situations." Decrees signed by the president in this vein became laws upon signing but were to be submitted to Parliament within thirty days of the first session of the National Assembly, who would then have the power to reject the laws. Whether the circumstances at this time qualified as an "emergency situation" was perhaps debatable. The main motivation of the president was perceived as the need to placate constituencies who had protested the Shia law, and they, in turn, tended to see the signing of the EVAW law to be more important than procedural issues.

The EVAW law was then duly sent to the Parliament for review and ratification. Supporters of the law became increasingly worried that it would suffer significant revisions at the hands of conservative MPs that would dilute the value of the law or even turn it into an instrument of repression of women. Some people suggested that it would be better to withdraw it from Parliament and keep it as a presidential decree for the time being—or to arrange a deal with the speaker to quickly introduce it to the plenary on a day when important conservative MPs were absent. But the Women's Affairs Commission in the Lower House, tasked with preparing the law for plenary debate, instead sought to follow due process. Its chair, Fawzia Koofi, distributed the law to all the eighteen parliamentary commissions, which would send representatives to the Joint Commission, where the law would be discussed before it was brought to general debate.

The parliamentary proceedings were also a final opening for international legal professionals from the Criminal Law Reform Working Group (CLRWG) to improve the EVAW law in technical terms. This was a joint Afghan and international group, chaired by the United Nations Office for Drugs and Crime (UNODC) and mandated to ensure consistency and coherence in the field of Afghan criminal law, where a number of standalone pieces of legislation were being introduced. The group had already submitted comments on the EVAW law earlier, when *Taqnin* had forwarded them a draft, but their comments had been mostly ignored. Now, having—in their words—"intercepted the law" in its new version, when it had been discussed at one of the regular gender coordination meetings for donors and aid agencies in Kabul, they were unsettled when they discovered that the law still contained technical flaws.[14] However, among the Afghan women's rights activists and MPs who had supported the law from its inception, there was little interest in introducing revisions at this point. They argued that the chief purpose of the law was to make a political statement: to create awareness of the problem of violence and abuses against women and to make a stand against impunity for such acts. Introducing changes now—especially if they appeared to come from foreign quarters—was too risky and could play into the hands of conservative opponents.

After the individual committees had submitted their proposed amendments, the law was discussed in Joint Commission meetings. Early on, a dividing line between the liberal and mainly female MPs and a smaller group of conservative male MPs, led by Qazi Nazir Hanafi from Herat, who mostly had jihadi backgrounds, became evident. As will be described in more detail below, discussions crystallized around three issues: the question of beating, which some claimed was sanctioned, up to a point, by the Quran and was therefore beyond discussion; the right of fathers to marry off their underage daughters; and conditions for polygamy. The atmosphere in the meetings became increasingly aggressive as a larger number of conservative MPs started to attend. In the end, the meetings were suspended, after a verbal fight between a representative from the Ministry of Women's Affairs, brought in by the Committee on Women's Affairs, and a male MP belonging to the jihadi group. Following an exchange of insults, the conservative MPs all walked out, declaring that an affront to one of them was an insult to them all. They refused to return to discussions until a personal apology was offered and until their remaining demands were met. These demands centered on waiving the need for a husband to get the permission of his first wife for polygamous marriages, amending provisions that could be interpreted as limiting a husband's prerogative in terms of sexual access to his wife, an exemption for fathers regarding imprisonment in cases of underage marriage, and the use of fines as punishments, which they argued was un-Islamic.[15]

The clashes in the Joint Commission gave ammunition to those who had suggested that the law was better left as a presidential decree and that the parliamentary process should be abandoned. They argued that the law risked being rejected outright, which would mean that the presidential decree that had enacted the EVAW law would become null and void. Even if this did not happen, the revisions demanded by conservative MPs could result in a much weaker law than what had been secured through the presidential decree. Key female MPs in the

Women's Affairs Committee, who insisted that the law should remain on Parliament's agenda, such as Fawzia Koofi and Sabrina Saqeb, were accused of using the parliamentary ratification process to put their stamp on the law and to claim credit for delivering it, even if this could mean losing the EVAW law altogether.

Western embassies were becoming similarly frustrated over the parliamentary process. They had lobbied parliamentarian powerbrokers such as speaker Yunus Qanooni to get the law approved in Parliament, but to no avail, and several members of the diplomatic community in Kabul told me that it might perhaps be preferable to leave it as a presidential decree for the time being.[16] By early 2010, the original supporters the EVAW law had succeeded in removing it from the parliamentary agenda. At this point, supportive government officials, women's organizations, and donors were already working to support the implementation of the law as it had been decreed, and reports of prosecutions based on the law were starting to trickle in.

Yet this was not the end of the parliamentary tussles over the EVAW law. In 2011, following the 2010 parliamentary elections, Fawzia Koofi reintroduced the law to the Joint Commission—many of the members of which were now newly elected MPs. Several of the questions over which there had been disagreement were reopened, such as polygamy and forced and underage marriage. As before, Qazi Hanafi and his legislation commission in Parliament[17] were the law's most ardent critics, and on some issues, fronts had hardened. Meetings were often conducted solely between Fawzia Koofi and Qazi Hanafi, with other MPs unclear about the exact process being made. When, in the spring of 2013, Fawzia Koofi stated her intention to introduce the EVAW law to a plenary vote, other MPs and civil society groups protested that they had little sense of whether the law would pass or be rejected. Despite their campaign to make Fawzia Koofi change her mind—or in other ways remove the law from the parliamentary agenda—Fawzia Koofi proceeded to introduce the law to the plenary on May 18, 2013. She had claimed in advance that she had persuaded Qazi Hanafi to be absent,[18] but if that was the case, she had miscalculated badly. Hanafi and like-minded MPs were there and made several inflammatory remarks, calling the law contrary to Islam and suggesting that its ratification would lead to revolution on the streets. After only fifteen minutes, speaker Abdul Raof Ibrahimi declared the debate over, saying that a special commission should be formed in order to investigate whether the law was in accordance with Islam.

Fawzia Koofi, badly discredited by the failed initiative, made no further attempts to introduce the law for ratification. Internationally, the truncated debate was reported as a sign that Afghan women's rights were in the process of backsliding (Sethna 2013; Arghandiwal and Aziz 2013). This was because the EVAW law—despite never having been approved in Parliament, had gradually come to gain the status, both internationally and nationally, as the singular most important achievement of the Afghan women's rights community. Significant funds had been allocated toward the dissemination of, training for, and monitoring of the law. It had featured prominently in Afghanistan's first CEDAW report, submitted in 2011, and its implementation was a high-up item in donor assessments of overall progress in the country. The fifteen-minute debate in Parliament was thus perceived by many as a massive setback. This was the case even if, technically, the debate had actually done nothing to change the status of the law one way or the other.

"WHAT IS THE BASIS FOR THIS LAW?" DISCURSIVE STRATEGIES AND HIERARCHIES

Having sketched the trajectory of the EVAW law from its initial conception to its possible demise, I now turn to the debates over its content. Below I explore which articles proved most contentious, the discursive parameters of the various forums where the law was discussed, and what this says about the intersections of gender and broader fields of power.

The Text of the EVAW Law

The law that was enacted as a decree in July 2009 and served as the basis of the discussions in Parliament consisted of forty-four articles. It enumerated twenty-two forms of violence against women and provided punishments for them, which ranged from fines and various lengths of imprisonment to the death penalty, the latter in cases where the victim was killed as a result of a sexual assault.

Forms of Violence Listed in the EVAW Law

1. Rape
2. Forced prostitution
3. Publicizing the identity of a victim in a damaging way
4. Burning or use of chemical substances
5. Forcing a woman to commit suicide or to self-immolate
6. Causing injury or disability
7. Beating
8. Selling and buying women for the purpose of or under pretext of marriage
9. *Baad* (giving away a woman or girl to settle a dispute)
10. Forced marriage
11. Preventing the choice of husband
12. Marriage before the legal age
13. Cursing, humiliation, or intimidation
14. Harassment or persecution
15. Forced isolation
16. Forced drug consumption

17. Denial of inheritance rights
18. Denial of the right to property
19. Denial of the right to education, work, and access to health services and other rights provided by law
20. Forced labor
21. Marrying more than one wife without observing Article 86 of the Civil Code
22. Denial of relationship

Of physical acts, the EVAW law named rape, statutory rape, immolation and acid attacks, beating, and violence leading to injury or disability as acts of violence against women. The punishments for these crimes were stipulated mostly by reiterating the punishments already provided in the Penal Code. However, whereas the Penal Code had been unclear about whether rape was a crime distinguishable from adultery (i.e., if one of the parties could be considered an innocent and violated victim of the act), the EVAW law differentiated between rape and adultery by using the term *tajavoz-e jinsi* (literally, "sexual violation") to refer to rape. Unlike *zina, tajavoz-e jinsi* was not a term originating in Islamic *fiqh* (on *fiqh*, see chap. 1, n. 2); it was a newer term in Afghanistan, used mainly in colloquial and media discourse to refer to rape.[19]

The EVAW law stated that if a person commits rape *(tajavoz-e jinsi)* of an adult woman, the offender "shall be sentenced to continued imprisonment in accordance with the provision of article 426 of the Penal Code," and if it results in the death of the victim, the perpetrator "shall be sentenced to the death penalty" (article 17).[20] It also stated that consensual sexual relations with an underage girl should be punished in the same way as rape. The law was therefore significant in making rape a crime distinguishable from adultery and in making statutory rape (sexual relations with a minor girl) a crime on par with rape.

As for punishments for causing injury and disability, the EVAW law merely reiterated specific articles in the Penal Code. In the view of some, simply referring to the Penal Code made parts of the EVAW law superfluous, since it was repeating punishments already provided in existing laws. However, many civil society supporters of the EVAW law argued that it was nevertheless important to have a law that specifically stated that punishments would apply equally if the victim of violence was female. In existing legal practice, this was often not the case, they argued, especially when a woman was abused by a family member.

In addition to the forms of physical violence already mentioned in the Penal Code, the EVAW law, more controversially, made a number of more minor offenses punishable. A person who beats a woman but causes no damages or injury was to be imprisoned for no more than three months (article 23), harassment or persecution of a woman was to be punishment by a prison sentence of no less than three months (article 30), and the same punishment was provided for those guilty of verbal abuse, degradation, and even cursing a woman (article 29).

As with the existing legal framework, forced marriage and *baad* (giving away a woman or girl in marriage as compensation or as a conciliatory gesture) were deemed punishable offenses. However, the punishments provided for these crimes in the EVAW law were considerably stricter, a minimum of two years imprisonment for forced marriage and up to ten year for the act of *baad*. Moreover, the EVAW law also criminalized underage marriage, selling a woman for the purpose of marriage, and preventing a woman from marrying according to her choice. The law also specified numerous other violations of the Civil Code and civil matters as punishable offenses. Polygamy in breach of the conditions set out in the 1977 Civil Code[21] was to be punished by a short-term imprisonment of no less than three months. Depriving a woman of her inheritance or property, denial of an actual familial or marital relationship to a woman (for whatever purpose), prohibiting a woman from pursuing an education or work, forcing her into isolation (for instance, by stopping her from seeing her parents), and forcing her to use narcotics were all to be punished with short prison sentences of one to six months. In addition, forced labor was to be punished with a six-month imprisonment, and forcing a woman into prostitution or to commit suicide was to be punished with prison for up to ten years.

Debates Prior to the Final Decree of the Law

Before the EVAW law was decreed in July 2009, it went through a number of changes.[22] For instance, the draft that had been prepared by civil society activists and UNIFEM, which had been handed over to the *Taqnin,* contained elaborate and quite radical provisions, such as protective rulings and restraining orders and the suggestion that domestic violence could be prosecuted without a complaint from the victim.[23] This draft also went much further in attempting to diminish the power of husbands over their wives. Article 53 made marital rape a crime, stating that "any intercourse with a wife without her consent is considered rape." It said that polygamy was to be subject to the approval of the courts, who would seek the first wife's approval, and in any case, a second marriage could be approved only if the first wife was barren, insane, or seriously ill. Violations would be punishable with up to five years in prison. The draft stated that rape victims could not be detained or tried for *zina,* and that husbands accusing their wives of not having been virgins when they married could be punished for the *hadd* crime of *qazf* (slander, false accusation of *zina*).[24] The draft also abrogated article 398 of the Penal Code, which made the killing of adulterous female relatives a minor crime.

MOWA was uncomfortable with many of these provisions. In interviews with me, MOWA staff recalled the civil society draft as being too far removed from Islamic law. The head of MOWA's legal department—one of the main initiators of the law—told me that she thought that the civil society draft had been influenced by foreigners (i.e., Westerners) and, as a result, did not sufficiently incorporate sharia. This, she felt, would reflect badly upon MOWA, who had officially submitted the law, and could put her ministry in conflict with the Supreme Court and the ulema council.

> Civil society made their own draft. They had included some input from foreigners and, as a result, the draft was not based on sharia. . . . Seeing that there was no reference to sharia, I refused to present this draft as a MOWA draft. . . . If we had accepted that, it could have created some problems for MOWA. What I suggested was that— okay, as we had already sent the MOWA draft [to *Taqnin*], I can help civil society to send a copy of their draft to *Taqnin* as well, [and] as [a] result, the final law will be even more enriched, as material from this draft could also be used.[25]

In the end, the law that was finalized by *Taqnin* in early 2009 was a much shorter and simplified version, and it did not include the more radical provisions from civil society. It also had some technical shortcomings, which was what most international agencies focused on in their subsequent work with the law. Representatives of UNIFEM, UNAMA, and UNODC protested what they argued was excessive and unenforceable criminalization, such as the inclusion of verbal degradation and cursing as crimes and up to twenty years imprisonment for sexual harassment like groping.[26] Some of the language in the law was impossible to work with, they said, such as the terms "forced prostitution" or "forced suicide."[27] They also wanted the EVAW law to explicitly amend existing provisions in the Penal Code when the two laws differed, arguing that not doing so would lead to a contradictory legal framework causing confusion for judges and prosecutors. Moreover, since the law focused only on crimes against women, U.N. legal advisors argued that it created a loophole in which sexual violence and assault against boys and men were effectively decriminalized. They suggested that the law be renamed the Law on Elimination of Violence against Women and Sexual Violence.[28] Additionally, they proposed that the law define rape in specific terms: "the penetration of the vagina, anus or mouth with an object or body part, accompanied by violence, threat or deceit."[29]

These suggestions were mainly rejected by the *Taqnin* and the Afghan women's rights activists who had been promoting the law. The head of the *Taqnin*,[30] an experienced and generally respected official who had worked in the Ministry of Justice for decades, explained to me that he had thought the suggestions to amend the Penal Code was unrealistic and would complicate matters, when there was an imminent need for the EVAW law due to the suffering of Afghan women. He also thought that the suggestion to include a physical definition of rape would have pushed the sensitivities of Afghan society too far. It would have been very embarrassing for the *Taqnin*, he argued, to present such phrases to, for instance, the Supreme Court.[31] Moreover, according to the view of the *Taqnin*, the EVAW law did not decriminalize sexual violence against boys and men, as this was already included in the Penal Code and still valid.

The Afghan women's rights activists who discussed the international inputs also objected to many of the suggestions. They argued that to specifically repeal or amend other laws would not be accepted by the *Taqnin* or the legislators and, as a result, the law would be rejected in its totality. For instance, one senior Afghan staff member at an international women's rights organization stated that the judges who had implemented the Penal and Civil Codes for years (and sometimes decades) believed that these laws "were written in stone" and would revolt against open attempts to amend them. He reasoned it would be unwise for the activist organizations to "make [their] intentions clear" by explicitly announcing that some of the articles in the EVAW law were, in fact, different from those of the existing laws. It was better to simply refer to the Penal Code—or, in the cases where the EVAW law differed from the Penal Code, to make separate provisions without specifically amending the latter. And since the EVAW law contained an article stating that it overrode all other laws, this would not be a problem.[32]

The disagreements between the international legal experts and the Afghan officials and activists reflected a different understanding of the purpose of the law. Whereas the former emphasized the need for a technically sound law and one that was in line with other laws in terms of punishments, the latter were focused on the symbolic and political impact of the law. They argued that given the widespread discrimination against women in Afghanistan, a law that was solely for them and that provided harsh punishments would go some way in rebalancing their position in society and the legal system, even if it could not be implemented in full.[33] This line of argument also testified to a top-down way of thinking about political change, a point to which I will return below.

"Good Women Do Not Need This Law": Discussions in Parliament

Many of the people who had supported the EVAW law were worried that it would meet with considerable resistance in Parliament, and as it turned out, their fears proved justified. During the autumn of 2009, seven meetings were held in the Joint Commission debating the law.[34] The Women's Commission, tasked with chairing the meetings and functioning as a secretariat for the revisions in Parliament, had added their own revisions to the law. These were minor and without consequences for the overall protection and rights afforded to women in the version that had been decreed that summer. Indeed, one of the members of the commission confided that some of revisions were silly and had been put there simply so that they could be easily removed in order to show flexibility to their adversaries.[35] In addition, the other commissions had reviewed the law, and some—three in total—had submitted proposed amendments in writing. Of these, the amendments submitted by the Legislation Commission of Parliament were the most comprehensive. Its representative in the joint discussions, Qazi Nazir Ahmed Hanafi—a former *mujahed* from Herat—emerged as the leader of the conservative MPs who sought

to block the law or amend it significantly.[36] The proposed amendments by the Legislation Commission, which would be the focal points of discussions in the Joint
Commission, centered around reinstating in the EVAW law the prerogatives of
husbands and fathers over their wives and daughters, justified by references to the
Quran and Islamic jurisprudence. They included objections to a set minimum age
for marriage, as it was argued that sharia law permits marriage of a girl when she
has reached maturity (i.e., puberty); the right of a father to marry off his underage
daughter without her consent; the right of a husband to demand that his wife not
leave the house without his permission; the right of a husband to beat his wife under certain conditions, as stipulated by sharia; and the right of a husband to marry
several wives, provided he observes justice between them.[37] The amendments also
took issue with the tendency in the law to impose prison sentences for actions
such as cursing or preventing a marriage, arguing that these matters should not be
criminalized and that, in general, the law risked "breaking up the family" through
excessive use of imprisonment.

The first item of controversy that arose in the discussions was the question of
beating or battery *(lat-e kop)*. Arguing that the Holy Quran prescribes beating as
a last resort in cases where the wife disobeys her husband, several MPs claimed
that article 5(7), which listed beating as a form of violence, was therefore contrary
to the Quran.[38] Although everyone present agreed that beating resulting in visible
injury was not permissible, the head of the Legislation Commission and others
contended that it was unclear whether or not the article also prohibited what they
saw as quranically prescribed beating, and, therefore, the article was problematic.
Going against the Holy Quran simply based on the wishes of a few random women
was unacceptable, the Legislation Commission stated in their submitted amendments.[39] While some protested this literal reading of the Quran and argued that it
was outdated, it was agreed that *beating* should be defined in such a way that it was
clear that it did not refer to the quranically prescribed disciplinary action. However, at a later meeting, when the head of the Legislation Commission was absent,
the article was quickly approved in its original form.

Another controversy in the discussions was over the marriage of underage girls
and the prerogative of fathers to arrange marriages for their daughters against
their will, an issue that resurfaced several times. With reference to the rights of
guardianship in Hanafi *fiqh*, it was suggested, first, that setting a minimum age for
marriage was against sharia and, second, that in cases in which girls were young
and wanted to marry "inappropriately," fathers were better positioned to make
decisions about their marriage and hence should be permitted to override their
daughters' choices and force them to marry someone more appropriate—(one MP
offered the example of a daughter wanting to marry a man of a lower class: "Do you
want to marry your daughter to someone smelly and dirty, someone who cleans
toilets?").[40] The amendment submitted by the Legislation Commission read: "If

the father is fully authorized [competent] and considers all aspects of the marriage and gives the dowry to his daughter, the girl's refusal shall not be accepted, as her foresight about the future is much less than her father's."[41] This text was not incorporated, but the Joint Commission agreed that "kind fathers and grandfathers" should be exempted for punishments for arranging an underage marriage.[42]

The question of the extent to which polygamy should be regulated—and to what extent breaches of such regulations punished—was another matter where the women MPs met with vehement opposition from the conservatives. In its written amendments, the Legislation Commission had stated, "Marrying more than more wife is not violence, it is a [natural] sexual drive (khast-e jinsi). Considering marrying more than one wife violence is contrary to the provisions of the Holy Quran."[43] Female MPs argued that the conditions under which polygamy could be permitted were not stricter than what was already stated in the Civil Code, though they conceded that two years' imprisonment for breaches—a suggestion they had themselves made—was perhaps somewhat excessive. At the time that discussions in Parliament broke down later that autumn, there was still no agreement on the article on polygamy.

Article 17, on rape, was contested by some of the conservative MPs, who argued that the punishment was too strict. In particular, they protested that the law undermined a husband's right to intercourse with his wife, even if there was no explicit mention of rape within marriage in the law. In general, the conservative male MPs questioned the need for stricter and better-specified punishments for rape (including a ban on presidential pardons on rapes and some other crimes). The background to the proposed ban on presidential pardons was a series of high-profile rape cases in which the convicted perpetrators had been set free by pardons issued by President Karzai or the opaque workings of the Supreme Court, after serving only a brief period of their sentence. Many of the women in the Joint Commission wanted to keep this ban in the EVAW law (and, in private, some even proposed the death penalty for rape). But the male conservative MPs argued that such a ban was unconstitutional. They also worried that because the law dealt only with rape and did not mention consensual zina, it suggested that the latter was not an offense at all.

As the discussions proceeded, different female MPs suggested some additional acts that should be added to the twenty-two forms of violence against women that the decree had listed. Two of these were readily accepted in the Joint Commission: the nonpayment of maintenance (nafaqa, a wife's allowance, normally to cover necessities such as food, clothes, and medicine) and preventing a woman from exercising her political rights.[44] A third suggestion, however, proved more controversial: honor killing (qatl-e namus). In fact, it was to be the issue over which discussions broke down. The Taqnin department in the Ministry of Justice had removed honor killing from an earlier draft, arguing that the crime of murder was already covered in the Penal Code. In Parliament, there were no suggestions to amend article 398 of the Penal Code, which reduced punishment for the killing of female family members and their lovers caught in flagrante delicto to a maximum of two years imprisonment. Everyone was apparently in agreement that there was such a thing as "real" or legitimate honor killing when a man discovered his wife or female relative in the act of adultery. Rather, the problem was over a man who killed his wife or female family member and then falsely or casually claimed that she had been engaged in an adulterous act. The representative of the *Taqnin* and the conservative male MPs contended that this act simply amounted to murder and was already covered in the Penal Code. To single it out as a special category of crime in the EVAW law was unprecedented in Afghan legislation and, moreover, actually amounted to eroding women's legal protection. Female parliamentarians and representatives of MOWA argued that because this kind of murder was so common, it should be included in the EVAW law so that the difference between legitimate and illegitimate honor killings could be explained, and the latter punished appropriately. As one female MP stated, "In so many cases, there was no [sexual] relation—there was no bed—but the woman was killed. This is a problem, and we should not ignore it. What is the punishment for those who kill their innocent daughter?"[45]

Eventually, in the last meeting, most participants agreed that in cases of honor killing, the EVAW law would state that if article 398 of the Penal Code was not applicable (i.e., if the woman was not directly caught in the act of adultery), the perpetrator should be punished for the crime of murder. This was a remarkable concession from the women's side—an agreement that men could take the law into their own hands when "real" honor was at stake. But before they could proceed further, one of the conservative male MPs declared that he did not agree with the proposed solution. Why this was the case never became clear, because the discussion suddenly escalated. A representative of MOWA quickly retorted that his agreement or disagreement did not matter, as the majority was in concord. The MP, infuriated, started insulting the MOWA representative: "You are a prostitute! You have given money to get this position. Unlike you, I am a representative of the people!" To which she responded, "You are the one who gave money to get your position! You gave banquets to get votes. I am a professor, a teacher. I do not care for illiterate men like you."[46] In a show of loyalty to a fellow *mujahed*,[47] the conservative male MPs all got up and left the room, stating, as they departed, "We shall see how you will be able to pass this law in the plenary." Bewildered, the female MPs apologized to the MOWA representative, but they asked her not to attend any further meetings. "These men are used to us," they said. "We know how to deal with them, but they do not accept outsiders."

In 2011, a year and a half later, when the discussions were reopened, many of the MPs were new, and the original decree from 2009 was used as the starting point.[48] It was the same issues that caused debate: underage and forced marriage, polygamy, and the question of "permissible" beating. In addition, following the 2011 controversy over the women's shelters (see chapter 4), the shelters had now become one of the issues where Hanafi's commission refused to compromise. Rather than by shelters, the commission proposed that victims of violence should be protected by parents or other *mahram* individuals,[49] under the supervision of a judge.[50] Although Fawzia Koofi later claimed that the Joint Commission, through personal meetings between herself and Hanafi, had reached agreement on everything but a minimum age of marriage, most of these issues resurfaced during the plenary debate in May 2013, where several conservative MPs protested the law's restrictions on polygamy, permissible beating, and forced marriage, as well as its references to women's shelters.

The discussions over the EVAW law had revealed particular discursive hierarchies and strategies. Occupying absolute authority in the discussion were references to the Quran and sharia. The female MPs made systematic attempts to ground their arguments in sharia, often emphasizing that they had sharia-based reasons for their claims. This was only partially successful, as none of them could speak Arabic or was thoroughly conversant in Islamic law, and the conservative MPs often outmaneuvered them. In the Joint Commission, the head of the Legislation Commission was often the only person present who was able to quote at length in Arabic and who claimed detailed knowledge of Hanafi *fiqh*. This put him in a unique position, and others frequently deferred to him because of it.

The frequent references to sharia effectively also undermined the authority of Shias. Many of the more liberal Islamic scholars in Kabul were Shia, often having studied in a more pluralistic scholarly environment in Iran, but their readings of *fiqh* were rejected by the Sunni MPs. When a Shia scholar was trying to make an argument about what Islamic law said about underage marriage, a Sunni MP responded condescendingly, effectively rendering him irrelevant to the debate: "My dear, you are Jafari. I care only for Hanafi and Maliki *fiqh*."[51] This was a barely concealed reminder to the scholar that, as a Shia, his historical place in the religious hierarchy of Afghanistan was one of insignificance.

During the plenary debate in May 2013, religious arguments were particularly pronounced. Many of the conservative MPs angrily spoke against the EVAW on religious grounds. One asked, "God *[Khudawand]* says that you can marry up to four wives. . . . What should we do—change God's law?"[52] Another, Mullah Torakheil, argued, "Mr. Speaker, This law is in contradiction with several aspects of the verses of the Quran. Article 3 of the Constitution explicitly states that those laws that are contrary to sharia and the sacred religion of Islam have no validity whatsoever!" Abdul Satar Khawasi even questioned President Karzai's judgment, given that he had signed a law so obviously in contradiction with Islam: "I am surprised. . . . Yet again, I am asking the presidential palace—how was possible that the president approved such a decree that contravenes sharia and religion? He has himself promulgated the Constitution, signed it into law, article 3 of the Constitution says that nothing can be contrary to the beliefs of the sacred religion of Islam. But even so, five or six of the provisions of the decree that the president signed are explicitly in contradiction and opposed to the word of God *[Kalamullah]!*"

The 2004 Constitution was another joint reference point for the discussions, and throughout the debates on the EVAW law none of the participants openly challenged the Constitution or any of its provisions. Indeed, as shown above, in the plenary debate, in particular, several of the opponents of the law invoked article 3 of the Constitution, which states that "no law shall be contrary to the beliefs of the sacred religion of Islam." Afghan laws written after 2004 normally started with a reference to specific articles in the Constitution as reasons for their enactment, and the EVAW law presented to Parliament did so as well. It referred to article 24, which stipulated the state's duty to upheld the liberty and dignity of human beings, and article 54, which obligated the state to protect the well-being of the family, the fundamental unit of society, and to eliminate traditions contrary to the provisions of Islam. Earlier, there had been suggestions to also refer to article 22, on gender equality, and article 7, on the state's obligation to abide by international treaties and conventions it had signed, as well as the U.N. Declaration on Human Rights. This had been rejected by the head of the *Taqnin,* probably to avoid making the law more controversial than it already was to the conservatives in the Parliament. Article 22 was, however, invoked by one of the conservative MPs when he protested the EVAW law's blanket ban on pardons for crimes covered by the EVAW law—he argued that this ban infringed on the rights of men.[53]

The 1976 Penal Code was also often defended by the conservative men. Some of them stated that the Penal Code provided a sufficient framework for violence against women, making most of the provisions of the EVAW law, if not the law itself, unnecessary. The 1977 Civil Code, on the other hand, proved less unassailable. When it seemed to contradict their interpretations of sharia, the conservative MPs declared that the Civil Code was of little importance to them. For instance, when many other participants in the discussions protested that the Civil Code prohibited underage marriage, one of the conservative male MPs retorted, "The Civil Code is not the book of Allah. The father has the right to marry off a girl whether she is young or old."[54] Some of the supporters of the EVAW law started to worry that, as a consequence of the parliamentary process, they might end up not only with a significantly weakened version of the EVAW law but also with an invalidated Civil Code, which, in many respects, provided women with rights in relation to marriage (see chapter 1). This, they argued, was a sign that the very idea of putting the EVAW law through Parliament had been a mistake from the outset.[55]

The women MPs were careful not to make references to human rights as a justification for the EVAW law. Likewise, the accusation that the law was in essence a foreign invention—"a gift from the foreigners" as one legal scholar had con-temptuously called it[56]—was never openly stated in the debates. Yet the possibility of such charges being raised—and the risk of their ramifications—existed as an underlying threat, of which all parties were well aware. There was a sense among some of the civil society activists who attended the discussions that the conserva-tive men were trying to tease out an explicit admission that the EVAW law was indeed "foreign" in origin when they repeatedly asked, "What is the basis of this law?" *(Mabna-ye in qanon chi ast?)*. If such a trap was laid, the women MPs suc-cessfully avoided it. Instead of referring to human rights or international con-ventions, they appealed to the importance of nurturing the health of the family, eradicating traditions contrary to Islam, and giving women the rights they were afforded according to sharia, in particular in relation to inheritance, the choice of a marriage partner, and education. The conservative men, in turn, built many of their arguments on claims that the law would "destroy the basis of the fam-ily," in particular, by putting fathers and husbands in prison. Some of them also expressed the sentiment, although less openly, that only immoral women were in need of the law: the kind of protection it provided was illegitimate and suspect. In one of the discussions, one of the conservative male MPs rather loudly muttered, "This law is, anyway, for the women of the street [i.e., prostitutes]. Good women living under the protection of Islam have no need for this law."[57] The statement reflected a commonly made assertion that women who left the house on their own were transgressors undeserving of protection or recognition. To feminist Afghans, both male and female, such sentiments were deeply offensive. As a female shelter manager stated to me in an interview: "In Afghanistan, what kind of woman is re-garded as deserving of their male relatives' protection and support? A woman who is obedient, loyal, always thinks about the name of her male relatives, one who is silent and tolerates everything. Not one who goes to court to complain, who goes public, who goes outside."[58]

Some hoped that the EVAW law could go some way in challenging the notion that women who ventured into public places without male escorts were forfeiting their rights to safety: "It's important that the EVAW law states explicitly that the government has an obligation to protect women in public places. Because there are these ideas in Afghan culture that good Afghan women are those who tolerate, who suffer, who stay at home and do not open their mouth. And that those who leave the house are not good women."[59]

The strategies at work in the negotiations over the EVAW law in Parliament had revealed a discursive field structured by Islamic terms. Justifying arguments by reference to the provisions of Islam was paramount. But the two sides approached their references to Islam in different ways. The supporters of the law argued that threats to the realization of "true Islam" were Afghanistan's internal conditions and harmful and ignorant traditions (or, occasionally, male power and patriarchy).

For the conservatives, on the other hand, the threat was cast in the form of foreign influence, which could undermine the otherwise strong Islamic foundations of Afghan society. Traditionally, it was alleged, Afghan women sensibly preferred to stay at home under the protection of fathers and husbands. The specter of women's increased visibility, promiscuity, mobility, and subversion of male authority was presented as a novel and dangerous break with these foundations, an unnatural development that could be explained only by atheism and by foreign contamination.

In any case, it was not as if the conservative MPs "won" the debate solely based on the merits of their argumentation. Underpinning the rhetoric of the conservative MPs were more subtle dynamics that made most of the female MPs unwilling to risk a full-on public confrontation and, in the end, led the supporters of the EVAW law to choose a more discreet way of promoting the law and supporting its implementation. In order to fully appreciate the power relations at work—and to assess the strategies that the supporters of the law employed—I turn from substantive debates to the processes through which the EVAW law was conceived, promoted, contested, and (in parts) implemented.

POLITICAL AMBIGUITY AND DISCREET LOBBYING

The process of drafting and advocating for the EVAW law revealed the constraints under which Afghan women's rights activists worked and the strategies they adopted as a result. MOWA existed in an increasingly tense relationship with the assertive and often more radical "civil society activists"—mainly staff in internationally funded aid organizations, along with a small group of government legal officials. Staff at MOWA had been unwilling to share the draft of the EVAW law with them until the day it was handed over to the Ministry of Justice. This upset many of the civil society activists and confirmed their opinion of MOWA as a nontransparent institution that would rather produce substandard work than consult others for help. More dramatic, however, was the sudden presentation of the third draft of the EVAW law, the one written by the then head of the Women's Commission in Parliament, Qadria Yazanpardast. As stated above, Yazanpardast claimed to me and to others that she had been unaware of the existence of the two drafts already produced and merely wanted to present Afghan women with a "gift" on International Women's Day, an occasion widely celebrated among urban groups in the country.[60] Others contested this, however, saying that her draft carried exactly the same title as the other drafts and was clearly an attempt to improve her meager record of achievements by appropriating the whole idea.

Divisions also appeared once the EVAW law reached Parliament. At that point, Qadria Yazanpardast, a Tajik MP and self-declared supporter of the jihad, had been displaced as the leader of the Women's Commission in an acrimonious leadership contest. In her place were two younger, more savvy female MPs, Fawzia

Koofi and Sabrina Saqeb, who played the lead role in attempting to steer the law through Parliament and defend it against conservative assaults. Like Yazanpardast before them, they had links to the opposition group in Parliament, but they were also perceived as being personally beholden to the powerful parliamentary speaker, Yunus Qanooni. They did not succeed in gaining the trust of other female or progressive MPs, who questioned Koofi's and Saqeb's personal commitment to women's rights and accused them of pushing through with a counterproductive process in order to be able to claim the EVAW law as their own legacy.

The competition, at times bitter, that existed between the various actors promoting the EVAW law reflected a broader set of dynamics in Afghan politics: personalization and individual competition.[61] Of this, more will be said shortly, but here I would like to suggest that the international aid given to women's activism was operating in such a way as to reinforce such dynamics. Jad points to the contradictions between NGOs and social movements and the way in which "the NGO structure creates actors with parallel power based on their recognition at the international level, and easy access to important national and international figures" (Jad 2004: 39; also see Jad 2007). Her analysis can be extended to any entity whose existence is largely dependent on international funding. International aid, as a bureaucratic practice, rewards time-limited achievements that can be formulated as the realization of objectives, targets, and benchmarks. Continued existence is dependent on the ability to "deliver" concrete "outputs" presentable in technocratic templates rather than the mobilization of large constituencies and coalitions. To some extent, this could explain the appearance of the three competing drafts and the seeming prioritization of personal aggrandizement and people trying to take credit for the law over the actual quality of the law being passed. For instance, MOWA—which, since its establishment, had been dependent on international funding and which recently had been under fire from both donors and civil society for a lack of tangible accomplishments—was understandably keen to protect the EVAW law as its own achievement and to see it realized sooner rather than later. This was presumably an important reason why, rather than going through a long process of carefully revising the law and anchoring it more broadly within the women's movement, MOWA was anxious to see the law ratified and implemented without delay. The third draft, the one submitted by the head of the Women's Commission in Parliament, was interpreted, similarly, as a strategy to demonstrate her individual achievement—even if it was at the cost of quality and collective gains.

The subsequent promotion of the EVAW law, once a single draft had been consolidated, took place through a small constellation of women's rights activists and diplomats. Rather than seeking broader alliances, in civil society or in Parliament, the law was fast-tracked through a presidential decree in a manner that reflected a small, externally dependent, and top-down women's rights movement more generally. When made aware of the technical weaknesses in the law—how it contradicted existing laws—the civil society activists and MOWA protested that such issues were of secondary importance. The most important objective was to get the law approved and to start implementing it, thus sending a signal that impunity for violence against women could not be tolerated.

This approach must be situated within the larger practices of lawmaking by decree referred to in chapter 1—devising and promoting a law in relative isolation and as a stand-alone piece of legislation was by no means particular to Afghan actors. As Hartmann and Klonowiecka-Milart (2011) point out, lawmaking by decree had become a standard practice among international consultants and aid workers in Afghanistan, who were often even more oriented toward the technocratic (and political) demands of demonstrable outputs than Afghan women's rights activists were. As reforms in the area of "rule of law" had gathered pace and large donor-funded programs were established in the country, international consultants and aid workers often became involved in what Hartmann and Klonowiecka-Milart fittingly term "résumé law reform" (2011: 282). In the field of justice sector reform in Afghanistan, as with the aid industry more generally, tangible results was what mattered—both in reports sent to headquarters and funders and on the résumés of staff and consultants, who typically were on short contracts. Drafting laws was an appealing activity in such a context. Laws were relatively straightforward to produce for expat staff, and they represented a concrete achievement. It was such rationales, rather than coherent efforts to improve the Afghan legal framework overall, that often drove the production of new laws. At other times, they originated in the specific preoccupations of small groups of Westerners or Afghans, resulting in stand-alone laws on issues such as money laundering, terrorism, anticorruption, and antinarcotics.

Many of these stand-alone laws had been conceived and drafted in their entirety by actors outside of the Afghan government. And then, through political pressure and informal lobbying, laws were typically enacted by presidential decree (Chaudhary, Nemat, and Suhrke 2011). In fact, I was told that the U.S. embassy had, one summer, sent an email out to various international aid organizations and actors in the field of the rule of law, wondering if anyone had suggestions for laws that they wished to see enacted as presidential decrees before the Parliament was due to return from their recess. (Once Parliament was in session, laws could not be enacted by decree but had to be presented to Parliament before coming into force.)[62] The drafters of such laws often did not amend or even consult the existing legal framework, instead merely "using as an transitional provision an omnibus clause that declared as abrogated any laws that were contrary without listing the laws and provisions that it abrogated" (Hartmann and Klonowiecka-Milart 2011)—a habit that produced incoherence and inconsistency in the legal corpus as a whole. Such practices also reinforced the opaque dynamics of legislative processes, where informal connections to the president and access to his gatekeepers were key determinants (Chaudhary, Nemat, and Suhrke 2011).

In the case of the EVAW law, these kinds of dynamics were particularly evident in the period leading up to its presidential ratification in July 2009. After the fiasco of the Shia Personal Status Law, which had embarrassed all NATO governments vis-à-vis their home constituencies by making it obvious that claims to liberate Afghan women could not be sustained, diplomats—particularly U.S. diplomats—took a strong interest in the EVAW law.[63] They thought that the EVAW law, which at that point was being reviewed in the Ministry of Justice, could to some extent neutralize the Shia law. This was also what many Afghan MPs, human rights officials, and, indeed, the minister of justice himself argued. As is evident from embassy cables, the U.S. embassy had repeatedly discussed the law with Minster of Justice Sarwar Danesh. A cable from May 2009 read: "[The political consular] told Danesh the Embassy had studied the EVAW bill and found it to be a strong piece of legislation. We were disappointed it was not moving through the Administration as quickly as we expected. We informed Danesh that [U.S. Ambassador-at-Large for Global Women's Issues] Verveer planned to visit Kabul in late June. We would welcome cabinet approval prior to her arrival. . . . Danesh pledged to work on getting the bill through Cabinet approval prior to the end of June" (Embassy of the United States Kabul 2009b).

Therefore, although the U.S. government did not want to take public credit for the EVAW law, as this would certainly have harmed its status by giving ammunition to those who sought to frame the law as a "foreign gift"—it also participated in (and reinforced) the kind of law reform where isolated, symbolic, and sometimes hollow achievements obtained through informal pressure and negotiations was pursued over more anchored, long-term gains requiring broader coalitions.

There were, however, other important reasons why such strategies prevailed. Chief among these was the dynamics in Parliament, described by Larson (2009) as a "culture of political ambiguity." This political ambiguity—or "a reluctance to disclose political allegiances" (12)—in turn hindered the formation of blocs and the articulation of platforms and made the development of a pro-women alliance that could secure legislation such as the EVAW law in Parliament difficult. It had several causes. Political parties and issue-based politics never had a strong position in Afghanistan. The electoral system after 2001 also discouraged the formation of political parties through the obscure system called the Single Non-Transferable Vote (SNTV), which recognized only individuals and not political parties (Reynolds 2006). President Karzai and many in his circle who had put forward this system argued that political parties and their divisive ways were to blame for the violence that had plagued Afghanistan since the 1978 coup (Humayoon 2010), a particular historical narrative that—incidentally—also favored executive power. Larson also argues that the importance of patronage politics served to discourage open and committed political allegiances, since this kind of politics depends on the possibility of shifting loyalties.

However, the most important reason for this political ambiguity, Larson suggests, was the lack of security. As she points out, Afghanistan had little history of political pluralism and tolerance of opposition (2009: 13), and the widespread caution about expressing political positions and allegiances should therefore be unsurprising. The members of the former jihadi parties[64]—who also dominated Parliament (Ruttig 2006)—had a comparative advantage in such a climate. Their leaders were widely believed to be able to exert intimidation and coercion. Even if such assumptions were often based on rumors, they nonetheless served to keep opponents in check.

For women, there were additional elements to these dynamics. Women were invested with particular importance when it came to assessing Afghanistan's observance of Islam. To the mujahedin, having been rehabilitated to power as partners to the U.S. invasion that overthrew the Taliban government, presenting themselves as the guardians of Islam was often a powerful way of demonstrating nationalist credentials and distancing themselves from the infidel military and diplomatic presence. Paradoxically, despite having returned to power through Western military force, they managed to boost their influence by tapping into popular resentment *against* the Western military operations. Positioning themselves as the authorities on Islam was useful to ward off other forms of opposition. When defending a controversial law that provided a blanket amnesty for the considerable abuses committed during the civil war (see chapter 1), the former mujahedin commander Abdul Rasool Sayyaf had notoriously stated, "Whoever is against mujahideen is against Islam and they are the enemies of this country" (BBC 2007). This ability to effectively to invoke Islam in confrontations with adversaries, combined with actual or rumored powers of coercion and violence, gave many conservative and mujahedin parliamentarians significant advantage. And, as elsewhere, women's appearance and conduct was an appealing measurement of religious adherence. Women who were seen to challenge the authority of conservative actors, whether directly or by defying gender norms, could find themselves the target of a particularly potent denunciation, one in which female and religious transgression was conflated.

I experienced these dynamics for myself when going to the house of the head of the Legislation Commission to interview him about the law and his views of it. At the end of the interview, the conversation turned to my own marital status, and there were some probing questions about my religious identity. As I was cast as a lapsed Muslim and unfit wife who had left behind my husband (of Pakistani origin) to pursue research in a foreign country, I suddenly found myself uncomfortably trying to pull down my long coat to conceal my legs completely. I recalled rumors that this man, during his time as a judge for the mujahedin, had ordered a number of executions based on religious non-adherence, and I started to feel uneasy—it was getting dark, and we were in the outskirts of Kabul. Although my sense of unease was passing and completely unfounded, it provided me with some insight into the powers of intimidation facing local women's rights activists.[65]

This sense of insecurity and intimidation was an often unstated yet obvious factor in the calculations and conduct of the Afghan promoters of the EVAW law. Many women MPs and women's rights activists were conscious of the risk of being labeled "anti-mujahedin" or being seen to openly challenge their authority. Some of the activists had suggested that in order to get the EVAW law through Parliament, it would be best to introduce it furtively and quickly on a day when the main jihadi and mullah MPs were not present, possibly through some kind of prior deal with the speaker, which pressure from the foreign embassies could bring about.[66] They were reluctant to meet the conservative MPs in open debate and felt that it was better to quickly and discreetly get a parliamentary ratification without drawing too much attention to the law or to themselves. The fear of arousing jihadi wrath also manifested itself in the actual debates in Parliament. Some of the women advocates of the law were careful not to appear too provocative or assertive, and it seems safe to assume that it was sometimes such concerns that provided their adversaries with much of their power, rather than the strength of their arguments. Compare the ways in which the two key MPs formulated themselves in the plenary debate over the EVAW law in May 2013. Fawzia Koofi, her voice somewhat hesitant, pleaded with her male colleagues to approve the law as a favor to their female counterparts: "Today I request the people's honorable representatives to view this law as a national need and vote for it . . . as a token of cooperation and friendship with their sisters who, shoulder by shoulder [for many years], have cooperated with them on so many issues." Qazi Hanafi, on the other hand, thundered that the approval of the EVAW law would be comparable to the aftermath of the communist coup of 1978, normally referred to by its Afghan date, the 8th of Saur: "If you ratify this law, which will make the shelters legal and permissible, you should expect similar outcomes to that of Hasht-e Saur,"—here he paused for dramatic effect—"and the [consequent Islamic] Revolution. . . . And millions more shall be martyred."

It was the anticipation of statements such as these that had made women MPs approach the speaker of the Parliament, Abdul Raof Ibrahimi, prior to the debate, in order to extract a promise that he would stop the debate if the tone became to inflammatory or if it looked like the law was in danger of being repealed. Ibrahimi kept his promise. He halted the debate, thereby returning the EVAW law to the same ambiguous status that it had held prior to the plenary debate.[67]

A LAW OF ONE'S OWN?

But in mid-2015 came what might prove to be the final blow to a separate EVAW law. It arrived not from Parliament, but from the new president, Ashraf Ghani.

A few years earlier, President Karzai had agreed that work would start on a comprehensive penal code that would incorporate the criminal provisions from approximately fifty different freestanding laws. As the drafting of the new code gathered pace, supporters of the EVAW law, such as prominent members of the Afghan Women's Network, started to advocate for the EVAW law to be kept as a separate piece of legislation. They argued that the EVAW law was a unique achievement and that to integrate its provisions into a general code would dilute protection for women. Like before, they contended that having a special law for women would send important political signals and be a tool of advocacy. Others, such as Ministry of Justice officials and U.N. staff, were somewhat baffled by this line of reasoning.[68] They countered that the EVAW contained significant technical weaknesses that made it problematic to implement, that it was unrealistic to expect prosecutors and judges to be able to refer to some fifty different criminal laws, and that there was no reason why the EVAW law's provisions could not be incorporated into a comprehensive penal code. Besides, the EVAW law remained a mere decree, and integrating its provisions into a penal code that would be presented for approval in Parliament would strengthen women's protection. The women's rights activists were not convinced. They lobbied the Ministry of Justice, the new vice president, the First Lady, and finally President Ashraf Ghani himself, who refused to commit himself to maintaining the EVAW law as a separate code.[69] To some of the advocates of a comprehensive penal code, the arguments in favor of separate EVAW law were so weak that they could not fully explain the women's rights activists' stance. They speculated that the considerable funds that had been distributed to aid projects devoted to the implementation of the law was an additional, if unspoken, consideration.[70]

Even if this was a rather sinister reading, it was true that the EVAW law had become central to the large aid programs dedicated to women's rights in post-2001 Afghanistan.[71] After the EVAW law was signed as a presidential decree in July 2009, it had quickly became the focus of the parts of the international aid apparatus that was orientated toward women's rights and legal reform. Donors funded the establishment of a special unit at the attorney general's office in Kabul, to be emulated in other provinces. These units, called the Special Units on Violence against Women, were specifically to investigate and prosecute cases of violence against women, and the unit in Kabul came to have more than half a dozen of dedicated prosecutors, who received top-up salaries through donor funds.[72] In addition, donor funds paid for training sessions on the EVAW law for judges, prosecutors, and other government officials; booklets that were produced and disseminated; and various conferences and meetings that were organized to discuss and promote the law.

Despite this, the impact of the law was uneven and difficult to ascertain. Some judges in Kabul stated that they were not applying the law, as they had heard it was under review in Parliament, and they were therefore unsure of its status.[73] During

2011, as various aid agencies conducted more training sessions, the law seemed to gain some level of traction. International donors were keenly tracing prosecutions and conviction numbers. A U.N. 2012 survey of twenty-two of Afghanistan's thirty-four provinces found that 1,538 cases of violence against women were registered with prosecution offices over a twelve-month period and that 225 of them resulted in convictions (UNAMA 2012). For sixteen provinces where more detailed information was available, it was found that 44 percent of the cases in which indictments filed were based on the EVAW law, meaning that the other 56 percent were indicted under the Penal Code.

The implementation of the EVAW law gradually became the focus of donor and international engagement with women's rights in Afghanistan. The law constituted a central issue during Afghanistan first CEDAW hearing in July 2013, with most member countries present urging the Afghan government to accelerate its implementation. In another indication of the central position the law had obtained, donors made a government report about progress in its implementation one of a key set of aid conditionalities ("hard deliverables").[74] When, in 2013, the Afghan government failed to produce the report, the government of Norway cited this failure as one of two reasons for why it would cut development aid to Afghanistan by almost 10 percent. Finally, in March 2014, the long-awaited report was published, covering the status of 4,505 cases that had been registered with either the police, the Ministry of Women's Affairs, or the prosecution over a one-year period.[75] The data suggested that at least 40 percent of the registered cases had been "solved" either through mediation or by the withdrawal of the case by the victim.[76] Only 361 cases (8 percent) resulted in some kind of criminal conviction, and a further 40 cases resulted in acquittals. (However, almost two-thirds of these 361 convictions came from a single province, Herat. Out of Afghanistan's 34 provinces, Herat was known for having a competent court system and a committed female chief prosecutor.) The rest of the total caseload, 2,129 cases, was still under processing.

CONCLUSIONS

In the next chapter, I delve into the background to this data, disaggregating both the statistics and the stories behind them. Here, I want to offer some initial reflections on the following questions: To what extent did the EVAW law challenge established gender orders and domains of governance? Did it entail a transformation whereby women were constituted as citizens under state protection and where family authority over women was supplanted by, or at least modified by, that of the state? As this chapter has sought to demonstrate, there can be no straightforward answers to these questions. The EVAW law as it was decreed did represent a potential reorganization of both women's subject position and the reach of state realms versus that of kinship. Had the decree been enforced in full by the courts, the result would have been a significant increase in the power of the government in overseeing and regulating sexual and gender relations, in underwriting women's protection and equal rights in marriage, and in punishing transgressions. As we have seen, however, as the law was reviewed in Parliament, attempts were made to amend it in a direction that would safeguard fathers' and husbands' prerogatives over women—by allowing fathers to marry off minor daughters and by establishing husbands' rights to beating and polygamy. Women were also afforded their part of the "patriarchal bargain" (Kandiyoti 1988); it was to be a crime for husbands not to provide maintenance for their wives.

But regardless of the final the text of the law, an equally important point is this—unlike the not too dissimilar legislation introduced by kings like Abdul Rahman Khan or Amanullah (see chapter 1), the EVAW law did not in any way represent the attempts of a ruler to curtail the power of kinship groups. This was not an attempt by the country's ruler to "modernize" society by emancipating its women from family control. Evident in the attempts to promote and implement the law were instead a constellation of foreign diplomats, activists, and pro-women justice officials, their efforts underwritten by the funds and infrastructure of aid agencies. While this constellation worked, in parts, through Afghan state institutions, this did not mean that there was a single, unambiguous, sovereign national power ruling over a single "public domain." Both the status of the law and its implementation was partial and tenuous. The legal status of the law was uncertain. It had neither been approved nor rejected by the Parliament, and it appeared to be in contradiction to other laws. Its presidential endorsement was offered up as a bargain. The minister of justice and the president had effectively offered to let two constituencies each have its own law—the progressive EVAW law for Afghan feminists and their allies and the Shia personal status law (which was, in many cases, in direct contradiction to the EVAW law) to the Shia clergy. Some of the supporters of the EVAW law appeared to endorse this—rather than engaging with the entire legal framework (and their political adversaries), they were content to be granted a law of their own.

In many respects, the EVAW law appears as a textbook case of Saskia Sassen's "neither global nor national" assemblage. As she states, "these assemblages cut across the binary of the national versus global. They continue to inhabit national institutional and territorial settings but are no longer part of the national as historically constructed" (2008: 61). In many ways, the promotion and implementation of the EVAW law was a case of the global working through the national. The law was drafted and promulgated through national institutions, submitted by the Ministry of Women's Affairs to the Ministry of Justice, and revised there before eventually being decreed by the president. Similarly, the implementation of the law happened through Afghan justice institutions—the prosecutors and the courts.

At the same time, as this chapter has demonstrated, these processes were to a large externally driven. The EVAW law, adopted partly due to Western pressure and enforced partly due to strong international involvement in monitoring and funding, in many ways brought Afghan women into a global protection order, where the guarantors were international organizations such as the United Nations. But if there was a global EVAW law assemblage working through national institutions, it should also be said that this assemblage was in no sense a totalizing, unidirectional force. Global templates intersected with local dynamics, dynamics that amounted to more than simply the formal procedures of national institutions seamlessly facilitating a global order. The processes traced in this chapter show that rather than being two contradictory forces, personalized politics and external reform attempts often worked together. Executive power was strengthened, because Western diplomats preferred to work with the cabinet and the president rather than the cumbersome and unpredictable Parliament when they wanted something done. This also gave President Karzai an opportunity to strengthen his power base through the granting of favors in an exchange of offerings and loyalty. The EVAW law was a gift to two of his constituencies—women's rights activists and Western supporters. At the same time, he also bestowed other gifts, such as the Shia law. Similarly, the emphasis placed on output and fundraising by the "NGO-ization" of women's activism also fed into personalized and patron-client politics. As I detail in the next chapter, the way in which the EVAW law was implemented also constituted justice officials as the patrons and benefactors of the victims of violence.

What clearly lost out in the EVAW law assemblage were the possibilities for more robust practices of democratic participation and collective mobilization. Supporters of the EVAW law decided that the price for parliamentary ratification of the law was too high. As we have seen, there were several aspects to this price. The conservatives in Parliament demanded significant concessions, which would have reinstated some of the authority of fathers and husbands over daughters and wives. But there was also a more general sense of uncertainty among women's rights activists about the prospect of confronting a political field that was stacked against them. They were well aware of sentiments—among certain male MPs and beyond—that the EVAW law represented an illegitimate protection claim: good and respectable women could rely on male relatives to shelter them from outside predations and for the same relatives not to subject them to violence. By implication, it was immoral women who were in need of the EVAW law. The category of "immoral women" was frequently also subtly stretched to include all Afghan women who questioned male authority in one way or another. This kind of gendered denunciation, infused with implications of religious and national betrayal, constituted a key political weapon in the hands of the jihadis and added to women's sense of vulnerability when operating in public debate and national politics. Instead of risking this hazardous terrain, the supporters of the law decided to fall back on more discreet strategies and on the support they had among sympathetic government officials and Western donors.

By virtue of it operating through transnational funding and pressure, the EVAW law assemblage was, in many ways, part of a technocratic global discourse about violence against women, one in which violence against Afghan women was rendered a global concern subject to the expert interventions of transnational actors and institutions (see introduction). At the same time, however, there was more to the composition and workings of the EVAW law assemblage than just another manifestation of a transnational governmental practice, underlining the point made in the introduction of this book that global power does not work in a singular direction. As we have seen, local politics shaped the framing and promotion of the EVAW law in particular ways, enabling and reinforcing personalized politics.

The international aid interventions in Afghanistan were also imbricated with broader geopolitical relations. The aid agencies involved in drafting, funding, and monitoring the EVAW law had proliferated on the back of a military invasion that had produced much starker international hierarchies than what could have been immediately visible through looking at the practices of organizations such as the United Nations and IDLO in isolation. In the processes examined in chapter 4, the controversies around women's shelters and the geopolitical dimension of external guarantees are brought into much sharper relief.

PART II

New Protection Mechanisms

3

Brokers of Justice

The Special Prosecution Unit for Crimes of Violence against Women in Kabul

A woman approaching the special unit for the prosecution of violence against women (the "VAW unit") in the outskirts of Kabul city will pass several checkpoints, road-blocks, and blast walls. Security has become tighter and tighter around the city, and with hardly any foreign troops moving around anymore, Afghan government build-ings are becoming a frequent target. In the spring of 2015, two woman prosecutors working at the unit were killed when one of the cars transporting female staff to their workplace was blown up by a suicide bomber. Nonetheless, work continues unabated—after the attack in 2015, the prosecution unit reopened the very next day.

If the woman is here to report a case of violence against her, she is likely to be ac-companied by a family member, perhaps her father or mother. Statistically, her case is most probably a claim of domestic abuse. The building she sees in front of her as she enters the compound has five floors, but only six rooms belong to the VAW unit. After asking around, she will find her way to one of the rooms. Her father, if he is with her, will want to speak on her behalf. First, she will be directed to the administrative office and will be told to submit a petition. A few days later, she will be back, and if she is lucky, her case will have been processed and will now be with one of the investigative prosecutors, who will be ready to take her statement. She will sit in one of the two rooms assigned to investigations. On a normal day, there will other complainants, witnesses, or suspects in the room, who, like her, are answering questions from the prosecutor assigned to their case. In each of the two rooms, there are supposed to be five prosecutors. Most of them will be sitting at their desks, but normally at least two will be absent, with their colleagues covering for them if the manager comes by to ask. Most of the prosecutors are male, and all of them are working with papers and pens only, despite the computers donated by the unit's chief aid donor only last year.

The chance that the woman's case will go to court is very small. It is quite possible that she has marks on her body from the violence, perhaps a broken bone or a strangulation mark on her neck. If she does, the prosecutor will refer her to the forensic medicine department, where she will get a certificate to be attached to her case file. The prosecutor will summon her husband in for questioning, and when he is there, the prosecutor will ask him why he is beating his wife. The husband might deny having beaten her altogether, though if he does, the prosecutor will tell him to stop lying—the marks are there. He might respond that he has only beaten her a few times, and it's because she has a phone relationship with another man or because she leaves the house without his permission. The prosecutor will brusquely tell him that "even a single slap"—no matter the circumstances—will earn him several months in prison under the EVAW law.

But then the prosecutor might suggest to the husband that if he is willing to sign a written guarantee, his wife might be persuaded to withdraw the claim. Or he might say to the woman that he has convinced her husband not to beat her again and that the husband will put this in writing. Her husband is young; he has made a mistake. Or his drug addiction has driven him to beat her. He clearly loves her. And where will it leave her to have her husband in prison?

If the woman refuses to withdraw her complaint and says she cannot live with her husband again, the prosecutor might suggest that she go to the family court for a divorce. He is likely to advice her not to withdraw her complaint until her divorce is secured. Perhaps this is what she wanted all along. Divorce is not easy to obtain for a woman in Afghanistan—she needs valid grounds, such as violence, to present to the courts. The woman may not be too concerned about whether or not her husband goes to prison, but she does want to obtain a divorce. Moreover, if she is to get her mahr *(dowry) from her husband, her only financial asset, she has to have a valid reason for the divorce. If she withdraws her claim from the prosecution, her husband will have no reason to grant her a divorce, and the court might refuse to issue one too.*

But perhaps the woman's family finally persuades her to withdraw her claim. Her husband has sent some elders to mediate. Her mother is worried about the stain on the family's reputation, and her father is concerned about his ability to feed her if she moves back to his house permanently. So the woman goes back the prosecution unit and says that her husband regrets everything and that she has forgiven him. The prosecutor, pleased that the case has been solved, asks her routinely if she is withdrawing the claim out of her own volition, and when she says yes, he tells her to come back if her husband starts beating her again. She never returns.

INTRODUCTION

The vignette above illustrates some typical features of how the special unit for the prosecution of violence against women (the "VAW unit") in Kabul operated and what the unit's cases most commonly looked like. The unit in Kabul was the first in the country, established in 2010. I attended the opening ceremony in March that year, in a small, packed conference room at the attorney general's compound. At that point, the unit had not yet been formally established, since the International Development Law Organization (IDLO)—an independent organization dedicated to the rule of law that works around the globe, which was the main initiator and donor of the special prosecution unit—had not yet been able to secure the unit's inclusion into the *tashkheel*—the official structure of the attorney general's office as an institution. The opening ceremony went ahead, however, and some six months later, that final issue had also been resolved. It was hoped that the unit, to be emulated in other provinces, would increase the prosecution of cases of violence against women. Female prosecutors, dedicated resources, and increased visibility would make this new branch of the legal system more accessible to women and more accountable to activists and donors.

Drawing upon a wealth of observational data, this chapter documents the everyday working of the VAW unit in Kabul. It argues that, by and large, the unit did not function quite as donors intended. More than 85 percent of cases registered there were closed prior to trial, often because the prosecutors were reluctant to pursue them. The prosecutors suggested to the women, that rather being left without a home and an income, they would be better off reaching some kind of agreement with their abusers, backed up by the prosecution itself. In some cases, however, it was victims or their families who did not want their petitions to proceed to court. A closer look at many of the cases reveals that women sometimes came to the prosecution office with intentions very different than seeing their husbands or other family members convicted and imprisoned. Some wanted a divorce, others wanted straying husbands to return to the marital home, and still others were seeking a government-sanctioned guarantee that the violence would cease. In some cases, the prosecution units simply became a tool used by families in conflict with other families or for the rehabilitation of reputation and honor. Complaints of rape or abuse, for instance, might be filed with the purpose of pressuring the defendant's family in matters of bride-price or compensation for elopement.

Overall, prosecutors, women, and their families bargained within a paradigm of gender norms in which rehabilitating the family unit and absorbing sexual transgressions into the framework of conventional marriage transactions were paramount. The VAW unit thus served to reaffirm the notion that acts of violence were family problems rather than criminal cases that belonged in the mainstream justice system. I suggest that this was a predictable outcome of the way in which the special prosecution unit operated—located, as it was, at the intersection of donor pressure, government indifference, and a lack of attention to (or disinterest in destabilizing) the broader relations that cast women's independent existence outside the family setting as deeply subversive.

This is not to say, however, that the VAW unit was of no consequence. To a significant number of women and their families, the VAW unit provided a novel recourse (and a resource) in the face of abuse, desertion, or unheeded responsibilities. Even if the VAW unit tended to adopt an approach of negotiation rather than the dispensation of justice, it was able to invoke at least the specter of criminal prosecution and, through this, sometimes secured women a better deal than what was available elsewhere.

THE SPECIAL UNITS AT A GLANCE

The rationale for establishing the special units had been fairly straightforward. With the EVAW law enacted in the summer of 2009, the special units were intended to serve as a focal point for the law's implementation. The initiative came from IDLO but soon received backing from other aid agencies and from Afghan supporters of the law. Having dedicated units within the justice system would provide women with a space where they would feel more welcome and where staff would both be committed to and skilled in dealing with cases of gender violence. It would also give donors a point where efforts of funding, training, and advocacy could be directed. All of this would bolster the enforcement of the EVAW law.

By the end of 2015 there were special units for crimes of violence against women at the prosecutor's offices in twenty of the thirty-four of the country's provincial capitals. In theory, each office was to process all cases of gender violence in that office's province.[1] Most of the units were supported by international aid. IDLO was the most prominent donor, providing top-up salaries and technical support, such as staff training in information technology and record keeping. It was, however, difficult to ascertain whether the rates of prosecution and conviction had increased, because neither the prosecution office nor the courts produced any data on this question. IDLO had attempted to establish an electronic database of cases, but it went unused. The U.N. mission's human rights section had, as described in chapter 2, published yearly reports between 2011 and 2013, but these reports could not give a full picture of how many—and which type of—offenses led to prosecutions or convictions (Shahabi and Wimpelmann 2015). The long-awaited 2014 report by the Ministry of Women's Affairs, produced after considerable Western pressure, provided more details. Based on data from twenty-six provinces, it suggested that 18 percent of all cases registered with the prosecution were referred to courts and that 13 percent led to a criminal conviction.[2] It also disaggregated these numbers according to type of offense. Unsurprisingly, cases of murder and rape had relatively high prosecution and conviction rates. Beating (*lat-e kop;* physical battery not leading to permanent or long-term injury) was, by far, the most commonly registered claim. It also was the offense with the lowest conviction rate, at only 11 percent.

TABLE 1   Calculations based on the 2014 report by the Ministry of Women's Affairs
(Afghan year 1391, March 2012–13)

	Total cases registered with the prosecution in 26 provinces	Percentage referred to court	Percentage convicted (of referred cases)	Percentage convicted (of total)
All cases	1,638*	18	72	13
Rape	96	50	75	38
Murder	84	48	70	33
Injury	41	39	56	22
Beating	971	14	76	11

* The number 1,638 refers to the total number of registered cases, and in addition to rape, murder, injury, and beating, it also includes a range of other crimes, such as forced marriage and harassment. The 1,638 number also includes a larger number of incidents not defined as crimes under Afghan law where women might nonetheless be filing a complaint (e.g., 145 cases of divorce and 242 complaints of non-maintenance) or be accused of an offense not codified in law (running away from the family home, 163 cases).

In 2014, I embarked upon a more detailed study of the VAW units in eight provinces together with two Afghan colleagues.[3] Our quantitative data confirmed the patterns in the MOWA report (Shahabi and Wimpelmann 2015). It also found some stark geographical differences in the percentage of cases referred to court. Particularly striking was the difference between Kabul and the other seven provinces. The prosecution unit in Kabul had registered the largest number of cases by far—two thousand over a two-year period, which amounted to almost two-thirds of the total caseload in the eight provinces and was the highest rate per capita. But it also had the lowest rate of indictment—13 percent. Even when disaggregated by type of offense, Kabul referred fewer cases to court than any other province.

In the remainder of the chapter, I provide an analysis of the intricacies of how the VAW unit in Kabul operated.[4] I suggest that the unit practiced a fairly open-door policy but, at the same time, was unable (or, in some cases, uninterested) in overcoming the structural relations that cemented women's dependence within the family unit. As such, it largely became a recourse for women whose martial or family situations had become intolerable, rather than a mechanism for dispensing justice as defined in the laws.

"DON'T YOU FEEL SHAME WHEN YOU BEAT YOUR WIFE?": PROSECUTORS REPRIMANDING HUSBANDS

In many of Afghanistan's more rural provinces, merely registering a case of gender violence at the VAW unit was a difficult exercise. According to Afghan law, only acts defined as felonies *(jenayat)* could be prosecuted by a representative of the state regardless of the will of the victim. This included murder, rape, injury by chemical substances, and "forced suicide."[5] For other acts, such as beating or forced marriage, a claim had to be submitted by the victim in the form of a written petition *(ariza)*. But in many provinces, women and family members attempting to file cases of violence often encountered prosecutors who either dragged their feet in registering their claim or sought to devise a "solution" through negotiations with family members without officially opening a file for the case. The reason to this reluctance was twofold. First, in rural provinces, the prosecutors were all male, and many had the attitude that VAW cases did not belong in the legal system at all, that the stains left on the family and the women's honor dictated that such cases should be solved within the family, with the women remaining within their marriages or families. Second, some perpetrators were able to influence the prosecution through bribes or political connections. As a result, prosecutors could sometimes be extremely abrupt with women who came to the VAW unit to register a case (Shahabi, Wimpelmann, and Elyassi 2016).

By contrast, at the VAW prosecution unit in Kabul, registering a case was relatively easy, even if it wasn't exactly straightforward. Complainants had to negotiate some administrative hurdles, such as writing a petition. For this purpose, commercial petition writers set themselves up outside the prosecution office, out in the open—simply with a chair and perhaps a desk. Upon the submission of the formal written petition, however, prosecutors would generally open a file—and without any particular requirements regarding evidence or the seriousness of the claim.[6] Neither would they, as was common in more rural areas, admonish women for daring to bring their "private problems" to outsiders in general and the prosecution in particular. The prosecutors in the VAW unit in Kabul would also make systematic efforts to bring in suspects. Complainants were given a summoning letter to hand over to the local police, who would deliver the letter to the suspect. If the suspect subsequently failed to show up at the prosecution, the police would be sent to identify his (or, less often, her) whereabouts and to bring him in.

There was a marked difference in the tone prosecutors used when interviewing the people involved in a case. When questioning a female complainant, prosecutors were normally oriented toward establishing facts and a sequence of events, often in some detail. By asking such questions, the prosecutors wanted to establish the truthfulness of the woman's account. In cases of beating, prosecutors would typically ask the woman when she had been beaten, where, how, and if there were any witnesses. As a rule, they would ask if the complainant had any physical marks and, if so, refer them to the department of forensic medicine. A review of the case files of some 160 claims of beatings showed that least 50 percent of the women did have physical marks documented by forensic examination, and these were often the victims of severe, repeated violence, which could involve broken bones, burns, and fingernails that had been pulled out. The majority of beating cases implicated husbands, and the prosecutors normally asked if the marriage had been consensual, and what had been the occasion or reason for the violence inflicted.

When subsequently interrogating male suspects, the nature of prosecutors' questioning often took on a mixture of fact-finding and reprimanding (as it turned out, this often to set the stage for subsequent mediation). "Why do you beat your wife?" one prosecutor demanded to know.

Husband:	"I only slapped her once."
Prosecutor (raising his voice):	"You have done a bad thing. Don't you know that one slap means three months in prison?"
Husband:	"My little daughter is one year old, she dropped my wife's cell phone in the water. My wife started beating her; she beat her twice—once when she dropped the cell phone, and later on she beat her again. I got angry, and I slapped her once, that was all."
Prosecutor:	"Why? Your wife is not your daughter; she is your wife. You have no right to beat your wife because she beat your daughter."

Most husbands would typically either flatly deny that they had beaten their wives, or they would admit to some beating but would suggest that they had good reasons. A common theme was that their wife had left the home without their authorization. One man said, "I have not beaten my wife; I have just hit her three times when she escaped the house. Most days when I got back from work, my wife would not be there. After two [or] three days, I would find her in some relative's house. I just have one thing to say: if my wife does not leave the home without my permission, I will not beat her."

Another man stated that he had only recently started to beat his wife, after she had begun to do things without his approval: "But she is my wife; she must be obedient to me. I am saying, 'Don't go alone to the male doctor for television [ultrasound] examinations; I don't like it.' But she does it over and over again. I keep telling her to inform me, so that I can go with her, but she doesn't."

Other men argued that they had reasons to doubt their wives' chastity and, therefore, to beat them:

I got to know this girl over the phone, and I fell in love with her. She told me her father would never agree to our marriage and our only option was to elope. One day we escaped as she was walking to school, and we had a *nikah* [wedding ceremony]. But after the *nikah*, I found out that this girl is not a virgin. That is why I started to hate her. I couldn't send her back to her father's house, because we were elopers. So I became compelled to violence, to beating her, but it was never very serious, only sometimes a few slaps, if I was very upset."

Prosecutors would generally not accept this kind of reasoning. They would assert that any beating, no matter the circumstances, was wrong and unlawful. Such reproaches did not necessarily mean that the prosecutors were ready to bring a case to court. But they would systematically set out to gather evidence. In addition to sending women for forensic medical checkups if they had physical marks of abuse, prosecutors would normally summon witnesses, especially in cases where the complainant and the suspect were not related to each other. In cases in which the two parties were married or otherwise related, it was often unnecessary for the prosecution to summon close relatives, since the relatives would accompany the complainant and the suspect to the office. In any case, the prosecutors often distrusted witnesses' credibility. They paid little heed to character statements and sought to scrutinize witnesses' accounts by probing into details, since they frequently suspected a witness had either been bought off or was conspiring with one of the parties to the case.

The prosecutors would not always trust complainants' statements either, in particular in cases of sexual violence. One prosecutor, when discussing a kidnapping claim, stated that the allegation could not be true, because the woman in question had not been attractive enough: "Look, she is not that beautiful, if someone is going to kidnap a girl, he'll definitively go for a good-looking one." Another prosecutor disbelieved a claim of forced sodomy (lawat),[7] saying that because it had happen so many times, it had to be consensual. Some prosecutors applied a rather absurd belief that a gynecological examination could distinguish between rape and consensual intercourse by establishing how the hymen had been broken. A hymen torn at the "top" (what the prosecutors referred to as "the upper side of the clock: 11, 12, or 1") suggested rape, whereas a hymen torn at the lower side ("the lower side of the clock: 5, 6, or 7") indicated the crime of zina (consensual intercourse). During the course of the fieldwork on which this chapter is based, there were a few cases in which women had been subjected to such "clock" examinations, although in none of those cases was the evidence from those exams used in court. DNA testing was not available in Afghanistan, and in any case, claims of sexual violence would typically be reported many days or months after it had taken place, so that medical evidence could not be obtained.

Overall, whereas prosecutors in Kabul sometimes distrusted women's account of sexual violence because of what they held to be "bad moral character," they would not generally say this to women to their face. Nor would they scorn women for other "bad" behavior or in any way suggest that they had deserved any violence inflicted upon them. Occasionally, however, they would ridicule men for acting in "unmanly" ways. In one case, a male prosecutor made fun of a man whose wife wanted to divorce him due to impotence. In another case, in which a wife was about to leave her husband, a female prosecutor told the husband to toughen up.

This man, whose case actually belonged to another prosecutor, had come to this female prosecutor for advice and help. Sobbing, the man said, "I love my wife, and I don't want to divorce her. Please *Saranwol sahib* [honorable prosecutor], show me a solution."

The prosecutor laughed, asking why his wife wanted a divorce.

"She says, 'I don't like you. I don't love you,'" the man responded, immaculately dressed in a striking turban, but still in tears.

"What kind of a husband cries over his wife?" the prosecutor wanted to know. "Just tell her, 'If you want a divorce, fine with me, [but] I won't give you a single *afghani* of your *mahr* [dowry].'"[8]

By and large, the question that determined if a case would go to trial was not the status of the evidence or even the seriousness of the charge. Instead, the prosecution of a case typically hinged on whether the complainant and the accused (as well as family members) could reach an agreement, either on their own or with the facilitation of the prosecutor. The efforts made to prepare evidence must be understood from this perspective. The main function of evidence was often to serve as leverage in the hands of the prosecutor to get the accused to agree to some of the terms of the complainant.

As mentioned earlier, the fact that so few VAW cases led to convictions was a concern for women's rights advocates, as well as Western diplomats. There was hardly an international donor conference or event related to women's situation in Afghanistan at which a discussion of the need for the Afghan government to step up its efforts to implement the EVAW law did not feature prominently. This insistence suggested—implicitly or explicitly—that higher conviction rates were mainly a question of the Afghan government's political will to apply pressure on the justice institutions to do their job properly:

> The problem is that neither Hamid Karzai nor current President Ashraf Ghani has taken meaningful steps to enforce the EVAW Law. An estimated 87 percent of Afghan women experience abuse in their lifetimes, and this continues today, while the law sits, largely unused, on a shelf. (Barr 2016)

> Today, on International Women's Day, the United Nations family in Afghanistan calls upon the Government of Afghanistan to take a stand and fully implement the Elimination of Violence against Women (EVAW) Law. . . . Providing appropriate support services for survivors of violence is important but it is not enough. . . . The most important thing is to put an end to the culture of impunity that prevails in Afghanistan and make the perpetrators of violence against women responsible for their crimes. The Government has to take the lead and ensure that the EVAW law is implemented. (UNDP 2013)

It is true that there was a lack of interest in large parts of the government to apply pressure to enforce the law, but that was not the only factor explaining the low conviction rates. A more complete explanatory framework must take into account the determinate contexts of women's lives (Agnes and Ghosh 2012: xiii) and those of legal officials. As Basu reminds us, "engaging with the legal realm always also entails specific entanglements with family and state, and [law] is metaphorically and metonymically working out those dramas" (2006: 45). In other words, a singular focus on a lack of political will could not accommodate the position of actual women arriving at the prosecution—not simply as autonomous individuals seeking the application of the law, but as social beings embedded in and constrained by intimate social and material relationships. Hence the objectives of the women (or their families) might not be the exact implementation of the law but, instead, the negotiation of a better deal within those relationships. Legal officials were similarly maneuvering within parameters of cultural expectations and material realities and, like the women, they did not always define the ideal outcome as the mere enforcement of the law.

In the sections below, I look into some of the most common types of cases registered with the VAW prosecution in Kabul. Reviewing the available information about cases registered over a two-month period, I attempt to detect patterns with respect to how cases were dismissed or withdrawn. I show that the reasons behind the large number of closed cases are rather complex and do not fit into a single category. What is abundantly clear, however, is that the high number of non-prosecuted cases makes more sense through a lens that understands people "to be moving themselves in and out of law in ways by which they can best optimize their social cultural and economic options" (Basu 2006: 71).

"MAKE HIM RIGHT AGAIN": CASES OF BEATING

In order to try to detect patterns with some level of accuracy, my colleagues and I decided to review available information about all cases registered with the VAW unit in Kabul over a two-month period in 2015—162 cases altogether. Of these, 105 cases were claims of beating *(lat-e kop)*.[9] Our research was able to retrieve some information about the status of 68 of these 105 cases. During our period of examination, 14 of the 68 cases were still ongoing, and 3 had been referred to trial. Of the 3 cases sent to court, 2 had led to a prison sentence of three months, whereas the last had been withdrawn by the complainant during the trial. The remaining cases of beating—51 altogether—had been closed. For 21 of the 51 closed cases, there was no additional information available, other than that the majority of the cases involved claims made by wives against their husbands. However, for the remaining 30 closed cases, more details were available.

More than half—16 of the 30 cases—were withdrawn after the complainant had obtained some kind of guarantee, issued by the prosecution, that the violence would not be repeated. It was not uncommon that getting such a commitment had been the explicit wish of the complainant from the outset. In one case, a middle-aged woman, wrapped in a large white veil and a rural dress, appeared in front of the prosecutor in tears, explaining that after more than twenty-five years of marriage, her husband had suddenly started to beat and abuse her, accusing her of extramarital affairs:

> I have six children; one of my daughters is married, and I even have grand children. . . . At this age, he drove me out of my home. It's been twenty days that I am living with my father. I don't understand what this man wants from me. It's my idea that he has been using drugs this last year, and that's why he has gone like this. Even in front of my five-year-old he humiliates me, calling me bad things. Please, Mr. Prosecutor, do this; make him right again (*o ra jor konid*, literally, "please fix/repair him"), and ask him—why has he been like this for the last one year?

The prosecutor told the husband to come inside and sent the wife out of the room so that he could take his statement, asking him, "What is the issue here?"

The husband, his hands shivering and his eyes brimming with tears, said with a trembling voice, "The Lord shames one person in young age and another in old age; it is certainly my destiny to be ashamed now. Twenty-five years of marriage, [but] before this last year, I did not even tease her. At home, she was always the husband, and I was the wife."

After advising him at some length, telling him not to ruin his life by taking drugs, the prosecutor asked him, "Well, do you regret what you have done?" The man repented deeply, and when the prosecutor asked him whether he would pledge to stop the abusive treatment—"You will not doubt your wife's character; you will not beat her; you will not humiliate her"—he agreed. His wife and her father were called back into the room, and she was asked if she would be willing to resume living with her husband if the latter would formally guarantee these things to the prosecutor. Yes, she enthusiastically replied, but then added that she wanted some of her relatives to come to the prosecution office and act as guarantors. This last-minute request brought some complications to what the prosecutor had thought was completed business. The husband, upon hearing his wife's demand for relatives to guarantee the reconciliation, turned to her and said in a new, abrupt tone: "Listen, don't try to be clever in front of Mr. Prosecutor; just agree with whatever he says."

> Woman: "See, Mr. Prosecutor! He is behaving like this with me in front of you; he is even worse at home. If we go back to the house, he will become the same person again."
>
> Prosecutor: "Do not fight! The issue is over. Your husband is giving you a written guarantee, he says, 'I am not going to beat her or doubt her.' . . . That's it; the problem is solved."

The woman's father interrupted him angrily: "No! Without relatives, it's not possible. The relatives should assure us and give us a guarantee."

Prosecutor: "What do you want the relatives for? I am taking his shop's license;[10] what else do you want? A written guarantee is better than some relative's assurance."

Woman's father: "If they go back to home; the same things will happen. Nothing will change."

Prosecutor: "Well, what do you want, uncle? Do you want [people] who have grandchildren to divorce?"

Women's father: "No! I don't want them to divorce. But still, relatives should come and assure us."

The husband, yelling to the woman's father: "You—do not interfere; you have ruined our life."

This led the prosecutor to shout at the husband: "This is not a place where you can fight! Stay silent, and talk when you are asked to." He then said to the women's father: "What are you going to do with the relatives? I am taking a written guarantee from him. The case file will be here with me. If he does the same things again, then you can come back. In that case, his punishment will be double; they call this repeat offender *(mojrem-e mutakarer)*."

After getting the husband's signature and fingerprint for the guarantee letter, as well as a copy of his shop's license, the prosecutor asked the party to leave. Six months later, when our fieldwork had finished, they had yet not returned.

In this case, the wife and her father had clearly approached the prosecution with the purpose of obtaining some leverage to change the husband's behavior. There was no indication that the woman had wanted to press charges and had then been prevented from doing so by the prosecutor. Even so, the somewhat rushed way in which the prosecutor dealt with the husband's guarantee suggested that he did not harbor any deep commitment to ensure the welfare of women victims. As human rights advocates repeatedly pointed out, there was no systematic mechanism in place to follow up with women who had withdrawn their claims, to prevent them from being subjected to further violence (UNAMA/OHCHR 2015; UNAMA 2012). Unless they returned to file another claim, they were assumed to be fine. Nevertheless, it was the case that what some women wanted (within the broader constraints shaping their choices) was some kind of intervention that would force the husband to stop the violence, rather than to see them prosecuted and imprisoned. This partly accounts for the high withdrawal rates.

In some of the other sixteen cases in which women had withdrawn their complaints, the women did indeed appear more motivated to see the law implemented and their abusers put on trial. Yet even in some of these, the women still settled for a guarantee and withdrew their cases. There were various reasons for this. Some had lost access to their children during the course of filing a case, perhaps having left them behind in their marital home. According to Afghanistan's family law, women are entitled to custody over sons until the age of seven and daughters until the age of nine (article 429). In practice, it was sometimes difficult for women to get the family courts to enforce this—and even more difficult to get judges to apply the provisions in the family law that allowed woman to be granted custody beyond those ages, if special circumstances applied.[11] To some women, the idea of going to court was so daunting that they chose to withdraw their case and be reunited with their children, even if that meant returning to an abusive spouse. Others stated that although they had originally wanted to pursue the case, they thought that their husbands showed sufficient regret and willingness to change their behavior. In these cases, it was difficult to ascertain exactly what had made the women change their mind. It was quite possible that they had been pressured by their husbands or in-laws.

In around half of the sixteen cases that were closed by way of a guarantee, it appeared that the prosecutors themselves had suggested to the woman that she withdraw the claim and reconcile with the perpetrator. In many of these cases, there was limited forensic evidence, or the woman was recently married, and the prosecutor judged it was better that her husband be given another chance. Whether prosecutors tended to suggest such a course also differed according to personal preferences. One of the female prosecutors displayed a particular inclination toward reconciling couples, often advising them to patch things up. In one case, a young woman around twenty years old came with her father to file a complaint against her husband. She complained that she constantly witnessed her husband flirting with other women in the most outrageous ways, and when she confronted him, he would beat her. The case was being processed by the female prosecutor's male colleague, but the female prosecutor nonetheless asked the complainant to sit with her so that she could give her some advice: "What are you going to do now? If you get a *tafreeq* [a divorce granted by the court][12]—you have a child—what will be his fate? And your husband regrets what he has done; just give him a chance." The young woman was crying, saying that she had given her husband so many chances, tolerating his behavior because of her baby, but he was not going to change. The prosecutor, however, persisted: "Well, I can see that there is regret. He is not a bad person; he is a very calm man. He is saying that he loves you. You give him one more chance, for the sake of your child. If he doesn't improve, we are here; you can get your *tafreeq*." In this particular case, however, the woman was not to be persuaded. Nor was she placated by the prospect of obtaining a divorce; she insisted on pressing criminal charges against her husband. But other women were more easily convinced. Moreover, some of the "guarantee agreements" (which were kept on file with the prosecution) also contained points that the woman should adhere to. For instance, in one such agreement, it was written that while the husband would never beat his wife again and would set up a separate household for her, the wife would wear proper hijab, refrain from going out without her husband's permission, and not misuse her cell phone.[13]

Yet not all the withdrawn cases were closed by way of guarantee that the abuse would end. Ten of the thirty beating cases in the sample were withdrawn after the victim had obtained some kind of civil claim or settlement through the family court or through a private agreement. Many of these women had arrived at the prosecution with specific demands in mind. One young woman wanted her husband to commit to paying her a certain amount of monthly allowance (8,000 afghanis, around US$130) and to set up a separate household for her, so she would not have to live with her in-laws. Once her husband had pledged to these two things, she withdrew her beating claim. Similarly, a woman withdrew her claim once she was assured of getting a divorce and the custody of her small children. Another withdrew hers after her brother-in-law had paid her 25,000 afghanis as a compensation for having beaten her.

Regardless of the strength of the criminal case before them, the prosecutors would summon the accused and try to broker a deal between him and the complainant. In a sense, the prosecutors defined their professional duty more in terms of "solving" disputes, rather than in implementing the law. In one case, a young woman had entered into an engagement with a man she had later found to have a controlling, difficult character. An engagement had no binding status in Afghanistan, and the woman had no marks from the beating she claimed that her fiancé had subjected her to, but the prosecutor still summoned the fiancé. Once there, the prosecutor got the fiancé to state that the engagement was broken, and the claim of beating was withdrawn.

At times, it was clear that the threat of prosecution functioned as a kind of bargaining tool for the woman. In these situations, their withdrawal of their cases cannot readily be interpreted merely as an expression of weakness or as an imposition on them by the prosecutors or their husbands or families. Instead, it is possible to argue that the prosecution provided women with a new form of leverage, which, comparatively speaking, strengthened their bargaining position. Moreover, this function extended to other types of scenarios too, where physical violence was of less importance to the complainant—or did not feature at all. However, it was also clear that in at least two of the ten cases, the complainant had filed an earlier complaint and had followed the prosecutors' advice to withdraw their criminal claims and simply pursue a divorce in the family courts. When the women got nowhere in the family courts, they came back to the prosecutors to file new criminal claims, saying that they regretted having withdrawn their earlier ones.

In the final four of the thirty cases, the victim returned and said she had forgiven the perpetrator and wanted to withdraw the claim. In some of these, it was difficult to tell what had made the complainant change her mind. Some women stated that elders had mediated; others provided no explanation. Most likely, they had been subjected to pressure from their families.

At best, then, the prosecution unit provided women subjected to beating with a new form of strategic leverage when it came to negotiating highly unequal rights in marriage and economic entitlements (Basu 2006: 71). In some cases, it might also have curtailed the violence inflicted on them. At worst, the prosecution unit reinforced gender norms in which women's responsibility to stay in their marriages overrode their physical safety, and similarly, in which the government's responsibility to uphold marriage took priority over its obligation to protect women from harm. Even in the best-case scenarios, however, the function of the special unit was far from empowering women as equal partners in marriage (Basu 2006: 71). Rather, women were negotiating a slightly better deal within highly unequal gender relations. That the prosecution units (at best) served to modify rather than suspend the "patriarchal bargain" (Kandiyoti 1988) was underlined by another type of claim that women brought: complaints that their husbands had abandoned them. In these cases, women came to the prosecution unit not with claims of violence but in an attempt to force their spouses to uphold their obligations as husbands by resuming marital cohabitation or by ending affairs.

"I AM LEFT WITH NO FATE": CHARGING HUSBANDS WITH ABANDONMENT

The largest single category of cases after beating was abandonment. Fourteen claims of abandonment (filed as *be sarneveshti,* literally "without fate") were registered with the VAW prosecution in Kabul over a two-month period. The legal grounds for these claims were unclear. Under the 1977 Civil Code, a husband is obliged to provide maintenance to his wife, but the failure to do so, or "abandonment," is not a crime under Afghan criminal law. Nonetheless, the prosecutors opened files on these claims and spent time investigating them, even if none of the fourteen claims led to indictments.

The details of the cases show that the VAW prosecution units had, to some extent, become an accessible resort for women whose spouses appeared to have disregarded their most basic responsibilities as husbands. Most married Afghan women were dependent on their husbands for financial survival, and social norms (and the Civil Code) dictated that husbands should provide for their wives. Interestingly, it appeared that women approached the prosecution to reinforce norms that more subtle forms of social control (family interventions or society's disapproval) evidently could not compel their husbands to adhere to. Many of these women found themselves in quite desperate circumstances. Yet from their accounts one could glean more than material difficulties—expressions of deep disappointment and anger about the way that they had been treated. One young woman came to the prosecution office with her mother and holding a newborn infant in her arms:

> Three months ago, while I was pregnant, my husband hit me and kicked me out of the house. Even before this, I was suffering from cruelty in my husband's house. His family used to say to me "You are a *zan-e mordarkhor*" (dirty woman, literally, someone who eats corpses or carrion). They humiliated me in any way possible. And then they brought me [to my father's house] three months ago, and they never came back for me. When I gave birth to my baby, my mother called them and asked them to come, but they didn't. Now my baby is eight days old, but my husband hasn't come a single time to see the baby. I have been abandoned."

Her mother continued, "When we were in the hospital, I called her husband and told him, 'Come, you are going to be a father.' But he did not come. This caused my heart so much pain. I do not want my daughter to get a divorce from her husband. I just want him not to leave her abandoned like this. Look at my daughter— she is like a flower; she is young; she is beautiful. Why should her life be ruined?"

In most of these cases, the prosecutors first tried to convince the husband to stay with his wife and fulfill his marital obligations. This was generally also what the women themselves wanted. Sometimes they also hoped to pressure a husband to cease an affair he was having with another woman or to stop him contracting a second marriage. However, even in these cases, the "abandoned" wives were insistent that divorce was not their preference. This was not surprising, given the enormous stigma and economic hardships faced by women divorcees. One woman, whose husband had sent her back to her parents' house when she protested his second marriage, said, "I don't want divorce; I will never ask for divorce, even if he marries a hundred women. I just want him to take me back home." Another woman came with a complaint that her husband was having an affair with a woman on whom he spent all his money. A few days before, she said, her husband had even taken this *khanom-e bad akhlaq* (woman of bad morals) for a trip to Dubai. Again, she emphasized that she did not want a divorce; she just wanted her husband to break off his affair. But attempts by the prosecutors to convince husbands to assume their marital responsibilities normally did not lead to anything. Typically, when confronted with the prosecution, they would opt for divorce, and there was little the prosecutors could do legally. "Divorce is a man's prerogative, and nobody can prevent him," as one prosecutor said to a despairing woman when she had to tell her that, rather than give up his affair, her adulterous husband had stated that he would end his marriage. However, in these cases, prosecutors would try ensure that the woman was paid her *mahr*, which is a wife's right when a divorce is initiated by the husband *(talaaq)* or granted by the courts due to certain faults by the husband *(tafreeq)*.

"MY FIANCÉ MARRIED SOMEONE ELSE WITHOUT TELLING ME": THE VAW PROSECUTION AS AN ACCESSIBLE RESOURCE

One of the more surprising aspects of VAW prosecution unit in Kabul was how it had become an accessible resource to women seeking to solve a range of problems in which violence featured only marginally, if at all. Given the importance of notions of privacy and shame in Afghan culture—and the indifference and misconduct of legal officials—many scholars have concluded that Afghans approach government justice offices only when absolutely necessary (De Lauri 2015; USIP 2010). However, many of the cases in the VAW prosecution in Kabul challenged this conclusion. This is not to belittle the difficulties faced by other people who approached the prosecution unit, many of whom clearly were quite desperate to find a solution to their troubles. Yet it was also evident that to some, the open-door policy of the VAW prosecution unit encouraged them to also seek help with problems that did not really center on incidents of violence, as defined in the law. One example, which certainly was at the extreme end of the spectrum, was of a young woman who arrived with a complaint that her fiancé had married someone else.

> My fiancé married someone else without telling me. . . . He used to live abroad. As long as he was there, he used to talk properly with me, and we had a good relationship. But after coming here, . . . I don't know what happened to him. One day he simply said, "I am in a relationship with my neighbor," and after that, he never called me again. Then I heard that his wedding ceremony is in so-and-so hotel. I went to his wedding ceremony. I talked to him and asked him why he was marrying someone else, and he just said "Can't you see it's my wedding? We will talk later." His brother hit me and asked me to leave the hotel.

"What did his brother hit you with?" the prosecutor asked her. "With his hand," the woman responded. One of his colleagues, listening in on the conversation, jokingly said, "Only his hand—a hand doesn't really count." The woman was quiet, and another prosecutor suggested, "You also go and marry someone else. You were just engaged—you were not married to him." The woman again did not say anything, smiling unsurely. The prosecutor continued, "Why have you been so lazy? He has married someone else—you also go and marry someone else. He is enjoying his life, and you are wandering around in the prosecution. . . . I feel pity for you." Hearing this, the woman started to cry. "You people can't understand my feelings," she said and left the room.

Other prosecutors criticized their colleague for the way he had talked to the woman, saying to him, "You cannot make fun of those coming here." The prosecutor whose case it had been then went and asked the woman to come back inside the room. "Well, what do you want us to do?" he enquired. "Do you want us to make him give *talaaq* to his wife?" The woman responded, "I want you to summon him here and ask him why he has done this to me." The prosecutor asked her to give her or a family member's phone number so that he could contact her if necessary.

Because the woman stated that she had been hit by her ex-fiancé's brother, the case was registered as a beating case in the records. She did not return, and the prosecutors did not follow up further. Her case thus appeared in the records as a withdrawn case. Without further examination, it would have appeared as part of the problematic trend of women being pressured by family members or prosecutors to withdraw their complaint. In this and quite a few other cases, however, the actual dynamics were quite different.

More generally, many of the complainants or their families did not necessarily think of the prosecution office as a place where one went to secure an actual punishment for a crime in accordance with the law. Some came with vague notions of just wanting some kind of solution, and many came with a specific objective in mind other than prosecuting the case, such as obtaining a divorce, a financial payment, or custody of children. The larger picture is, of course, that Afghan laws and social practices granted women very few possibilities to obtain such rights. The VAW unit, therefore, provided some correction to a very uneven playing field, where women's access to fundamental rights was severely restricted. In some roundabout, unexpected, and limited way, the VAW prosecution unit could be said to serve as a tool of legal empowerment.

"HERE IS YOUR HUSBAND, AND HERE IS YOUR FATHER. CHOOSE ONE OF THEM.": RAPE AND KIDNAPPING

Over the two-month period, 7 claims of rape and sexual assault, and 4 claims of kidnapping (which involved sexual crimes) were registered with the VAW prosecution unit in Kabul. By the time our fieldwork in the VAW unit was completed, some seven months later, there had been no recorded convictions among these 11 cases. For 3 of the rape cases, there was no information available. One case had ended with withdrawal, as the complainant stated that she was going abroad for medical treatment and could no longer pursue the case. In 2 cases (one of which involved a father, and the other a brother-in-law), the suspects were indicted, but the cases had not yet proceeded to trial. The final case had gone to trial, but the rape charge was dismissed, and both the complainant and the defendant received suspended prison sentences for *zina* instead. This case involved two young relatives, and the woman eventually confided that the relationship with her cousin had been consensual. Although she had wanted marriage, her parents had forced her to approach the prosecution unit with rape charges instead, after they had failed to convince the man's family to provide a *baad* to compensate for the humiliation the premarital affair had caused the family. The prosecutor also thought that the relationship had been consensual and thought the best solution was a *nikah*. He argued, however, that as long as the family of the young woman did not agree, he had no option but to send the case to court and the suspect to jail. Before the trial could conclude, the woman arranged to see the judge privately, and she confided that she had been in a relationship with her cousin and that it was her family who had forced her to go ahead with the trial. The judge applauded the woman for her bravery and sentenced the couple to a three-year suspended imprisonment for adultery. For as, as the judge said to his colleague, "The girl and the boy seem to be in love, and being in love is not a bad thing."

A similar dynamic was evident in one of the kidnapping cases, but this case was closed before being sent to trial. A young couple had eloped, whereupon the sister of the woman filed a kidnapping claim against the man. The prosecution summoned all parties for questioning. The woman who was alleged to have been kidnapped stated that she had married the man of her choice and that her family was upset because they had already promised her to an older man who would pay a handsome bride-price. Although there appeared to be no grounds for a criminal charge, the prosecutor was not content to simply dismiss the case; he wished to see the parties reconciled, too. Protracted and detailed negotiations took place in the prosecution office, down to the exact kilos of meat and rice that were to be provided by the groom's family for the wedding feast. However, in the lead-up to the wedding party, relations between the two families again broke down. The prosecutor summoned the parties one more time and simply told the woman to chose between her own family and her husband there and then: "Here is your husband, and here is your father. Choose one of them. Do not fear; no one can say anything to you. You are in a government office—no one can beat you. Say whatever you want." After some hesitation, she walked over to her husband, and her family left in anger. The case was dismissed.

The three other kidnapping cases did not lead to convictions either. Two were dismissed and referred to the family court for divorce, and the final case was sent to court, where the defendant was acquitted. In all three cases, during the course of the alleged kidnappings, the complainant had been married to the accused, although whether the marriage had been consensual or not was disputed.

That many of these claims of kidnapping and rape turned out the be about something very different—families seeking compensation for their loss of control over their daughters' sexuality—should not, in any way, be taken to suggest that there were few actual cases of rape and sexual assault in Afghanistan. The loss of "virginity" under any circumstances, forced or not, was associated with such stigma (and outright danger) in Afghanistan that a large number of rape cases went unreported. Moreover, the sample of cases presented here is too small to determine whether they might be representative even of the rape cases that were registered with the prosecution units. What the cases discussed above illustrate, however, is that the prosecution units could become vehicles for family agendas that had little to with women's rights. In these cases, dismissal or acquittal cannot be understood to mean a setback for women's position per se—in fact, quite the opposite, since when the prosecutors dismissed these cases, they were siding with women against family claims over their bodies. In other words, dismissal rates must be treated with some caution.

Interestingly, the prosecutors in the VAW unit in Kabul showed little interest in charging anyone for consensual sexual activities. Sexual intercourse before and outside marriage *(zina)* is punishable in Afghanistan by up to fifteen years in prison. Elsewhere in the country, women were sometimes also prosecuted for "attempted *zina*" or even for "running away from home" (see chapters 4 and 5). In the cases covered by this research, there were several instances where it appeared that women (and men) had committed acts of *zina,* but if this was the case, the concern of the prosecutors was to see the individuals involved married or otherwise to caution against immorality. One woman even got the prosecutor to call her lover—the father of her unborn baby—and tell him to face up to his responsibility. There were no examples of the prosecutors in the VAW unit in Kabul initiating investigations of *zina.* This was in contrast to the prosecutors in some of the rural provinces, who would sometimes boast about how their investigations of rape had uncovered acts of *zina*—cases in which women who had filed claims of rape suddenly found themselves accused of crimes instead.

BARGAINING UNDER THE SHADOW OF THE LAW?

The VAW unit in Kabul displayed many similarities with the various alternative dispute-resolution mechanisms and specialized civil courts for women set up in other countries in the region, such as India and Bangladesh. In these countries, delays and corruption in the formal legal systems, as well as class and gender barriers, have led feminist groups to push for the establishment of "women's courts" or other arbitration mechanisms (Basu 2011). These bodies, which deal with a great number of domestic violence cases, are intended to provide women, especially poor women, with a safe space where they can speak freely about their marital and other difficulties, using their own language, in a nonjudgmental environment.[14] Research has shown, however, that in practice, these institutions, despite their feminist foundations, have displayed an overwhelming tendency to reinscribe gendered norms (Vatuk 2013; Basu 2011). Women's existence outside of marriage is considered problematic, if not impossible, and the focus is on the restoration of family life—and thus on getting both parties to amend their behavior. In some instances, officials in these institutions will threaten men with criminal prosecution if they don't take part in the reconciliation negotiations, but these threats are often defused by the fact that the main objective is to reconcile the parties. At the same time, as indicated by much of the literature on these bodies, the underlying cause for the inability to transcend such gender expectations is not always ideological prejudice but is often the realization that for many women in abusive marriages, there are few options available. Vatuk cautions that before judging these bodies too harshly, one should keep in mind that the problems of domestic violence that they are trying to address on a case-by-case basis are intrinsically linked to the structural issues of male bias and gender discrimination that characterizes society as a whole (2013: 97).

Although the Afghan VAW unit in Kabul, as part of the criminal justice prosecution, was intended to be a different kind of institution, it displayed many parallels to the specialized civil courts and dispute-resolution mechanisms in neighboring countries. Like these bodies, the VAW unit was unable to overcome the structural relations that situated women as dependents within the family unit. And like these bodies, the VAW unit thus largely became a recourse for women whose marital or family situations had become intolerable, rather than a mechanism for dispensing justice as defined by the laws. Yet within those larger constraints, it is still possible to argue that the Kabul VAW unit served to strengthen many women's bargaining position. Generally speaking, the VAW unit was not unique among legal institutions in Afghanistan in prioritizing settlements between parties over the application of the law. It is well known in legal research on Afghanistan that legal officials—presiding over both civil and criminal cases—often seek to reach agreements rather than to make decisions strictly based on law (De Lauri 2015). To a significant extent, a key function of the VAW prosecution unit in Kabul appeared to have been to include cases of violence against women into this preexisting practice. In other words, the dedicated prosecution units have made it possible for more claims of violence against women to enter into the criminal justice system, but without necessarily subjecting these cases to prosecution. As one of the cleaners in the Kabul prosecution unit muttered to herself with disapproval (after having scorned a complainant for making too much fuss about a missing file): "Don't know where this Violence [the VAW prosecution unit] came from. . . . In our time, any kind of dispute would be solved at home. . . . These days, even if husbands push their wives with a finger, they come running to the Violence unit."

The dismissive attitude of the cleaner notwithstanding, she was correct in her perception that the prosecution unit in Kabul provided (some) women with a novel resort—one with a very low threshold—in case of abuse or difficulties. This was a far cry from how the supporters of the EVAW law, both local and international, had wanted to see the new prosecution units operate. They argued—correctly—that a low conviction rate sent signals of impunity and that many women could be at increased risk after their claims had been dismissed or withdrawn. Indeed, there was no evidence of a systematic follow-up of women who had withdrawn claims or obtained a "guarantee" from the prosecution. The general message given to such women was simply "come back if it happens again."

Moreover, in Kabul, women were at least generally welcome to register their claims, with prosecutors starting initial proceedings. In rural provinces, women were met with a much more aggressive attitude, with officials denouncing them for being "bad women" and refusing to open files without significant pressure. There, the attitude that cases of violence against women did not belong in the justice system and that no decent woman would bring her "problems" to an outsider was very much in evidence still. Moreover, the open-door policy in Kabul, in turn, also meant that some cases were registered for reasons that had little to do with women's protection. Particularly in cases filed as rape and kidnapping, families would sometimes bring false charges in order to restore their reputation or to obtain a bride-price. Nonetheless, I would like to suggest that in some instances, the inclusive policy in Kabul provided some women complainants with new forms of leverage. Because claims of gender violence and abuse had not featured much in the criminal justice system at all, the ability to apply the threat of criminal sanctions increased the bargaining power of women vis-à-vis their abusers. This enabled some women a greater chance of obtaining some limited rights—such as divorce, child custody, or some kind of formal recognition that the violence that they were subjected to was unlawful and illegitimate.

CONCLUSIONS

The low prosecution and conviction rates of cases of gender violence were disappointing to many of the supporters of the EVAW law. They saw it as a sign that the government was lacking in commitment or even pandering to conservative constituencies. This was certainly part of the picture, and, as shown in chapter 2, the political buy-in of the EVAW law was incomplete at best. To some extent, the dedicated VAW units represented an attempt to solve the problem of missing national will by placing part of the legal implementation under direct global management. The VAW units—particularly the unit in Kabul—became a focal point where donors could channel money and training efforts and, up to a point, monitor performance.

Yet, as this chapter has emphasized, to view a law's implementation simply as a question of top-down enforcement offers a limited perspective. Laws and justice are ultimately filtered through a host of social relations before becoming concrete possibilities in individual lives (Agnes and Ghosh 2012: xiii). Especially when there is a considerable gap between legal frameworks and the lived structures of kinship and gender, it makes sense to view legal institutions as a space where rights and obligations between people—women, family members, and perpetrators—are negotiated, and where the law constitutes one reference point rather than the overarching framework (Agnes and Ghosh 2012: xiii). Applying this perspective makes it easier to grasp both the limitations of the Kabul VAW unit *and* the small difference it sometimes made. As the examples in this chapter illustrate, the withdrawal of claims did not simply occur as a result of the ideological prejudice of officials who believed that cases of gender violence were not criminal offenses. Rather, withdrawals took place against a composite backdrop of concerns and objectives by women, perpetrators, families, and officials. Although larger structural relations narrowed women's options, it was not always the case that withdrawing their complaint was simply the result of an imposition. In many instances, the prosecution unit in Kabul served to empower women in a limited sense—by offering them leverage in pursuing objectives other than punishing the perpetrators in accordance to the law. Arguably, there was a common thread running through the way in which the EVAW law was promoted and enacted—and the way in which it was expected to be enforced. Both entailed a mode of intervention that attempted to circumvent, rather than transform, complex political and gendered landscapes. Both, nonetheless, were filtered or somewhat appropriated by localized practices of mediation and patronage, so that the ultimate impact was curtailed.

4

With a Little Help from the War on Terror

The Women's Shelters

As long as there is violence against women, . . . when a girl has no place at her father's house, which should have been the place of love and mercy; when she has no place at her husband's house, which should have been a place of dignity; when she is not treated according to the rights and dignity that Islam has given to a woman, then she must have a place where she can take refuge and her life can be saved, and shelters are these places.[1]

The girls running away from their houses and seeking refuge in shelters are of the kind who seeks to realize immoral and unhealthy desires, desires contrary to our society and against our culture. These are girls wishing to be free to do whatever they want.[2]

This chapter focuses on the controversies in Afghanistan over the space, both literally and metaphorically, for women to leave their homes and families in cases of abuse. Between 2001 and 2014, more than two dozen women's shelters were established in the country, providing a living space for women and girls who could not—or for security reasons, did not want to—live with their families. As it was highly uncommon, if not altogether unheard of, for women to set up accommodation on their own outside of family or marital dwellings, the shelters were, by their very existence, radical establishments. They unsettled government practices and popular discourses that cast women running away from their homes as transgressors and even criminals. They also problematized the domestic domain as a potential site of abuse, from which women had a legitimate right to seek protection. As the shelters gradually established themselves in the post-2001 landscape, a series of negotiations unfolded over the conditions under which women could legitimately "escape" from home and take up residence in a shelter. At stake were the interests that kinship groups and society at large could claim in the movement, chastity, and propriety of women—and how such interests could be secured in practice through surveillance mechanisms over women's mobility and conduct.

At the same time, I argue that the controversies over the shelters revealed deeper social and political fault lines. The women's shelters operated through donor funding and donations from abroad. As they drew upon international networks and resources, they were, at least in part, constituted as transnational institutions. This enabled the shelters to act fairly autonomously of the Afghan government on many counts and to challenge or circumvent attempts by Afghan government officials to regulate, supervise, or co-opt them. However, the international leverage and resources that the shelters were able to mobilize could be sources of frustration, suspicion, and resentment. To many Afghan officials, and to the conservative media and politicians rallying against the shelters, the fact that the shelters were funded and supported by foreigners meant that the women residing in them were out of control in three ways: beyond family control and outside both government and national supervision. In other words, the shelters were regarded as a challenge to the institution of the family, to the government's authority over the foreign-funded civil society, and finally to Afghanistan as a sovereign Islamic nation. Such anxieties formed the backdrop to the government's 2011 attempt to nationalize the shelters by placing them under government administration. As I will explain, the contestations over the shelters became enmeshed in broader issues of competing models of service provision, popular discontent with NGOs, and finally the U.S.-led war against the Taliban.

THE "RUNAWAY WOMAN" AS A TRANSGRESSOR

When human rights workers visited Afghan prisons in the months after the 2001 invasion, they found that the majority of female detainees were held for reasons related to "moral crimes": "There were about 300 women confined in Kabul jail. . . . The majority were . . . detained for a variety of offences related to family law such as refusing to live with their husbands, refusing to marry a husband chosen by their parents, or for having run away from either the parental or the matrimonial home. It appears that these women have no access to lawyers, have no information on their rights, if any, and are generally left in jail until their respective relatives intervene" (Lau 2003).

Being incarnated for having run away was a gender-specific predicament. Only women could "escape from the house" (farar az manzel); men simply went out, left, or, in some cases, abandoned their families. Broadly speaking, constructions of "running away" as a female-specific crime or subversive act hinge upon a gender order in which women are considered legal minors. Women are the wards of household heads, husbands, and families who have claims over them and to whose supervision and protection they should be returned. Women's outings to public places (anywhere outside the house: the street, the bazaar, or the houses of relatives) are thus subject to permission *(ijaze)* by elders, husbands, or male relatives.

The kind of gender order that renders unaccompanied women in public places potential runaways whom the authorities are duty-bound to arrest is not only hierarchical (in the sense that women are subordinated to men and family elders) but also segregated. Outside space is constructed as male space, where men socialize and engage in business, trade, and politics, whereas women remain trespassers. As interlopers in public spaces, women must limit their forays to what is strictly necessary and with a clear purpose. Unaccompanied women who move around at leisure or without legitimate reasons are suspect and seen as potentially threatening to the social order. The head of a juvenile detention center in Herat patiently explained this to me as a response to my somewhat disingenuous question as to whether there were any boys in the center who had been arrested for running away. Boys, he said, could not be said to "run away": "When a boy leaves and come back after two or three days, no one in the family considers that to be a problem. A boy can walk alone on the street in the night; nobody's going to stop him to ask him what his business is or where he is going. The police take notice of a girl or woman walking alone on the street in the night with no obvious aim, but they won't notice boys in the same way. According to our traditional beliefs, if a girl is gone for three [or] four days, it will be a big shame for her family."[3]

The underlying principle in this is the stake others, namely a woman's family and male guardians, hold in her sexuality and her reproductive capacities. In post-2001 Afghanistan, doubts over a woman's virginity or fidelity could potentially be raised whenever her chaste behavior and nature could not be positively verified by reputable witnesses. Women who had spent unaccompanied time outside of family domains might fall into a category of questionable virtue. From a systemic perspective of public morality and social order, that is, the overall upholding of a gender order that recognizes kinship claims on women, single women at large in public spaces or living beyond family surveillance are deeply unsettling. If tolerated, the entire system of social regulation of female sexuality might collapse. As it turned out, this was exactly what many feared the shelters might bring about.

In the years following the overthrow of the Taliban, government practices generally accommodated family sovereign claims over women, although in fluid and unpredictable ways. During the Karzai presidency (2001–14), the number of women imprisoned for moral crimes was several hundred at any one time, according to government figures.[4] But moral crimes was a broad category; it encompassed both *zina* (premarital or extramarital intercourse) and the more vague crime of running away. While the Penal Code made *zina* a punishable crime for both sexes, there was no reference in the legal framework to any crime of running away. Families, judges, and the police often asserted that, regardless of the written legal framework, the practice of detaining runaway women was in accordance with Islam. In fact, however, governments in Muslim countries have dealt with women runaways in quite different ways, as recent literature has shown. Mir-Hosseini (2010) points out that while all the classical *fiqh* schools construct a marital relation in which women are placed under the protection and domination of the husband in an exchange relationship—in return for *nafaqa* (maintenance: food, shelter, and clothing), a wife is obliged to observe *tamkin* (obedience), but the exact meaning of *obedience* differs. For some legal scholars, obedience is primarily understood as sexual obedience, a husband's right to his wife's body. If the wife requires her husband's permission to leave the house, it is because of his rights of sexual access to her. To go out without his permission would be to infringe upon his rights to this access and she would be declared *nushuz* (disobedient). Others have interpreted the duty to obedience more broadly, as opposed to only in sexual matters.

Furthermore, the exact conditions under which women have been housebound in Muslim societies have been shown to vary. And even more variance has been found in the degree to which this has been enforced by institutions of law. Sonbol (2003) examines the Egyptian concept of the "house of obedience" *(bayt al-ta'a)*, which she points out is a modern practice. The house of obedience is a precept under which a judge could order a woman to be forcefully sent back to her husband if her petition for divorce was rejected in court. Sonbol argues that prior to the codification of personal law in the late nineteenth century, legal practice was more flexible. Egyptian women were able to negotiate their own marriage contracts and could include clauses giving them significant mobility, the ability to get divorce, and so on (Sonbol 2003). As a general rule, a judge would not order—and even less, force—a woman to live with a husband if she refused to do so. Sonbol claims that the nineteenth-century promulgation of personal laws in Egypt, while ostensibly a mere codification of sharia, actually incorporated patriarchal gender relations from Europe to greatly enhance the husband's power over his wife compared to existing legal practice. The new laws, in effect, gave the husband absolute right over his wife and the *bayt al-ta'a* was an official enforcement mechanism to that end (Sonbol 1998; see also Cuno 2009; Tucker 2008). This Egyptian law also became a model for other codified personal laws across the Middle East, such as in Yemen, where, until recently, the *bayt al-ta'a* was enforced by the courts and police (Shehada 2009).

The Egyptian example serves to illustrate that there is no single Islamic or *fiqh* position on women's right to leave the home and certainly no uniformity in types of government enforcement. If Islam cannot serve as a deterministic analytical device, it follows that historical variation has existed also in Afghanistan, although the limited research on gender boundaries in earlier periods makes it difficult to assess how much. However, as detailed in chapter 1, judges and legal officials who had been working since the 1970s and 1980s recalled that the government rarely prosecuted people for *zina* in those years, and it certainly did not detain women for escaping the house. The mujahedin government started to arrest runaway women, and incarcerations for *zina* also increased. Yet even compared to those stricter conditions, the Taliban government's infamous orders that women could leave their house only in the company of a *mahram* and only if completely veiled were a radical new imposition. In their rigidity, Taliban gender policies effectively usurped kinship power. The question of permission for women to leave the house was no longer left to the discretion of families or husbands; it was subject to the uniform dictates of the government, which also took it upon itself the right to punish women directly (Cole 2008). As Malikyar reports from the Taliban's 1996 takeover of Kabul: "The new rulers of Kabul assigned a number of militia men to the streets, markets and mosques, bestowing them with a mandate to carry out on-the-spot punishments on violators. On 2 October, two women, spotted in full veil on a Kabul sidewalk, were beaten with a car radio antenna. When asked for the charges, the militia men stated that the women did not have a good reason for leaving their homes" (1997: 396–97).

The Taliban's attempts to impose their singular gender regime was part of their larger project of imagining and enforcing a political vision counterposed to the West and to the urban depravity (as they saw it) and violent chaos presided over by the PDPA and the Rabbani-led mujahedin government, respectively. It was also an assertion of rural, Pashtun power over urban, non-Pashtun groups, forcing the latter to adapt practices more associated with the former (Cole 2008).

After 2001, government policies on women's mobility and public presence became much less restrictive, and more fluid and open-ended. Nevertheless, women and girls were detained, charged with, and convicted for *farar az manzel*, signifying that the Karzai government was accommodating family sovereign claims over women and had not embarked upon a total break with the mujahedin and Taliban governments of the 1990s. Except for in the large, more liberal cities (Kabul, Herat, and Mazar-e Sharif), women—particularly women in their teens or twenties—who appeared to be travelling on their own were usually considered suspicious and apprehended by the police. In some cases, women were tracked down and arrested after the police had received reports from their families that they had run away. Yet the outcome of an individual case of running away was never certain. If the police did not suspect adultery and thought that the woman had acceptable reasons to flee, they might refer her to a shelter. In other cases, women would be detained and investigated. Once detained, women were typically subjected to hymen examinations ("virginity tests"). Unmarried women who failed this test could be found guilty of adultery by default.[5] Others could be found guilty of the act of running away or the intention to commit *zina* based simply on the fact that they had left their home on their own and without family permission. Typically, the prison sentence for running away would be one to five years, whereas *zina* could be punished with between five and fifteen years in prison.

The significant number of incarcerations of women based on charges of running away in the post-2001 period gradually became the focus of both Afghan women's rights workers and the gender and legal reform aid agencies. They protested that running away was not an offense according to Afghan criminal law; only *zina* was criminalized.[6] Elaborate training programs were developed to inform legal officials of the actual limits of the law. In response, many judges—if they engaged with such appeals to legality at all—referred to article 130 of the Constitution, which stated that Hanafi jurisprudence could be applied when no other laws did.[7] Alternatively, many changed the charge of running away to "running away with the intention to commit *zina*." Eventually, the Afghan office of the International Development Law Organization (IDLO), the intergovernmental organization active in the field of women's rights and the legal system that had initiated the special prosecution units, solicited the opinion of the Afghan Supreme Court on the matter, which responded by issuing a directive in August 2010.[8] The directive stated that in order to determine a runaway case, the first step was to consider the following questions:

1. Is the runaway a female? Is the runaway single or married?
2. What was the cause and motive for running away?
3. Has the runaway escaped to the house of relatives or strangers?

Stating that it concerned itself with female runaways only, the Supreme Court further listed three scenarios, differentiated on the basis of whether there had been violence or not, and whether the woman had run away to a relative or "legal intimate" *(mahram)*. It concluded that if a woman had experienced violence and was running away to a relative or legal intimate, this would not be considered a crime, "because it is the right of every individual to stay safe from cruelty or torture." Moreover, if a married woman ran away to a relative or legal intimate, but for no "religious or legal reason," this was deemed not to be a criminal issue but a civil one, and only the husband could launch a complaint against the wife. However, if a woman, married or single, ran away to the house of a "stranger" (a category that included any nonrelative, not necessarily people the woman didn't know) rather than to relatives or to state authorities, even if she ran away due to family violence, this act was prohibited and punishable, because, the court reasoned, it could result in crimes such as adultery or prostitution. The Supreme Court's directive referred to a principle of Islamic jurisprudence called the Prohibition of Means: "Any action that leads to what is prohibited is prohibited. That is why running away [to a stranger] is prohibited and is punishable."

The Supreme Court's directive illustrated that what was under discussion was not only the validity of the grounds for running away, but also the *mode* of doing so. Effectively, it identified a danger in the prospect of women being outside family

or government surveillance. This hinged on a strong connection being made between women's mobility and freedom and their sexual availability. The directive
said women were incapable of being entrusted with their own virtue—therefore,
women who had been outside the supervision of authorized guardians could no
longer be considered positively chaste. Although men could also be arrested for
zina, it was not considered problematic per se for them to travel or live on their
own or to go to the houses of "strangers." For women, these acts were deemed
crimes in themselves.

The fact that escaping from the house was considered such a subversive act is
critically important for understanding the controversy over the shelters. Shelters
enabled women to leave their families and reside in a space where, in the imagina-
tion of many Afghans, they were completely at liberty to indulge in immorality. As
Qazi Hanafi, MP, said on a television program in 2011: "[A shelter] is a place where
youngsters want to go to fulfill their immoral desires, those that they cannot fulfill
at home, where they are monitored and controlled by their parents."[9]

Given such sentiments, it is not surprising that the shelters increasingly found
themselves on a collision course with conservatives. The first shelter had been registered in Kabul in early 2003, initially in response to the deportation of single
Afghan women from Iran. They were a novelty in Afghanistan. During earlier
times, women subjected to abuse would seek refuge with other family members,
neighbors, or in some cases, local leaders. During the communist era, a number
of women, if they could afford it, also lived independently.[10] Mary Akrami, whose
organization set up the first shelter, argued that the shelters responded to a new
need in Afghanistan, brought about by the upheavals of war and the accompany-
ing impoverishment and dislocation.

> "When I returned to Afghanistan [after the fall of the Taliban], there were women on
> the street, at night, who had nowhere to go. I don't remember it was like this before.
> Other family members or neighbors would take in women with problems at home.
> Now, family members were too poor, and neighbors were strangers to each other. . . .
> When I set up the shelter, even my friends and family were against what I was doing.
> They said that shelters are against our culture. But I told them: it's not in our culture
> to have women on the street either."[11]

By the end of the decade, there were nine registered shelters in the country.
The majority of these were run by Afghan women's NGOs, receiving funds from
a variety of sources, including U.N. agencies, private donations, and international
NGOs.[12] Two were run by directly by UNIFEM, although these were technically
short-term referral centers, from which women would move to long-term shelters
in the capital. Four of the shelters were in Kabul and would each typically house
between forty and fifty women. Provincial shelters, located in the northern, eastern, and central parts of Afghanistan, could accommodate around twenty women

each. Shelter residents had quite different backgrounds. Some were single women deported from Iran or Pakistan; others had fled forced marriages, threats, or violent abuse. Yet others had been placed in the shelters after the police had acted upon reports from neighbors about family violence—in some cases, violence so severe that it could only be described as torture. Foreign women had also stayed at the shelters, including citizens of Pakistan, Iran, and European countries.

At the same time, the shelter managers were well aware of the fact that some of their residents were potential criminals in the eyes of the authorities and sections of the public. By the time the Supreme Court directive was issued in 2010, such considerations had already informed the admittance procedures of several shelters, as became clear in my conversations with shelter staff in Kabul and provincial capitals. However, the exact practices that the shelters developed in response to this dilemma differed. In theory, women were not supposed to go directly to the shelters (whose location was not to be disclosed), but to MOWA, the Afghan Independent Human Rights Commission (AIHRC), or the police, who would then refer them to the shelters. But one shelter manager in Herat explained that a lot of women in her province were unable to come to the shelter because the police would accuse them of adultery and begin a criminal prosecution instead. If a woman failed to go directly to the authorities or to a close relative's house after she fled her home, she was liable to be prosecuted for *zina* or running away. The response of this particular shelter manager in Herat was to attempt to systematically inform local women of what she perceived to be the parameters set by the law. Using the example of a driver breaking the speed limit and then claiming ignorance, she contended that it was the duty of women themselves to know how the law worked. Women seeking to leave their families because of abuse had to make sure they would come directly to the authorities. A woman should not spend even a single night at a more distant relative's house or anywhere else, which would create a gap of time in which she was unaccounted for.

According to the manager of a referral center in Jalalabad—a kind of short-term shelter that would send women on to shelters in the capital—the police and this center had an understanding that the former would subject all women to hymen examinations before they were allowed to go to the center. Unmarried women were allowed to go to the shelter only if they were found to have intact hymens; those who did not were arrested and could be prosecuted for adultery. This was a way of giving the shelter legitimacy within the local community, and, the shelter manager said, it was also in accordance with the protocol they had signed with MOWA.[13] Staff members at the local MOWA office, however, confided that when they suspected sexual relations between a young man and woman who were eloping, they would try to contact the family directly and arrange for a *nikah* (wedding ceremony) so as to keep the couple out of reach of the police and their medical examinations.[14]

Other shelters, notably those run by the organization Women for Afghan Women (WAW), were more defiant. They stated that they would admit women even if they had come directly to them without referral—regardless of their prior history.[15] This stance fed into anxieties among conservatives and others that the shelters were some kind of moral void into which women could escape and where they could behave without regard for social norms and propriety. The statement by Qazi Hanafi, MP, quoted at the beginning of the chapter succinctly articulated such concerns. Allegations such as Hanafi's, which circulated widely in Afghan media, formed part of the backdrop for the sudden announcement by the minister of women's affairs in 2011 that the government would take over the administration of the shelters.

"WHAT HAVE BEEN RUN BY NGOS NOW BELONG TO THE GOVERNMENT": ATTEMPTS TO NATIONALIZE THE SHELTERS

On February 15, 2011, the minister of women's affairs, Dr. Husn Banu Ghazanfar, held a press conference in Kabul at which she stated that the women's shelters would henceforth be run by MOWA. In a series of rather nebulous formulations, the minister made several accusations against the shelters and laid out the reasons why MOWA was better positioned to run them. The background to the new regulation, she stated, was a ministerial commission that had reviewed the shelters and had uncovered "serious problems and many violations." When asked for further clarifications, the minister mentioned a lack of order and discipline, chaos, no follow-up of the women's legal cases, and disregard for the protocols that MOWA had drawn up for the individual shelters.

The question of who would run the shelters was also presented as a matter of national sovereignty and self-reliance. Minister Ghazanfar referred to a donor conference held in 2010 at which the Afghan government had asked the international community to channel money through the government. "What have been run by NGOs now belong to the government. We are ready to be responsible and should stand on our own feet." The minister further stated that the budgets of individual shelters were completely out of proportion to their activities, implying that some were involved in corrupt practices. Questioning why the shelters needed to spend a total of US$11 million on 210 residents, she declared that MOWA would be able to run these shelters much more cost-effectively. The minister also said that there were rumors that were discrediting the shelters, but that they would find less fertile ground if the shelters came under government control. The minister did not specify what these rumors were, but they generally consisted of allegations that shelters were immoral places harboring prostitution, extramarital sex, and drug abuse and that they were encouraging women to leave their families and husbands. When probed, the minister stated that she had no evidence that such things had taken place in the shelters, but she added that neither did she have any evidence to the contrary. In any case, she said, the takeover by MOWA would stop such rumors, as the ministry's staff would be present in the shelters and constantly report back to the ministry.

The press conference was the culmination of long-running tensions over the shelters involving the government, conservative politicians, the international donor community, and the NGOs running the shelters. The statements made by the minister illustrated the many dimensions to this conflict. Indeed, the press conference was a microcosm of them. One axis of tension concerned the conditions under which women could leave their families. Although the formal requirement was that admittance to the shelter was only through referral from the government or AIHRC, some shelters admitted women directly. Such open-door policies undermined the possibility of screening out those women who were not deemed worthy or in need of protection. To the conservatives, they opened up the possibility for any woman to leave her family, engage in adultery on the way, and take up residence in a place where no questions were asked. But some women's rights activists and shelter managers were also uneasy with the open-door policy adopted by a few shelters, which they regarded as an obstacle to a broader acceptance of the shelters in Afghan society. To these activists, adhering to the stricter admittance procedures would provide some reassurance that those residing in shelters had legitimate protection needs, demonstrating that the shelters were providing a necessary and legitimate service.[16] When faced with the unilateral declaration by MOWA that the shelters would be nationalized, however, all the shelters joined together to form a united front in the ensuing confrontations.

As the press conference indicated, MOWA's decision to take over the shelters was the result of other considerations as well. Minister Ghazanfar spoke about how Afghanistan, as a sovereign country, should no longer tolerate the fact that large portions of its development aid were channeled directly to NGOs. Whether the government or the NGOs should run the shelters was made a litmus test of whether the country was recognized as an equal and sovereign nation state in the international community and, particularly, by its Western allies. But the skepticism toward NGOs was also rooted in preferences for welfare and social services to be more tightly regulated and implemented by the state, as well as a growing antagonism toward the aid industry in general and "Westernized" female NGO personnel in particular. In order to show how the shelters had become entangled in all these additional dynamics, the next section details a few events leading up to MOWA's nationalization attempt.

"WHAT HAPPENS IF WE LEAVE
AFGHANISTAN": BIBI AISHA

In the spring of 2010, when I visited a shelter in Kabul run by WAW, the staff told me that one of their residents was a girl from the province of Uruzgan whose nose and ears had been cut off by her husband. The main reason I had visited the shelter that day was to try to retrace the complicated story of a woman named Fereshta, who had run away from her family and whose tragic fate is detailed in chapter 5. The girl who had been disfigured by her husband did not feature much in our conversation, but a few months later the world would come to know her as Bibi Aisha. On the cover of *Time Magazine,* her mutilated face was accompanied by the headline "What Happens If We Leave Afghanistan."[17] The *Time* cover revived debates both about the war in Afghanistan and about the appropriation of Afghan women's suffering as an argument for supporting the U.S.-led military operation. The magazine cover was rightly criticized for constructing an irrefutable and uncomplicated relationship between saviors and victims, between Western withdrawal and the mutilation of Afghan women. In fact, the linkages of Aisha's husband with the Taliban—which the logic of the article associated with the mutilation—proved vague at best and, as was widely pointed out, the presence of NATO countries had not prevented the violence against the girl. More generally, by making the fate of women like Aisha directly dependent on the West's willingness to commit to continued armed operations—and by depriving the maiming of Aisha of all context save this direct relationship—the magazine was a model example of how "discourses of salvation—of saving Muslim women from Muslim patriarchal law—are sutured on to a specific civilising mission, one that involves *giving* women their democratic/secular rights" (Siddiqi 2011: 77).

But the publicity surrounding the *Time* cover also fed into the growing controversy in Afghanistan over the shelters. In some circles, the cover was viewed as a national humiliation. The case came to represent the impotence of the Afghan people vis-à-vis the international community. For instance, Amina Afzali, the minister of labor, social affairs, martyrs, and the disabled, expressed her displeasure with the shelters' high profile in discussing abuse. She referred in particular to the case of Bibi Aisha, who had been taken to the United States for facial reconstruction, which had humiliated Afghanistan in the eyes of the world. Other countries, if subject to similar scrutiny, would also have been shown to have such extreme cases, she contended (A. J. Rubin 2011).

The photograph and the publicity surrounding it also reinforced the skepticism in some of the other shelters toward WAW—the organization running the shelter where Bibi Aisha had lived. WAW was founded by expatriate Afghans in New York in 2001. It proved very apt at fund-raising, lobbying, and arranging high-profile gala events in the United States. WAW also espoused an uncompromising stance on women's rights. However, among other shelters and their supporters, there was a measure of frustration over WAW. Questions had long been raised about its policy with the media. The fact that WAW permitted journalists to publish photographs of the shelter residents was criticized in particular, given that Afghan women who allow photos of their faces to be circulated are often stigmatized in conservative communities. Other shelters limited media access on the grounds that their residents were both deeply traumatized and in need of anonymity for protection. The location of some of the WAW shelters was an open secret in Kabul, and women were allowed to go out and visit their families. WAW also appeared to be paying little heed to its protocol with MOWA, which called for regular reporting and admission only through referral. Other shelters claimed that WAW's lenient ways were undermining the standing of the shelters as a whole, making them vulnerable to populist backlash as well as government antagonism. The Bibi Aisha cover made these sentiments resurface. It might be easy for WAW to spirit one or two women away to the United States, but all Afghan women could not be sent into exile, one women activist complained.[18] She worried about the ramifications that the publicity of the Bibi Aisha case had for the legitimacy and acceptance of the shelters in the communities where they were located.

Like the controversy over the government regulations for the shelters a few months later, the Bibi Aisha cover highlighted the transnational alliances that many Afghan women's advocates had established. These sometimes entailed a framework of action in which the main target of advocacy was NATO countries and their populations, who had to ensure that their politicians would do the right thing and not "abandon" Afghanistan. NATO governments had to stand up to Karzai and his warlords, to mercilessly defeat the Taliban, and to keep supporting and funding Afghan women. Such a reductive framework made Afghanistan a homogenous field where the sources of women's oppression were interchangeable—local patriarchies, the Taliban, warlordism, and Afghan culture were collapsed into a singular threat that only the West could defeat. This framework could not accommodate the trade-offs, negotiations, and compromises that other Afghan feminists at times found necessary in order to mitigate continuing dependence on the West. Nor did it easily allow for a scrutiny of the new relations of domination created by the international military forces. In fact, the publication of Aisha's photo coincided with a surge of targeted operations involving frequent night raids and the detention and killing of suspects, creating widespread fear and anger among many Afghan groups.

The fallacies of "the rhetoric of rescue" and the discursive effects they produce have been amply analyzed elsewhere (Abu-Lughod 2002; Butler 2009). My point here is to show how such discourses appeared in contestations about concrete gender issues *within* Afghanistan. For instance, WAW espoused a clear political position that called for a continued NATO presence and was uncompromising toward any strategy other than military defeat of the Taliban. After the announcement of the surge and the increase in U.S. troops in 2009, WAW had issued a press release declaring its support for this policy.[19] The following year, referring to how the picture of Bibi Aisha had laid out the bleak future of Afghan women should Western troops leave Afghanistan, its country director, Manizha Naderi, told a *New York Times* journalist, "That is exactly what will happen. People need to see this and know what the cost will be to abandon this country" (Nordland 2010).

As the controversy over the shelter regulations moved into international arenas, a similar logic was articulated. Calls for the United States and other countries to honor their pledges to Afghan women were made synonymous with a resolute stand against the Taliban, and thus the defense of women's rights was made dependent upon continued international military presence.

NASTO NADERI'S CAMPAIGN AGAINST THE SHELTERS

Fanning the backlash against the shelters around the turn of the decade was the relentless anti-shelter campaign of Nasto Naderi, a journalist at Noorin Television, which was affiliated with the political party Jamiat-e Islami.[20] Known as a formerly reputable journalist who had inexplicably turned into a populist reporter with questionable journalistic standards, Naderi had for a long time been running what he claimed to be an investigative exposé of the shelters. His television show *My Homeland (Sarzamin-e Man)* was widely watched. One of his early programs on the shelters had shown footage of an orphanage falsely presented by the show as a shelter. The program showed several young women gathered in a room in the purported shelter, and Naderi had implied that they had been forced into prostitution by international aid workers.

A later program, which aired just hours after the MOWA press conference, featured a story about a girl who had fled her family after her father had killed her lover. When we met a few months later, Naderi claimed to me that this "very beautiful" girl had caused the death of twelve people and was therefore a criminal who did not deserve to be in a shelter.[21] In reality, she had run away after her affair with the boy was discovered. Her father had killed her boyfriend when the latter refused marriage, which led to a cycle of revenge killings that claimed the lives of twelve people. In his feature about this story, Naderi stated his intention to go to the shelter where the girl lived the very next day, film crew in tow, to confront the shelter staff on live television about housing such a girl and to "show the faces of these activists."[22] Horrified, the manager of the shelter—run by an Afghan NGO—mobilized her supporters and networks. They contacted the U.S. embassy,[23] and—as later narrated to me by Naderi—"then Karl Eikenberry [the U.S. ambassador] called the minister of interior, and the minister of interior told the chief of my television channel: 'don't make a program about this woman again.'"[24]

Unsurprisingly, Naderi argued that this constituted an undue interference into media freedom, and the event only served to reinforce his claims that the shelters were ultimately a foreign product. Mixed into these spurious and speculative broadcasts was Naderi's rhetoric, drawing upon the established vocabulary of the jihadis' antifeminism (see chapter 2), which painted women's increased mobility as a threat to national independence and Islam and, thus, to the historical achievements of the mujahedin. Naderi declared that the shelters were an abomination and an insult to the establishment of the Islamic Republic of Afghanistan,[25] which the former mujahedin commanders had sacrificed so much for: "The shelters are not acceptable for our people who have fought 30 years to put the word Islam in front of Afghanistan. We live in an Islamic country. . . . But some NGOs come and want to make another way for our country" (Abi-Habib 2010).

Yet interspersed with all of this were elements of more substantial, if ultimately deeply flawed, criticism of the aid industry. In military combat trousers, a tight T-shirt, and a bandana, Naderi and his similarly clad colleagues in the television station had the air of urban vigilante militias, out to protect ordinary Afghans from the predations and injustices of NGO women and their international collaborators. Echoing the charges made by the minster of women's affairs, Naderi told me that the anti-shelter campaign had been motivated by what he called an "NGO mafia" that was exploiting women for its own gain. He claimed that while all women in Afghanistan needed help, those running the shelters were merely using the image of the downtrodden Afghan women to raise money for themselves and to further their careers. How was it possible, Naderi asked me, that so much money could be spent with so few results? And how could the shelters justify spending ten thousand dollars a month on a building that housed five or six women when other women were starving in the streets outside? These statements were not substantiated by evidence, but they undoubtedly carried some local resonance. Naderi also played on popular perceptions, reinforced by the Bibi Aisha case, that the shelters pitted women against their families and encouraged them to leave their homes, and even their country, upon a whim. He complained to me, "They say you should leave your family, go to the shelter, and if you have a big problem, you can just go to the United States or Europe [for asylum]. No NGO is talking about how the women can live with their families."[26] This statement ignored the fact that some of the shelters were involved in or supported reconciliation between shelter residents and their families. Upon written promises that the families would not harm them, women would go back to their marital or natal homes, though sometimes with tragic consequences (see chapter 5).

Despite their inaccuracies, *Sarzamin-e Man*'s tirades against the shelters gave force to government and popular skepticism about them. Following Naderi's cue, other television channels started to air programs about the shelters, often including personal attacks on the shelter managers and others, such as officials at AIHRC, who had supported them. Eventually, as the public outcry escalated, the ulema council of religious leaders declared that the shelters had to be closed down, and upon the orders of the Vice President Marshal Fahim, MOWA was tasked with drafting new regulations that would bring the shelters under government control.

VICTORY FOR THE SHELTERS

At some point in early 2011, a draft of the new government regulations on the shelters was presented to the Criminal Law Reform Working Group (CLRWG) in the Ministry of Justice, tasked with reviewing all laws and regulations related to criminal matters.[27] Members of CLRWG alerted the shelters and activists, who found the draft deeply unsettling.[28] In particular, they objected to article 4, which stated that all shelters would henceforth be run by MOWA: "The Ministry of Women's Affairs shall be responsible for the administration of the protection centers. To administrate protection centers established by non-governmental organizations (NGOs) the Ministry of Women's Affairs shall appoint 2 of its female employees as the director and deputy director to the protection center."[29]

The draft also provided for an admission committee that would consist of representatives from relevant ministries, the Supreme Court, and AIHRC, who would supervise the running of the shelters and, when appropriate, refuse admission to some women. Furthermore, this committee would refer "women and girls who had been compelled to leave their house" for a forensic medical examination (i.e., a virginity test). Article 8 stated that women and girls suspected of or accused of crimes would not be allowed into the shelters and that residents were not allowed to leave the compound of the shelters. Shelter organizations and women activists feared that this would mean that the ability to accept women who were suspected of moral crimes would be even more constricted.

These provisions clearly reflected the ongoing tension between protection needs versus the dangers of adultery and anxieties over unsupervised women. MOWA representatives argued that the regulations were an attempt to secure legitimacy for the shelters and that a framework of government monitoring would provide reassurances (or recognized proof) that the women living in shelters were still chaste. The head of the legal department of MOWA explained to me: "Most men in this country are very conservative when it comes to the issue of women. To those men who regard themselves as Muslims, for their wives to go and live in a shelter, when nobody knows what's going on in those places, . . . it is never acceptable."[30]

In short, the draft regulations laid out an official monitoring regime to prevent women's shelters becoming black holes where women's conduct and chastity could not be controlled and verified. They were also designed to create some local anchoring for incidents related to individual admission. Many shelters were under strong pressure to return women to their families who attempted to claim them back. In one case unfolding during the development of the regulations, even a current minister was said to be applying pressure to retrieve a female relative from a shelter.[31] MOWA, meanwhile, claimed that an admission committee at the local level would strengthen the authority of shelter decisions to admit women and make it more difficult for families to challenge them.

The shelters protested these and other elements of the regulations. They argued that government-run shelters and an admission commission would actually be less able to withstand pressure from relatives and that MOWA was not institutionally equipped to run the shelters. On February 2, 2011, WAW issued a strongly worded press release, warning that the proposed government regulation endangered NGO funding of the shelters and conceded to the Taliban and their sympathizers in the government.

> [The proposed regulation] would give the Ministry of Women's Affairs (MoWA) control over the few existing shelters in Afghanistan, all of which are run by non-government organizations (NGOs). These shelters are funded by international foundations and governments, not one of which has authorized any branch of the Afghan government to assume control of them. . . .
>
> WAW has taken a strong stance against negotiating with the Taliban. All past and recent history—the accumulation of vicious threats and violent acts against women, their stance against education for girls—is undeniable evidence that regardless of what they sign during negotiations, the Taliban will not honor women's rights once they gain control of a territory. WAW sees MoWA's audacious move as an attempt to appease the Taliban and ultra-conservative members of the government.
>
> NGOs have made progress on women's human rights in Afghanistan. In fact NGOs are the main defense against the obliteration of those rights in the country.[32]

Meanwhile, discussions in Afghanistan took place through CLRWG, where shelters and women activists were invited to provide their input. Although this process seemed to be making progress,[33] alarming articles about the regulations, detailing their content and quoting the concerns of the NGOs running the shelters, appeared in the international media.[34] Critics also linked the proposed regulations to ongoing efforts by the government to interest the Taliban in peace talks. Nader Nadery, a well-known human rights campaigner from AIHRC, stated that the government was restricting women's rights for this purpose: "[The government officials] are sending these signals [to the Taliban] that: 'look we have made these changes and look we are putting some restrictions, we are taking on board some of your concerns.' It is a very, very wrong policy. If you give in more, in advance of any talks, you feed into the confidence of the Taliban, so that they will come and dictate their terms. They will not accept the constitution; they will not accept the gains of the past nine or 10 years" (Farmer 2011).

A few days later, the fronts hardened further with the press conference given by the minister of women's affairs. She presented the regulations in their original form, without the revisions arrived at in the CLRWG. Although more sympathetic observers argued that the minister's aggressive tone was designed to placate conservatives,[35] some of the shelters interpreted her intention as whipping up anti-shelter sentiment in order to assert MOWA's control. They found her accusations of corruption in the shelters to be irresponsible, especially since she had been unclear about what she meant—*corruption* in Dari can mean both *moral corruption* (*fesad-e akhlaqi,* which is a euphemism for illicit sexual behavior) and *financial corruption* (*fesad-e idari,* literally "office corruption"). Indeed, *fesad-e akhlaqi* was employed by Nasto Naderi later that day, when he declared his intention to visit one of the shelters and expose its activities on live television.[36]

The mistrust between MOWA and the shelters also reflected generational and ideological differences. In post-2001 Afghanistan, support for the state welfare model of the communist era remained influential, since many people from the urban middle class who were staffing government positions had also been bureaucrats under the communist government. Furthermore, the notion that the state should be a provider and benefactor, running welfare programs and intervening in markets had a certain resonance among the urban population as a whole. These ideas, however, ran counter to the dominant paradigm for the provision of social services in the international aid community that financed the shelters and for the ways in which the shelters were currently run, through NGOs. This paradigm entailed relying on non-state actors as subcontractors for provision of services. Doubtlessly, there was also a certain amount of resentment and even jealousy among MOWA staff toward the Afghan "NGO women" running the shelters, many of whom had made a name for themselves on the international conference circuit about Afghanistan and had received international awards and scholarships.[37] Their proficiency in English and in the vocabulary of the aid industry, as well as in delivering the project proposals and reports it required, stood in stark contrast to the somewhat hapless state of much of MOWA, where the skills valued by the international aid industry were much less in evidence.

In the weeks following the MOWA press conference, international mobilization against the regulations gathered pace. At the forefront was WAW, which set up an online petition demanding that President Karzai withdraw any law "that wrests control of Afghanistan's women's shelters from the local Afghan NGOs that have founded and run them and transfers it to the Ministry of Women's Affairs." The Afghan Women's Network, the umbrella network for women's organizations, wrote a passionate open letter (in English) entitled *To The Gatekeepers of Women's Honor.* The letter denounced the Afghan government for allowing a non-transparent and incompetent process to take over the shelters and for hypocritically accusing shelters and their supporters of undermining national honor by exposing human rights abuses against women. In reality, it was the government itself that was damaging Afghanistan's international reputation by turning a blind eye to the abuses committed against women, often by its own officials. Letters about the shelters were sent to Western embassies in Kabul from citizens in their own countries, and three U.S. senators wrote to the Afghan president, reminding him of the sacrifices the United States had made for Afghanistan and calling the proposed regulations "a grave mistake." The assistant secretary of state of the United States followed with a more cautiously worded statement, expressing concern over the regulation and encouraging the government to allow the NGOs to operate the shelters independently.[38]

As the international storm intensified, President Karzai eventually backed down. Claiming misunderstandings, he said the regulations were to be redrafted, along the lines of the suggestions already put forward by the CLRWG. This new draft would allow the NGOs to continue to run the shelters and incorporated their protests about admission committees and other issues. In contrast to earlier controversies, such as those over the Shia Personal Status Law (see chapter 2), the Afghan women activists were unanimous in their approval of the end result.[39] There was also a feeling of confidence: they had wielded influence and could shape government policy in a positive way. As one Afghan human rights official happily told me, "They [the government] are listening to us women activists, because they know that we are able to make trouble and noise if they don't."[40]

In the international diplomatic community in Kabul, not everyone considered the victory to be so clear-cut. A U.S. diplomat later told me that she thought the Afghan women activists had been too quick to mobilize international opinion. They should have tried to reach an agreement with the Afghan government first: "In this case, the women activists went straight to the *New York Times*. . . . They rely too much on international media. This kind of strategy is going to do some long-term damage. . . . Afghan women's rights activists should focus more on negotiations, less on uncompromising public statements."[41]

Judging from the timing of the press statements and international newspaper coverage, which appeared in parallel to the discussion over the shelter regulations in the CLRWG, the shelters and their allies had not exhausted the path of negotiation before mobilizing international outrage.[42] It was the storm of international reaction that made the Afghan government backtrack on its declaration to nationalize the shelters. As the controversy over the shelters was brought into the transnational sphere, however, the parameters of the debate changed. More than anything, the attempts to take over the shelters were presented as a deliberate strategy to appease the Taliban, as a first step on a slippery slope of bringing the militants into the government. The West was condemned for abandoning its commitment to Afghanistan and for not staying the course, which translated into fighting for Afghan women by defeating the insurgents and not making any concessions. In fact, there was nothing in the background or actions of the main advocates of the takeover—the minister of women's affairs or Nasto Naderi—that suggested they harbored a wish to bring the Taliban back into power. But in the polarized situation in which the shelters were now immersed, there was little room for the other kinds of criticism (however flawed) that earlier had emerged earlier, such as alternate visions of how to deliver these services or the limitations of the NGOs regarding accountability.

CONCLUSIONS

As we have seen, attempts in 2011 to place the shelters under government administration spoke to the anxieties over the possible ramifications of unsupervised women. At stake were both individual families' authority over women and society's ability to enforce female modesty and propriety. At one level, therefore, the controversies over the women's shelters in Afghanistan centered on the sovereign claims that families could make over women (and the entire gender order that underwrote those claims). The shelters directly challenged the notions that women were the wards of their families and that the government and public institutions were duty bound to honor such claims by detaining women who appeared to be defying family authority by traveling alone. By opening up a space into which conventional forms of social regulation of women's conduct could not reach, shelters were seen as undermining family control over female sexuality. The initiative to nationalize the shelters was an attempt to accommodate such anxieties by establishing an official surveillance regime (or a guardianship system) that, through admission policies and the day-to-day monitoring of the shelters, would (re)constitute shelters as spaces where social regulation over female sexuality and mobility could be maintained. While some of the shelters were quietly addressing such demands on a case-by-case basis, having such concessions formalized and uniformly imposed by the government was unacceptable to the shelter managers and their international supporters.

The controversy over the shelters signified a logic of drawing up boundaries between good women, worthy of protection, and those beyond the pale of respectability. A woman's sexual purity was to serve as a measure of her eligibility for protection, based on the familiar notion "that the most important thing to know about a woman is her chastity" (Miller 2004). Moreover, in Afghanistan the parameters of respectability were extremely constricted, as shown by the Supreme Court directive that rendered all women outside family or government supervision criminals. The shelters did not challenge the validity of such a distinction between respectable and immoral women, at least not in Afghan public discourse. Instead, they adopted one out of two strategies. Some tried to expand narrow notions of propriety, by renouncing, for instance, the claim that shelters were places of moral corruption and by underlining the existence of cases of abuse so severe that the women had valid reasons to live in shelters. In other words, rather than questioning the distinction between good and bad women per se, they maintained that the women residing in nonfamily settings were not bad. Secondly, some of the shelters, notably those run by WAW, circumvented the moral/immoral categorization by exiting the Afghan public domain altogether. Instead of directly confronting constructions of sexuality that sorted women into those deserving and those undeserving of protection, they leaned on transnational support to operate independently of the scrutiny of Afghan government officials and conservatives.

As the struggle over the shelters intensified, it was reframed as a litmus test of the Western commitment to earlier pledges to help Afghan women versus Afghan sovereignty. Embedded within these competing prisms were opposing visions of state domain and statehood; an older welfare (and often paternalistic) model of the state was confronted with a neoliberal, privatized model. In this context, the shelters appeared as foreign space in a double sense, defying the regulation of both the state and of Afghan society more broadly.

The shelters' success in thwarting government attempts to nationalize them indicated the consolidation of an effective transnational alliance around women's rights in Afghanistan. Yet the international financial and political support to the NGOs running the shelters served both to empower and to constrain them. It brought them victory, but it carried some costs, by entangling the shelters in the contested space of the ongoing war, the presence of the international military forces, and possibilities of negotiating with the Taliban. The transnational support structures used by some NGOs generated new hierarchies of power. In rallying Western support against the Afghan government's nationalization bid, some of the shelter organizations argued that permitting the Afghan government to take over the shelters was tantamount to capitulating to the Taliban. As I have shown, the effect was to flatten the context in which the backlash against the shelters had emerged, reducing the criticism against them to a mere expression of Taliban extremism, to be defeated by Western military resolve.

To a greater extent than the EVAW law (and the specialized prosecution units), the shelters could be said to work outside, rather than through, Afghan government institutions. Although the EVAW law had been promoted and implemented with external funds and support, it nonetheless came into existence with the appearance of being a bona fide national product. Its supporters, both Afghan and international, were at pains to erase any Western traces from the law, whereas the shelters were more starkly transnational. They defied closer government regulation by mobilizing international support. In the shelters, Afghan women were explicitly protected by virtue of international funds and pressure, not by Afghan government institutions.

Almost four years after the attempted nationalization, this bargain was quite durable. The shelters remained autonomous. Furthermore, by the end of Karzai's final presidential term, in 2014, the number of shelters in Afghanistan had tripled, with close to thirty shelters in nineteen provinces. Run by NGOs, the shelters remained completely funded by international aid, but in a less ad hoc way. Their expenses were guaranteed up to at least 2017 through a shelter fund to which the U.S. government and UNWOMEN were the main contributors. Managers reported a more cordial relationship with MOWA and even with the police. The local police were now more likely to let women stay in shelters even if they were suspected of moral crimes, at least until their cases came up in court. At the same time, there were no shelters in the unstable, conservative parts of the country in the east and the south. In these areas, women who were abused typically faced the difficult choice of enduring the pain or fleeing by entering into an illicit relationship. The number of women imprisoned for moral crimes remained in the hundreds, and the Supreme Court still refused to change its stance that women who ran away from home might be punished for attempted adultery.

PART III

Individual Cases

5

Runaway Women

This chapter investigates the controversies surrounding three young women who embodied the role that had implicated the shelters in so much controversy—that of the "runaway" woman.[1] I learned their stories only after hearing of the violence later inflicted on them—murder, rape, and stoning. Only when I started to retrace the series of events that had preceded these violations did it become clear that all three women had first run away from abuse at home. Moreover, it became apparent how framing "escaping from the house" as a subversive act strongly bore on the women's options and directly made them vulnerable to the violence that was later inflicted upon them.

In the following discussion, I explore the trajectories of the three women, as well as the competing interpretations and assessments of their actions and the actions of those around them. Rather than focusing only on the formal justice system, I expand my lens to map how multiple legal orders intervened in the three cases at different moments. I employ the idea introduced at the beginning of this book, namely, that what is considered violence or a violation can tell us a lot about prevailing gender orders and other forms of power in a given context. By probing the fault lines revealed in these three episodes as they were taken up by very different mechanisms of justice, I ask the following questions: How were these series of events defined and spoken about by various groups of people—relatives, religious authorities, government officials, and the women themselves? What kinds of claims about violations or transgressions were recognized by public institutions, whether these were *jirgas* of elders,[2] government courts, or Taliban councils? Just as importantly, what was *not* recognized or named as offenses?

Posing these questions makes it clear that in both government and nongovernment forums, the loss or infringement of family or kinship sovereignty over female sexuality—as could occur when a woman runs away or engages in illicit relations—counted as a central violation. At the same time, this was not due to some predetermined cultural script, but a more tenuous construction, actively forged out of contingent struggles. A runaway woman was not automatically the main culprit in all cases; family honor was not always a key reference point. Alternative forms of intervention existed and were sought out, with various degrees of success. In other words, whether a runaway woman was, in the end, treated as a criminal to be punished by public authorities, a fugitive to be returned to her family, or a victim of abuse entitled to protection was, in most incidents, an open question. Nonetheless, the stories of Nafisa, Fereshta, and Siddiqa show how difficult it was for individual women to escape family abuse when state and non-state mechanisms aligned to cast women who left their family settings as inherently suspect. Even if some women might receive a sympathetic hearing when they finally reached a governments court, the paths they had to take to escape from abusive situations typically involved difficult choices that left them irrevocably tainted in the eyes of their communities and the law itself.

THE POLITICS OF SHAME

During the Afghan year of 1387, in the winter of 2008–09, a judge in a conservative Pashtun district in central Afghanistan was entrusted with a task he would later feel he failed at. The judge's cousin was looking for a girl to be his second wife, and the family of the prospective groom approached him for help. The judge accepted the task, and when he heard that Mohammad Ajmal, a local farm laborer, had a good and decent daughter, he sent his female relatives to see the girl. They came back with reassuring reports—Ajmal's daughter, Nafisa, was a good and hardworking girl—and the engagement was soon confirmed. The judge received from the groom-to-be a new suit as a token of appreciation for his efforts. But later on, after the ensuing scandal, he reflected on whether he should have been more thorough in his investigation. People had come to blame him for the scandal that followed, he later recounted. They said he should have asked more questions: Did the girl love someone else? At the very least, was she happy with the marriage? But, as he asked, how was he to have thought of such things? The custom in investigating a prospective bride was to send women to visit the girl, and the kind of things they would look for was whether she makes tea and looks after the guests properly, and of course, if she is beautiful. "It did not even occur to us that she could have a relationship with someone else. She was a Pashtun girl—how could she have a relationship? That Ajmal's daughter was completely without morals *[bad akhlaq]*—how were we suppose to know?"[3]

Nafisa, in fact, proved deeply unhappy with the engagement. She was only six-teen, and her fiancé was forty, considerably older. She was also to be his second wife. Nafisa's family was poor; her father had causal employment as a farm la-borer. The bride-price, reported to be around 250,000 *afghanis*, the equivalent of US$5,000, played an important role in her betrothal. As was customary in many circles, once the engagement had been confirmed through a *nikah* ceremony, her fiancé was granted nocturnal visiting rights.[4] This kind of arrangement, referred to as *namzad-bazi* (literally, "engagement play"), was often—or could be—a time of playfulness and excitement when couples got to know each other in an air of quasi-illicit mischief.

This was not Nafisa's experience of *namzad-bazi*. She proceeded to make con-tact with a young man working in the village as a servant. As Nafisa said when she was interrogated later on, "I was forced to marry someone. . . . He was an old man. I became friends with Amin, and I wanted to be with him. He became the one I loved. To run away was the only option I had."[5] Amin was the cousin of the host of a radio program, and Nafisa had called the program with her cell phone to place a song request. The radio host had passed on her phone number to his cousin, and Nafisa and Amin had struck up a kind of courtship over the phone. They then met in person and agreed to run away and get married. Theirs is not an unusual story—since the arrival of the cell phone network, many Afghan girls have attempted to escape unwanted marriages by seeking out men to elope with over the phone. But Nafisa and Amin's intention to escape to relatives in Pakistan was thwarted en route, in the eastern city of Jalalabad, when they were reported to the police by the manager of a hotel where they were staying. They were detained and sent back to their home province, the scene of the crime. In court, Nafisa was sentenced to serve seven years in juvenile detention for running away and *zina*. Amin received a similarly lengthy prison sentence, although his sentence was re-duced to two years after an appeal.

In the couple's village, Nafisa's fiancé and his family had been outraged when they heard of the elopement. They immediately went to Nafisa's father, Ajmal, who agreed to hold a *jirga* to settle the matter. For two days, the proceedings went on, presided over by two elders from each of the families' tribes. The discussion centered around one issue: under whose supervision had Nafisa been when she escaped, and therefore, whose shame *(sharm)* was it that this event had occurred. The fiancé and his family demanded two *baad*: one girl as a replacement for Nafisa and one girl as reparation for the dishonor that Nafisa's family had caused the fiancé with her elopement. But Nafisa's family rejected this demand. Ajmal ar-gued that the fiancé had been visiting her, spending time with Nafisa in her room. Therefore, he should have known about her relationship. Eventually, the elders reached the decision that one *baad* would suffice. She was to be Nafisa's younger half sister, Ajmal's daughter by another wife. The mother of this girl found the arrangement deeply unjust. It was Nafisa and therefore also her mother who had proven themselves to be the spoiled *(kharab)* ones; why should she and her daughter have to suffer the consequences? Her protests were to no avail, however, and after two days, she gave in. Nafisa's half sister was to be handed over to the fiancé within ten days.

Meanwhile, Nafisa was in the juvenile detention center in the provincial capital. A senior official arranged to have a room for himself in the compound of the detention center, under the pretext that he could not travel back to his house in Kabul on a daily basis. This was a violation of the rules, but his subordinates dared not protest. Through deceit and threats, he sexually abused Nafisa, and she became pregnant. He had told her that he was in a position to influence her legal case, and at first, Nafisa told no one about what had happened. But when the prison attorney came on one of his regular inspections of the detention center, she spoke out, as he later recounted.

> I went to Nafisa's room and asked for permission to enter. . . . When I asked her whether she had any difficulties with the juvenile rehabilitation center staff, she started crying and she was unable to talk for two minutes. I understood that she had a problem, so I insisted that she tell me. She said, "Something has happened to me that I cannot tell you." Then she started crying again and said, "The [senior official] has raped me. . . . He called me to his room, and when I went there, he asked about my case. I told him that I had escaped to Jalalabad with Amin. Then he said, 'I will ensure your freedom. I will marry you to Amin, and if he does not want to marry you, I will.' After he had said this, I went back to my room. After one hour, Jalaluddin, who was his abettor, came to my room and said, '[the senior official] wants to see you in his room.' When I went to his room, he locked the door and tried to hug me, but I didn't let him. I told him, 'But you are like my *mama* [maternal uncle].' He said, 'Who cares for the *mama?*'" and he threatened me with his pistol and tightly closed my mouth with his hand, and after that I couldn't do anything, and he raped me."[6]

After his initial shock and disbelief, the prison attorney arranged for Nafisa to make a statement in front of all the detention center staff, and then, in front of a judge. The senior official was subsequently taken into custody. At the primary court, he bribed the judge with a sum of around US$20,000 and was acquitted. It was at this point that I first heard about the case, through the lawyer who had just been assigned to defend Nafisa during the appeal for the charges of running away. At that point, the first trial of the senior official had concluded, but Nafisa was still being held in the juvenile center in the provincial capital, the location where she had been raped. Her lawyer and human rights officials were trying to get her transferred to Kabul, amid speculation that she would be released and killed through collaboration between the senior official and her family. The United Nation's human rights section and the Afghan International Human Rights Commission (AIHRC) had also become involved. Since the case was sensitive and the girl's life appeared to be at risk, these organizations decided to involve themselves in a discreet manner and to not make public statements about the case. The United Nations would contact the Supreme Court about the release of the official, and the AIHRC would press the Ministry of Justice, which had jurisdiction over detention centers, to transfer Nafisa to Kabul. The lawyer, as he explained the case to me, spoke of his frustration with the lack of progress about these things, but a month later, Nafisa had been moved to the juvenile center in Kabul, and the official was under arrest again, awaiting trial in the provincial court of appeals. After a few months, he was sentenced to twenty years in jail, the absolute maximum sentence. The prosecution had based their case on article 17 of the EVAW law and articles from the Penal Code on the misuse of office.[7]

A few months after this, I had negotiated the permits required to visit the juvenile detention center in Kabul,[8] where Nafisa was serving her seven-year sentence. I glimpsed her at the end of the long corridor, heavily pregnant. She looked at me from a distance, hesitated, and then turned back. The guards told me she did not want to speak to anyone. Four other girls volunteered to share their stories of how they ended up at the center. They were mostly around fourteen or fifteen years old, and their accounts were similar to Nafisa's. All four girls I spoke to in depth had fled unwanted marriages or engagements, either to older men or to their cousins. I sat with them one by one in the corner of a brightly decorated and surprisingly pleasant common room. They talked hurriedly, as if worried that time would not permit them to tell their whole story. One, when engaged to a man in his forties, had left home and had been taken in by an elderly woman. "At first," the girl said, "the woman treated me like a daughter, but soon she attempted to force me to sleep with a man for money." The girl tried to escape back to her parent's house, but the police picked her up and took her to prison. She had been detained for five months and thought she would go to court for the first time the next week. Meanwhile, her uncle had visited her and promised that if she returned to her family, she could marry a man of her choice. Another of the girls I spoke with had been engaged to her cousin in childhood but had run away with another young man right after her engagement party. They arrived late to the city of Mazar-e Sharif and decided to spend the night outside a shop. However, the shopkeeper discovered them and called the police. At first, she was put in a shelter, but when her father told the police she had a fiancé and had run away, she was sent to the detention center. The courts had decided that she should spend a year in the juvenile prison. After that, however, she would be free to marry whomever she wanted. Her eyes brightened as she spoke of her boyfriend, who was also in prison. She whispered about how much she loved him and hoped to marry him when they were both released.

The girls also said that Nafisa was always fighting with the staff, who thought her insubordinate and difficult. It could well be that this was the reason we were unable to meet. At this time—inexplicably, to the human rights officials who had been following her case—Nafisa had been assigned a new lawyer from a different legal aid organization. The new lawyer appeared to take little interest in her case and was impossible to track down for an interview. He was thought to be less committed to Nafisa's case than to the money that came with it.[9] But even if Nafisa could have her sentence overturned or reduced, her life was in ruins, and her most likely prospect for the foreseeable future was to live in a shelter.

Still, what had happened affected everyone involved. None of the families recovered its standing. Amin's family, afraid of revenge from both Nafisa's family and her fiancé's family, moved back to their province of origin. For Nafisa's family, the shame was the worst, and they eventually moved to another province in a different part of the country. This was not surprising to people who had followed the case. "People will shame [phivar] this family; they will say 'you are a family who cannot control or protect your women,'" said one.[10] The fiancé and his family did not emerge unscathed either. Although friends and neighbors tried to console them, the family still felt that their standing had been severely damaged. "After a few days, people came to us and said that the shame [sharm] is related to her father. 'You do not need to be upset. . . . She escaped from his house and not yours.' . . . But we don't have any kind of relationship with this family anymore. People and the tribe [quam] are blaming us, [saying] that we allowed this to happen. Because of this incident, we have lost our honor [izzat] in the community."[11]

The fiancé was no doubt aware that he was an object of mockery in the area. People spoke of how Nafisa had used the cell phone he had bought her to make contact with Amin and how it was the day after one of his overnight visits that she had run away.

The jirga proceedings were criticized from several quarters. Local jirga "experts," men who were reputed to be particularly knowledgeable about the traditions and rules of resolving conflicts, were dismissive of the way that the people involved had conducted themselves. They argued that the people in the jirga had been ignorant of real Pashtun traditions. They had completely failed to deal with the two people who had escaped. It would have been more appropriate for Amin's family to give a girl in compensation for Nafisa. Moreover, the two elopers should have been found, and the fiancé's family should have had the option of forgiving them or killing them.

> "Oh, it was not a good and proper jirga, especially because Ajmal [Nafisa's father] was not a powerful man. The subtribe that this man belongs to is one of the weakest subtribes. And his subtribe did not support him in this case. If he was capable, if he understood how jirgas worked, he would not have accepted [the demand] to give another daughter to this man. This is how he should have formulated himself: 'My daughter was not only engaged, she has had a nikah. She was your wife, so the problem is not mine. If you want to kill them, it's up to you.'"[12]

This would have launched a challenge to the fiancé to admit "ownership" over Nafisa, an ownership that would have implied that he alone was responsible for rectifying the situation and thereby vindicating his own reputation. Another *jirga* expert concurred, saying that in this case, the best solution would have been to kill the eloping couple. But, he contended, the people on the *jirga* did not follow this principle, because they did not actually seek to restore the rights of the people who had been wronged. He concluded that, since the people on the *jirga* were weak, they instead sought to make peace between the two parties. He also blamed Amin for what happened with Nafisa after she was arrested: "What happened was very shameful, but [it is] connected to what had happened earlier. The boy has to be blamed for both. If he had known about Pashtun traditions, he would not have accepted [the demand] to give the girl to the government. He should have escaped to an area where there was no government presence, where he could have asked for protection. What he did [is that] he turned a Pashtun girl over to the government."[13]

A government official also disputed the *jirga,* but as he was a trained religious scholar, his objections were based on religious grounds. He argued that the girl, a married woman, should have been stoned, and the boy should have been punished. The problem with the *jirga* was that neither of the guilty parties (the elopers) were punished and, moreover, that an innocent person (the sister given in *baad*) was penalized in their place. He said that Nafisa had made many mistakes. If she had disagreed with the engagement, she should have gone to the authorities to complain, not run away in secrecy with a man and without telling anyone.

In fact, however, elopement was often the only attractive option open to girls who found themselves in a situation like Nafisa's—married or engaged against their will. If they chose to go to the authorities, there was a good chance that they would just be sent back home—and that was if they were not intercepted and detained by the police even before reaching a government office. Leaving with a man offered them protection along the way. A couple was less likely to arouse suspicion than a young woman traveling on her own. It also promised a future, since single women without family support were often condemned to a life in a shelter or an unfavorable marriage arranged as a last resort. Ironically, then, constraints were stacked against them in such a way that young women saw embarking upon an affair as their only option—the most grievous transgression in the view of their communities and the government. The directive from the Supreme Court, prohibiting women from leaving their homes in the company of non-*mahram* men (see chapter 4), in effect often closed off the option of appealing to the authorities to escape abusive situations and coerced marital unions.

Unlike the others who commented on Nafisa's case, the religious scholar faulted Nafisa for what had happened in the juvenile detention center, arguing that the senior official had offered her a bargain for her freedom in return for sex. He stated that she had "agreed to this intercourse, without regard for laws or traditions," and only when the official had failed to fulfill his promise did she make accusations of rape. On the other hand, many government employees pointed out that Nafisa should not have been the only female staying in the juvenile center. A few people argued that the chief of the Department of Women's Affairs (DOWA) in the province was to blame for this. One female official from the province stated: "In our environment, a mother is responsible for her daughter, to keep her safe and to control her. When a woman has a legal case, DOWA is responsible for her. But the head of DOWA [in Nafisa's province] has her own issues, and there is no activity of DOWA in this case. Look, both the boy and the girl are in prison, and nobody has helped the girl."[14]

The former head of DOWA in Nafisa's province said that when she held this office, she would bring women in difficult situations to her home:

> There was a girl from an insecure district who came to the governor's office, and she was referred to me so that I could find a solution. Her problem was that she had no brother, and she was in a land dispute with her cousin. I brought her to stay in my house. People from [her district] were coming to me and threatening me. I said, "I don't have any special interest in this case. I have no young son, and my husband is very old. I am just solving her problem." . . . She was in my house for several days, and then there was a meeting of elders, who decided that she could marry anyone she wanted and that nobody had the right to deny her this. Many proposers came forward, and she chose an MP. Now she is living with great honor in her husband's house.[15]

But the present head of DOWA protested that she had security problems and had repeatedly asked for a women's shelter to be built in the province. She could not take anyone in to live in her own house because of threats and insecurity. In other provinces, shelters sometimes served a dual function; the police would place women they had arrested in a shelter when there was no special women's section in the prison or detention center or when there were no other women detainees. This comment by the head of DOWA shows that the distinction between protective spaces and places of detention was blurred and reinforced the notion that women fleeing violence or abuse were criminals. However, the suggestion that the head of DOWA should, by virtue of her personal and political abilities and connections, serve as a protector of women, was an accurate reflection of how the office was functioning in most provinces. When the head of DOWA was a forceful personality with a political and family background enabling her to withstand pressure, the office could be an important ally to women who were in disputes with their families. In provinces where the DOWA chief lacked political clout or took less personal interest in these matters, the local DOWA office was of little help and sometimes even assisted families in pressing their claim over women. The latter was the case in the province of Parwan, where, as related below, DOWA was one actor in a series of events eventually leading to the death of Fereshta, who had fled a forced marriage with her cousin.

THE KILLING OF FERESHTA

Fereshta, from a village in Parwan near the provincial capital Charikar, north of Kabul, had been engaged to her paternal uncle's son in childhood, and Fereshta's brother to her fiancé's sister. When Fereshta's father was martyred during the jihad, her mother married her late husband's brother, and the family moved into his household. As she grew older, Fereshta began to dislike the idea of marrying her cousin, with whom she was now living in the same house. Many who spoke about her case later on suggested that it had been unseemly to expect her to marry a boy she had grown up with; she now looked at him like a brother. Perhaps there was also a looming conflict within the family; the engagement between Fereshta's brother and the sister of Fereshta's fiancé had already been broken, and the girl had married her maternal cousin instead. Whatever the case, when Fereshta turned twenty, she was told in no uncertain terms by her stepfather and uncle that her engagement would not be broken and that she would marry her cousin, whether she wanted to or not.

When she started to protest her impeding marriage, she was beaten, and her wedding eventually proceeded against her will. Fereshta's mother, her striking features painted with grief, later spoke bitterly to me of how her daughter's wedding had been a cheap, rushed affair. The cousin, who was illiterate, was widely thought of as an unworthy match for the attractive and articulate Fereshta, who had completed nine years of school. On the evening of the *nikah*, Fereshta was given a sedative, and the marriage was consummated while the bride was unconscious. Her grandmother, who played a pivotal role in the attempts to make Fereshta submit to the match, reportedly told Fereshta when she regained her senses that she was no longer a virgin and that she therefore had no choice but to stay in the marriage.

But Fereshta rebelled. Some forty days after her wedding, she left the house and headed south to Kabul. She traveled with her neighbor and boyfriend, but once in Kabul, she went to a shelter run by Women for Afghan Women. The shelter took her in and started to look at the possibility of invalidating her marriage or getting her a divorce. Meanwhile, Fereshta's grandmother appeared in the Kabul offices of the Afghan Independent Human Rights Commission, presenting a formal letter issued by DOWA in Parwan. The official who received the grandmother later told me, "The letter introduced the grandmother of Fereshta saying, . . . 'Fereshta has run away, but she is married. Please offer her your assistance so that she can find her granddaughter and take her back to Parwan.'"[16]

Attempting to strengthen her story, the grandmother explained to the officer at AIHRC that Fereshta was not only married but also pregnant, and being young and innocent, she had been tricked by another man, with whom she had escaped. The officer decided to call the various shelters in Kabul, and once she found out which one Fereshta was at, she asked her to come to the AIHRC office, where her grandmother was waiting. When Fereshta arrived and saw her grandmother, she immediately started to shout at her, saying how she had been forced to marry her cousin despite declaring that she had not wanted to. The AIHRC staff decided that the case was more complicated than the grandmother had led them to believe, so they asked the grandmother to return to Parwan and let Fereshta go back to the shelter.

A few days later, however, when Fereshta had been hospitalized for an appendix operation, the police arrived. How the police knew that Fereshta was at the hospital was never clearly established. It was speculated that someone in DOWA or at the hospital had tipped off the family, who had mobilized the police to arrest her. On the basis that Fereshta was married and had run away, the police arrested her and took her to the juvenile prison in Parwan, the scene of the alleged crime. The prosecution put together a case whereby Fereshta was charged for running away while being married, with reference to article 130 of the Constitution, which grants judges permission to apply sharia in cases in which no other laws applied (see chapter 4).

Fereshta's grandmother, uncle, and self-declared husband appeared in court, now accusing her also of having aborted a child. Rather than having her imprisoned, they wanted her returned to them. Fereshta's defense lawyer, impressed by the way she was able to present her case, supported her by arguing that the marriage had been invalid and that there was no evidence of Fereshta having committed *zina*. The judge proceeding over the case agreed and ruled that Fereshta should be released. She had been punished enough, and there had been no proof of adultery. She was alone when she came to the shelter, and she was alone when she came to court, the judge later stated to me. He had felt no need to probe the matter further. He also regarded the marriage as having been forced (though there were no attempts to incriminate anyone for this) and recalled how Fereshta, "wise and beautiful," had been unjustly paired with an illiterate husband.

Having been acquitted both in the primary court and the appeal court,[17] Fereshta moved from the detention center into the shelter in Parwan. Shortly afterward, a "reconciliation agreement" was brokered with the help of DOWA and the local shelter. Such agreements were commonly used throughout the country in cases in which a woman had fled her family. Arranged by shelters, AIHRC, the police, or the courts, family members would normally sign a letter guaranteeing a woman's safety, and she would move back into the house she had escaped from or would live with other relatives. In Fereshta's case, she went to live with her maternal uncle in a household different from that of her mother, uncle, and husband, and this maternal uncle acted as the guarantor of her life.

A few days later, however, this uncle invited Fereshta for what she thought was a reconciliation meeting with her husband's family. Perhaps hoping that this was an occasion to settle matters with her extended family, she went. After the food had been served, when it was getting dark, Fereshta declared her intention to return home to her maternal uncle's house. Defying her grandmother's and other relatives' protestations, she made her way out of the compound, but as she reached the gate, she was killed by two shots from a single-barreled shotgun. The police, alerted by neighbors hearing the shots, arrived promptly at the scene. There they found Fereshta's body and most of the family members, whom they arrested. Her husband and her father-in-law were not among them, having fled immediately after the murder. Nor was Fereshta's mother, who had been sent away days before the dinner party.

In the trial that followed, an elderly and frail relative of Fereshta—her grandmother's brother—figured as the perpetrator. He had voluntarily confessed to the murder, although Fereshta's mother and others claimed that the main culprits had been the husband, his father, and the grandmother and said that the old man was put forward as the scapegoat. His age meant that he was expendable as a breadwinner and that he was unlikely to be executed. To further mitigate the charges against her elderly brother, Fereshta's grandmother showed a video in court. It was of a woman dancing lecherously and appearing drunk. In a bid to portray Fereshta as a woman of loose morals and therefore make her murder less of an offense, relatives claimed that this girl on the video was her, something that was refuted by witnesses called in by the court. This and other attempts to justify the murder failed to convince the judge. The elderly granduncle was sentenced to sixteen years in prison for Fereshta's murder, within the maximum range of sentencing, although it was not the sentence that Fereshta's mother, now estranged from the rest of the family, told me she had wanted. As she publically declared following the verdict: "This horrible man had no right to kill my daughter. The government must avenge my daughter's blood by sentencing this man to death."[18]

A STONING IN KUNDUZ

On August 15 of the same year, a crowd of around two hundred men gathered near the bazaar of Mulla Quli, a small settlement in the Dasht-e Archi district of Kunduz. They were assembled for the stoning of Siddiqa and Abdul Qayam, who had confessed to the act of adultery. Sometime later, a cell phone video emerged, showing in gruesome detail what had happened that day.[19] Before the crowd, a Taliban mullah declares in Pashto: "When a married woman commits adultery, she will be struck by stones—this is called *sangsar* in Arabic. The women you see here today committed adultery with this man. She has admitted this herself not once, but many times. . . . Islamic law will be enforced here in Kunduz, by the grace of God. They will both be punished, these two people."

Siddiqa, who has been placed waist-deep in a hole in the ground, is then struck by stones thrown by the crowd. Her blue *chadari* gradually stains with blood until a large rock hits her head, and she slumps over. Subsequently, Qayam, a tall young man dressed in a fresh, white *shalwar kameez,* is brought before the crowd. He is blindfolded, and as he crouches on the ground, a rain of stones hits him. Eventually he collapses facedown on the ground, barely visible through the dust whipped into the air as the stones continue to strike him.

News about the stoning in Kunduz broke almost immediately and shocked much of the country. But Dasht-e Archi, along with other districts in Kunduz, had fallen to the Taliban, and beyond condemning the stoning, there was little the government could do. Like Nafisa and Fereshta, nineteen-year-old Siddiqa had faced a marriage against her will, although in her case, it had not yet been consummated. Siddiqa had appealed to Qayam, a married driver whom she knew through her brother, to escape with her. Together they eloped to relatives in Kunar Province. But their bliss proved short-lived. Hearing the news of their escape, a large number of men from Siddiqa's family, an influential and rich tribe, surrounded Qayam's family home, threatening to attack the house and kidnap its women, unless Siddiqa was returned to them. Qayam's family consequently convinced the couple to return, and over the phone, the former *woleswal* (district governor) guaranteed their safety. Qayam's relatives immediately set out to broker a deal that would settle the matter with Siddiqa's family, who had been greatly affronted by the elopement. A settlement involving a substantial amount of money and another girl from Qayam's family was agreed upon, and frantic efforts to collect the money ensued. Meanwhile, the couple found themselves turned over to the custody of the local Taliban. They confessed to adultery, perhaps thinking that their resolve would lead their community to accept the match, but instead they were sentenced to death by stoning by a committee of Taliban ulema. With Qayam's family still scrambling for the last *afghanis* to settle the case, Siddiqa and Qayam were stoned and killed by a large group of villagers and the Taliban, with no protests from Siddiqa's family. When the horrific images filmed by someone in the crowd emerged a few months later, it led to renewed calls for government action. However, the government never managed to fully reestablish control over Dasht-e Archi, and years later, no arrest had been made.

THE VIOLATIONS THAT MATTERED

The three sets of events in this chapter all became issues of governance. They involved attempts at dispute resolution, punishment, or redress through fora and mechanisms outside of the immediate family, even if the institutions that dealt with the incidents were of a very different nature. Fereshta's family mobilized DOWA, AIHRC, the police, and the courts in their attempts to retrieve Fereshta. They claimed that she was a married woman, implying that the government there-fore had an obligation to return her to them. Fereshta, on the other hand, retorted to state officials that her family had been wrong in forcing her to wed her cousin and that her marriage was invalid. The elopement of Nafisa and Amin became a state matter at the point when they were arrested by the police in Jalalabad, a routine government action on suspicion of elopement. But to Nafisa's family, the government did not appear as an ally, but rather as an irrelevant or alien institu-tion, and perhaps out of reach. Once official bodies had detained their daughter, they made no attempt to contact her or follow her case in any way, and neither did Nafisa's in-laws. Instead, the central violation that preoccupied those in Nafisa's home area was the failure of her family to deliver their part of the engagement agreement between the two families when Nafisa ran away with Amin. However, the forum through which this conflict was settled was also public, even if informal and outside government scrutiny.

The stoning in Kunduz did not involve the Afghan state in any significant way. Instead, a group of Taliban insurgents who had recently taken over the district were the main governing force intervening in the case. From a distance, the ston-ing looked like a brutal, top-down imposition of Taliban justice on a community that was already in the process of sorting out the dispute in a more conciliatory way. Qayam and Siddiqa had been stoned for *zina* following the intervention of the Taliban, who had insisted on applying sharia justice despite the fact that nego-tiations over a settlement between Qayam's and Siddiqa's families were still ongo-ing. As such, the episode could be understood as a classic example of contestations over legitimate authority, not unlike a case from the 1980s described by Edwards (2002), in which a Safi woman was stoned to death for adultery by mujahedin commanders contrary to the wishes and sentiments of her tribe.[20] But, as I will show below, it quickly became evident that the conflict dynamic in Kunduz was more ambiguous than a matter of mullahs and their brutally rigid religious dogma imposing themselves over tribal authority, which is how Edwards reports that the local community perceived the Safi stoning. Notably, in Kunduz, the family of Siddiqa voiced no protests over the execution of their daughter.

Despite the three cases being subject to interventions from different kinds of institutions, all of them featured the loss or infringement of family sovereignty over female sexuality as a central offense. In Fereshta's case, her family, led by her grandmother, went to government agencies asking them to return her to them. Fereshta's departure was framed as an illegitimate act of escape in which the gov-ernment had an obligation to restore the runaway. The subsequent dynamics lead-ing to Fereshta's arrest and return to Parwan was difficult to pin down, given the tragic outcome. Widely considered an unjust killing, it was not surprising that the various people involved tried to dissociate themselves from the events preceding it—and certainly from the act of sending Fereshta back to her family. In particular, the head of DOWA, a woman in her late twenties, who had later brokered the guarantee with the maternal uncle with whom Fereshta was to live, was extremely reluctant to talk about the case. She repeatedly cancelled our meetings, usually saying she had to go to a workshop at the last minute. This is also what she had said one day when I showed up at her office to speak to her assistant and found her at her desk. She then unenthusiastically agreed to an interview, in which she claimed to remember nothing about the case.

Nevertheless, it seems that the first port of call for the family following Fereshta's escape had been DOWA, who then evidently equipped Fereshta's grandmother with the letter that asked for the authorities' cooperation in retrieving her grandchild. The family, having discovered Fereshta's whereabouts due to the intervention of AIHRC, then got the police in Parwan to send a request to the police commander of the Kabul central zone to find her and bring her back to Parwan. Up to this point, the government had recognized the family's claims on Fereshta by acting on their demand to bring her back to Parwan, but the events that followed showed that the state was an ambiguous guarantor of family claims over women. In the last phase of her life, government institutions sided with Fereshta. She was released from prison, and the court did not recognize the family's absolute power over her. Finally, when she was killed, the court sentenced her granduncle to sixteen years in prison for her murder.

In the other two cases—Siddiqa's stoning in Kunduz and Nafisa's elopement—there were no calls on the government to assist the families in maintaining authority over female relatives. There were several reasons for this. The district of Dasht-e Archi in Kunduz was outside government control, as illustrated by the government's inability to arrest anyone later on, despite the outrage that the stoning had produced. Nafisa's family, by contrast, was living in an area with greater government presence, but they were poor and probably unable to call on the government to retrieve Nafisa and return her to them in the way the much-better-connected family of Fereshta had done. Nevertheless, the offense against kinship prerogatives over female sexuality figured as the central violation in these two episodes too.

The case in Kunduz appeared, at first, to be framed as a different kind of violation: Abdul Qayam and Siddiqa were punished for the offense of *zina*, a crime against God. (The act of stoning, in turn, was what was considered as the main violation in Afghan and international media). But upon closer examination of the events surrounding the stoning, a more ambiguous picture emerges, a picture in which the family's sovereign rights over their daughter also played a part. Once it was clear that Siddiqa had eloped with Qayam, two hundred men of her Turkmen tribe surrounded his house, threatening to enter it and take away the women inside unless Siddiqa was returned. In their view, by eloping with Siddiqa, Abdul Qayam had stolen a woman from her family and tribe, thereby launching a direct attack on their standing in the community.

And a lot was at stake. Siddiqa's grandfather had been Mulla Quli, the namesake of the village itself. For such an important family to be seen as unable to keep their women under their protection and control, to appear vulnerable to unauthorized access, might have been nothing less than intolerable. Later on, when Taliban started to investigate the case, it was articulated in a different way, as the crime of *zina,* a crime against God, rather than an offence against Siddiqa's family. But the latter's agenda proved not entirely different from that of the Taliban.[21] When Qayam and Siddiqa arrived back to Dasht-e Archi in Kunduz—begged to do so by Qayam's family, who were under siege by Siddiqa's tribesmen—Siddiqa's family refused to let her stay under the protection of the former *woleswal* (district governor), who had given the couple a guarantee that they would be safe if they returned. The former *woleswal* was from the same tribe as Qayam and was therefore not considered trustworthy by Siddiqa's father, who insisted that she and Qayam stay with a village mullah while negotiations between the families took place. It was this mullah, considered a Taliban sympathizer, who opened the door for the Taliban to start investigating the case. Nothing suggests, however, that Siddiqa's father opposed the intervention by the Taliban. A member of Qayam's family later claimed that Siddiqa's father had said, "I shall hand over my daughter to the Taliban and will ask them to do what religion orders," doubtlessly knowing that her execution might be the outcome.[22] The local researcher who carried out the data collection in Kunduz (I could not travel there, since the area was under Taliban control) opined that to Siddiqa's father, the preferable outcome was the couple's death: "I believe that in our culture, this [an elopement] is a very big shame. It is about the honor of the tribe. Even if ten girls had been offered as reparation, I believe he would do the same [not accept a reconciliation agreement with Qayam's family]."[23]

The events in Kunduz bring to the foreground how gender relations are forged out of contingent struggles and alliances. In terms of the end result, there appeared to be a convergence in how Siddiqa's father and the Taliban sought to solve the case. This concurrence between family assertions over women and the regulation of sexuality by public authorities is not unusual. Historically, Islamic (and other) legal traditions have often incorporated ideologies that place great emphasis on controlling female sexuality and protecting paternity. Yet, as previous chapters have shown, this is not a given, since the arrangements sanctioned in Islamic legal practice have varied over time and in different places, including how official bodies defined and enforced punishments for the crime of *zina*. Mir-Hosseini and Hamzić argue that in the early twentieth century, as Muslim countries modernized their legal systems, the application of classical Islamic law generally became confined to family law. *Hadd* punishments, including stoning and lashing for *zina*, while rarely explicitly abolished, became legally obsolete (Mir-Hosseini and Hamzić 2010: 21). However, with the resurgence of Islamist political movements toward the end of twentieth century, many countries saw attempts to "re-Islamize" criminal law, particularly as new leaders, who often had come to power through military coups, sought to derive political legitimacy from a declared project to restore the Islamic credentials of society. In this manner, a return to classical *fiqh* in penal law was presented as a purification of society, returning it to a stage of "pure Islam," prior to Western contamination.

For instance, in Pakistan, Zia ul-Haq promulgated the infamous Hudood Ordinances in 1979 after seizing power through a coup d'état. One of these, the Zina Ordinance, criminalized extramarital sex and instituted *hadd* punishments for those offenses under certain conditions (Lau 2007). It thus formed an important part of General Zia's declared purpose of taking power: the need to cleanse Pakistani society and make it more Islamic. But the divinely ordained regulation of sexuality, in turn, provided a vehicle for those who wanted to reinforce sovereign rights over daughters and wives. Khan finds that, in practice, the Zina laws in Pakistan became an instrument family members used against women who had married without their permission or otherwise defied the family's claim over their bodies (S. Khan, 2006). More generally, Mir-Hosseini and Hamzić suggest that the criminalization of women's sexuality enabled through the revival of *zina* laws "provided contemporary patriarchs with an efficient and novel means to further assert their control" (2009: 12).

By and large, a similar pattern can be identified in Afghanistan. As the legal system became codified and modernized, starting with the *nizam-namas* of Amanullah in the 1920s (see chapter 1), *hadd* punishments were assigned a largely symbolic place in criminal law. Although literature on this question is scarce, it seems it was rare for government courts to use stoning and lashing as punishments for *zina* in the twentieth century. Only with the emergence of the mujahedin and then the Taliban came the call for the revival of such "Islamic" punishments. Again, there is little data on the degree to which *hadd* was actually implemented during the Islamist governments of the 1990s, and there is certainly little knowledge about the extent to which families concurred with physical punishments for adultery when these were ordered by government officials with explicit reference to sharia. The stoning in Kunduz, however, illustrates a similar dynamic to the cases found in Pakistan: the congruence between familial and Islamic injunctions against female sexual autonomy, through an alliance in which patriarchal claims and an aspiring sovereign power—the Taliban insurgents—found common ground. Because even if Siddiqa's family approved of it, there could be no doubt that the stoning was not just about the transgression of Qayam and Siddiqa—it was also a strong political message that the Taliban was in charge in the area and that they were uncompromising in implementing Islamic tenets.

But this alliance of kinship with public power—through a public execution of an adulterous couple—had a fragile hold. The stoning horrified many Afghans. There were certainly several elements to this reaction. The fact that the stoning could take place, and the subsequent inability of the government to punish or even prosecute anyone for the act, had political implications. It showed the impotence of the Afghan state and the international coalition supporting it, and it starkly raised the specter of the reemergence of a Taliban-controlled Afghanistan. But there was also a strong reaction to what appeared, at least at a distance, as a brutal, impersonal imposition by a body outside the family, the village, and the local community. The killing of an adulterous daughter or wife (or one alleged to be so) by her family or husband was a fairly common occurrence in Afghanistan, but a public execution for adultery by a government body—in this case, rebels aspiring to state power—was not.

Yet paradoxically, even if the stoning in Kunduz generated strong reactions, few (if any) Afghans would publically denounce the *principle* of stoning adulterers. The protests against the Kunduz stoning were on procedural grounds. The investigations had been too quick, the stones thrown at Siddiqa and Qayam had been too big, and the punishment had been carried out outside legal channels and by unauthorized actors. The reluctance to take a public stance against stoning per se testifies to the hegemonic position of classical *fiqh* in post-2001 Afghanistan. There was little political space to explicitly challenge the notion that the laws of Islam were immutable and that Afghanistan, as a Muslim country, had to uphold them. But even if it appeared politically impossible to repudiate stoning in principle, there were no significant calls for the government to stage public stonings or lashings of adulterers.[24]

Thus the Afghan government formally recognized state-implemented Islamic punishments for sexual transgressions, but in practice, it relegated to families much of the power to police sexuality in general and female sexuality in particular. A remarkable feature of government policy was how the moral regulation of women was subcontracted to families, given that women could commit a crime simply by inhabiting spaces outside familial supervision. In post-2001 Afghanistan, the mere sighting of a woman traveling without her family could, according to the Supreme Court directive, serve as a legal basis for arrest. In a sense, the Afghan government acted in a way that upheld a system in which no women could be "at large," outside of family supervision, without valid reasons. As such, government complicity in facilitating family control over women was potentially even more significant than in Zina Ordinance–era Pakistan. In the latter, family members had to make an accusation of actual *zina* in order to have government institutions do their bidding (S. Khan, 2003).

At the same time, the government was far from coherent when it came to reinforcing family authority over women. Rather than a singular government policy, what emerges from the three cases is an extremely fluid and contested field. In the case of Fereshta, the government paid only partial heed to the family. Against their wishes, the court refused to find Fereshta guilty of any offense, and it did not agree to send her back to her family, at least not directly. Instead, it was broader societal constraints that made Fereshta go to live with her family—the standard assumption by certain shelters and government officials was that women should be returned to live with their families if at all possible. And when Fereshta was murdered for having refused to submit to her family's wishes, the government promptly intervened to punish what was largely seen in her province of Parwan as a case of a family having overstepped their prerogatives and conducting an illegitimate killing. Although many felt that the sentencing of only one family member for the deed was insufficient, since the murder appeared to have been a collective undertaking, the court verdict at least signaled that family claims over their women were far from absolute. Allegations that Fereshta had an immoral nature resurfaced in the trial, presumably to make her murder seem more justified. But the judge rejected this line of argument and sentenced the designated murderer to sixteen years in prison, which must be considered a clear statement that the killing of Fereshta had been a serious offence.

If the murder of women at the hands of their families was, in most instances, a clear transgression, forced marriage was not treated as a clear offense. Instead, legal practice and public discourse tended to treat it as a regrettable tradition. The EVAW law had made forced marriage, whether of an adult woman or underage girl a crime punishable by up to two years in prison. Before that, the 1976 Penal Code also stated that marrying an adult woman against her will was to be punished with a short-term prison sentence. But forced marriage appeared only marginally as a violation in the three cases discussed here. All of them contained instances, sometimes several, of marital unions that were coerced, yet there were no attempts to prosecute or punish anyone for this. If anything, forced marriage appeared as an unhealthy tradition, not as a punishable transgression. This was even the case regarding Fereshta, who was from Parwan, the most liberal of the three provinces. In Parwan, the fate of Fereshta was widely reported as a warning of the risks of forcing a daughter to marry someone against her will. Fereshta's family was cast as ignorant of the principles of Islam, which prohibits forced marriage *(estevaj-e ikhbari)*.[25] Talking about the case on radio, the chief prosecutor in the province reasoned that it was this ignorance and the failure to adhere to the rules of Islam that was to blame for the family arranging the marriage against Fereshta's will, which, in turn, led to the dispute and eventually to Fereshta's death. Similarly, Afghan legal experts speaking in the media about the case blamed the lack of legal awareness and called for workshops, especially in remote districts, to facilitate understanding that could prevent other women from becoming victims in the same way.[26] Local mullahs also referred to the case as an example of how forced marriage was reprehensible.

Thus, even if the EVAW law was in force by the time of Fereshta's marriage, there was no suggestion of prosecuting Fereshta's family for forced marriage. Nor was this a possibility in the other two cases. This fitted an overall pattern in Afghanistan—any conflict that occurred because of a forced marriage was typically pursued, if at all, through the family courts, where requests for a divorce or an invalidation of the marriage were heard. Forced marriage was generally treated as an issue of civil law, not one involving a criminal act. The only case of criminal prosecution for forced marriage that I encountered in this period was from Herat Province—a father was accused of "selling" his four underage daughters to finance his drug addiction. AIHRC staff in Herat told me that they had come across this case and alerted the authorities, who had arrested the father and started to prosecute the case. The head of the commission's Herat office, echoing conservative MPs in Parliament, stated that the marriage of these four girls had been contrary to Islam: "So according to Islam, when a daughter has not reached the age of majority [puberty], there are two requirements if her father is to arrange her marriage. There must be no objective of making money, and the father has to exercise kindness. He has the right to give away his daughter, but only if it is with kindness. In this case, the father did not show kindness. And he was a drug addict, so he was selling his daughters."[27]

The question of financial motivation marked a fault line in the discourse on forced marriage. Marrying daughters off for overt financial profit amounted to a greater offence than simply marrying them off against their will. The latter was sometimes considered within the rightful prerogatives of fathers, who were purported to decide in the best interest of the girl. Indeed, during the debates over the EVAW law in Parliament, it was argued that fathers should have the right to marry off underage girls, even if the girls did not agree to the marriage. As described in chapter 2, in the revision of the law agreed upon by the parliamentary Joint Commission, fathers were exempted from punishment for forced marriage. Marrying off a daughter purely for pecuniary gain, on the other hand, was denounced as a crude and self-interested act. The distinction carried an obvious class dimension, underlining the link between "honor" and status. Selling a daughter without any pretense was an act reserved for the destitute, something that those better positioned could afford to avoid.[28]

In the aftermath of both Nafisa's and Siddiqa's elopements, *baad* (or the prospect of *baad*) featured as a means of reparation, even though it was widely acknowledged that *baad* was not consonant with state law or Islamic law. In fact, since the time of Amir Abdul Rahman Khan, central governments had tried to eradicate the practice by explicitly outlawing it. Even the Taliban government had, in a short decree on women's rights, made it an offense.[29] Both the Penal Code of 1976 and the EVAW law made *baad* a separate crime with stricter punishments than those for simple forced marriage. Yet while *baad* was not publically condoned, it nevertheless surfaced as a standard "solution" to cases where women had been illegitimately appropriated. In the cases of Siddiqa's and Nafisa's elopements, *baad* was used as the immediate restitution of the rights of those who were deemed to have been wronged: the family who had lost a bride. This illustrates the way in which marriage practices, to a large extent, were understood as transactions between families. And in turn, this understanding of marriage shaped the ways in which gender violence was defined.

CONCLUSIONS

The trajectories of the cases discussed in this chapter suggest that as cases of gender violence became public matters, they were predominantly articulated as violations of family and male "honor." The gender relations that the Afghan government and other public institutions were called upon to sanction were often of a kind where kinship has recognized authority over women and, in particular, female sexuality. At the same time, public acknowledgment of these claims was by no means guaranteed, and individual cases often took the form of a tug of war, with highly unpredictable outcomes. The government might routinely arrest runaway women at the behest of their families, but it did not necessarily pay heed to family claims over women in court. What these micro-struggles over the definitions of gender violence and over the right (or obligation) to adjudicate and avenge these incidents tell us is that legal regimes are highly context specific. Although such regimes are cloaked in assertions of indisputable and unambiguous truth, they emerge out of temporal alliances and accommodations and are embedded in political relations. For instance, the case in Kunduz reminds us of the importance of Dina Siddiqi's warning against "timeless, decontextualized Islam" that "does not bring into view the complex and historically specific ways in which national and international vectors of Islamization articulate with politically economy and rural structures of power" (Siddiqi 2011: 82). As the events surrounding the stoning suggested, local patriarchs might find an ally in military actors contending for territorial control, whereas to the latter, the spectacular and brutal public display of "Islamic justice" was part of an active project to demonstrate power. At the same time, religion could be invoked very differently, to limit the power of families and husbands over women by appealing to the need to eradicate harmful traditions contrary to Islam. Objections to forced marriages like Fereshta's were also framed in this way. In other words, even if gender violence was often defined in ways that subordinated women to male guardians, this must be considered an active accomplishment that needed maintenance and reinforcement through the forging of new articulations and the upholding of old ones. As the discussion in previous chapters shows, the idea that the state should be obligated to reinforce families' authority over women by apprehending runaway women as criminals was contested and tenuous, having surfaced as part of the political projects of the Taliban and the mujahedin.

On the other hand, even if women were not returned to their families by the direct order of courts, legal and social practices nonetheless often combined to produce this effect anyway. As the case of Fereshta showed, there was a stigma linked to women traveling and living independently. This made it possible for authorities to arrest Fereshta at her family's request and later to broker an agreement to send her to live with her family. The problematization of female autonomy through both state and non-state mechanisms worked against these three women from the outset. To Nafisa and Siddiqa, the most obvious—and perhaps the only—option they could see was to escape with another man. They both lived in conservative, insecure provinces where it would have been difficult for them to travel unnoticed on their own. Siddiqa and Nafisa might both have been truly in love with the men they escaped with, but it is easy to imagine that, in general, when the only option to escape abuse is to elope with a man, women are extremely vulnerable to exploitation. Yet regardless of the women's situations, many authorities were unforgiving about the fact that the women had run away or committed *zina*. Neither in these nor in other cases did the authorities or the courts see their circumstances as mitigating factors.[30] As the local representative of AIHRC said about Siddiqa: "This girl was the granddaughter of Mulla Quli, yet she did not respect her grandfather's honor? Even if the Taliban was not right, she should have been punished in some way, by the courts."[31] Nafisa also met widespread condemnation, although one young justice official was more sympathetic: "I asked her if she had sexual intercourse with her fiancé, and she said 'Yes, one or two times. And two or three times with Amin.' Then she started to cry, and I realized she was just a child, and it was because of her age that she made those mistakes."[32] Through a combination of luck and strategy, Fereshta was able to stay clear of such pitfalls. Having gone straight to a shelter, admitting to no physical relations with her boyfriend, and being fortunate enough to have a committed lawyer and to encounter a sympathetic judge, she was released from prison.

The stories of these three women also provide an important additional indicator as to why the EVAW law was so sketchily implemented and why so many cases that should have led to criminal convictions (according to the law) instead resulted in mediated solutions or withdrawal. The social and official landscape was stacked against female autonomy, reinforcing the idea that only under exceptional circumstances could women be permitted to live outside of family settings, and if so, they were mostly confined to shelters. A woman living on her own remained generally unheard-of in Afghanistan and normally invited rumors of her being of "questionable character" to the extent that her safety could be at risk.[33] This left women with little bargaining power in cases of abuse, and it certainly discouraged them from pursuing claims against their families.

Upholding Citizen Honor?

Rape in the Courts and Beyond

INTRODUCTION

Given the strong legal and social regulation of women's sexuality in Afghanistan, as well as how this issue has been tied up with social status and "honor," it is unsurprising that there has historically been a great reluctance to report cases of rape.[1] Women themselves would risk being ostracized by both family and society, and they could also be charged with *zina* or other moral crimes. To families, going to the authorities with a complaint of rape could signal weakness—an admission that the family was incapable of settling its own affairs. The successful regulation of female sexuality has been considered a key locus of family and kinship power, to be jealously guarded against outside involvement. Extramarital sexual relations have been highly shameful for a woman and her family, often irrespective of the consent of the woman. Not only would her status as a wife or prospective wife be ruined or significantly diminished, but the public knowledge of such a crime would also severely taint a family's reputation—it would be seen as unable to protect (or police) its women.

Yet over period of a few years, Afghanistan witnessed a number of high-profile rape cases in which public mobilization for government intervention led to assertive state action. Around 2008, a number of families went on national television with demands that the government punish their daughters' rapists. Harrowing television clips showed the young girls and their families wailing and weeping, crosscut with footage of male family members calling for justice. The cases attracted considerable attention and support, and later, human rights workers and activists cited them when they campaigned for the EVAW law to contain strong provisions on rape. In the years that followed, popular mobilization took place around several other cases of rape, protesting government indifference and forcing a response from the authorities. Perhaps the most compelling example was in late 2014: in Paghman, a suburb of Kabul, a group of women had been forced out of their vehicle, separated from their menfolk at gunpoint, and subjected to multiple rapes. Once the event became publically known, growing outrage quickly led to the arrest of a group of suspects. In unusually speedy trials, five of the suspects were sentenced to death by three courts (the primary court and two rounds of appeals), and then executed by hanging, all within a time frame of less than two months.

At first glance, it would appear that these cases signified a dramatic redrawing of relations of gender and governance in Afghanistan, a redrawing brought upon a reluctant government by mobilization from below. Two sets of shifts seemed to be involved in this redrawing. First, the cases signaled that there was popular demand for state protection of women against (some forms of) sexual violence, and that rape was no longer solely considered a private, shameful matter but instead a criminal violation against women. The prospect of such a shift, which essentially positioned women as rights holders vis-à-vis the state, was underlined by the fact that some of the victims in these cases appeared in public and spoke about how they had been assaulted and how they wanted their perpetrators punished. In other words, in their public appearances, they appeared as citizens who had been subjected to a crime. Second, the public demands for state intervention seemingly entailed a shift in relations of governance in the sense that the government was being invited into a new domain, one that had previously been largely delegated to families—the regulation of sexuality. The potential long-term implication of this was the constitution of rape as site of state power, subject to the interventions of law and bureaucracy.

In this chapter, I discuss a handful of these high-profile cases in order to assess the extent and exact nature of these shifts. I ask whether the new "openness" surrounding rape in Afghanistan meant a changed position for women, wherein rape meant a violation of their bodily integrity as opposed to an affront to their male relatives' honor. I further ask whether we can gauge from these cases the contours of a stronger Afghan state. My answer to both questions is a qualified no.

"THE PRESIDENT IS SELLING PEOPLE'S HONOR"

In the spring of 2008, Sayed Noorullah of Sarepul Province started a public campaign to get the Afghan government to punish his niece's rapists. His teenage niece, Bashira, had been tricked into a house and raped by two young men, one of them the son of Haji Payenda, a powerful former commander and currently an MP in the province. When attempting to report and pursue the case in Sarepul, Noorullah had been beaten and intimidated by local government officials. However, he was not one to give up easily. He appeared on national media, demanding that the government take action. The threats continued. Upon the intervention of local human rights workers, the case was eventually moved to Kabul, where Noorullah again spoke on national television, cursing President Karzai, Parliamentary Speaker Qanooni, and other officials for failing to address the case:

> I am the father[2] of a thirteen-year-old girl who was kidnapped and then raped by the son of Haji Payenda, a member of Parliament. . . . Several times, through Aryana Television and other media, the issue has been made known to all the government officials and even President Karzai. . . . All the ministers, all the Parliament members are aware of the incident and know everything. . . .
>
> I have just one question for Mr. Karzai: For the sake of God, if this had happened to your daughter, what would you have done? Then would you have felt my feelings? Only two days ago, you sacked the attorney general,[3] and since then, all the offices that I approach reject me by saying that even your attorney general has been fired. Today in the public health office, even the prosecutor who is dealing with my case tells me to go away and that now that the attorney general is no more in office, "no one is going to listen to your stories anymore." Was there justice only in the attorney general? By sacking him, did his office, his laws, and everything also vanish? Is there no system anymore? Should we just abandon our case and mind our own business? Once again I am repeating it: if this would have happened to your daughter, Mr. Karzai, Qanooni, Chief Justice, and Attorney General, would you have tolerated it? Would you have just watched?
>
> If we are traitors, if our case is unfair, and if our accusations are false, Mr. Karzai, if you have any *gheirat* [honor, courage], then please kill us and drive over us. If you don't have any *gheirat,* then may God's curse be upon you and your whole clan, whoever you are.[4]

Meanwhile, another family from the same area also went on television, and in a disturbing television clip, recounted how their young daughter had been raped by five government officials. The cases were becoming a major embarrassment for the president, who swiftly fired senior police officials in the province and summoned Noorullah for an audience, during which he promised to personally follow up the case. Eventually Payenda's son was sentenced to twenty years in jail at the primary court in Kabul. The case, however, was not over. As it was coming up for appeal in the courts, Noorullah reported continuing intimidation and interference, and he continued his media campaign. Eventually, senior parliamentarians and confidantes of the president brokered a deal. The families of the victim and the perpetrator were to reconcile. Declaring himself exhausted by the threats, and for the sake of his family's safety, Noorullah agreed. In return, he would get a *baad,* a girl given in compensation, who would marry his son; a guarantee on his life signed by the elderly Sighbatullah Mujadiddi, a friend of Karzai and the former leader of the Upper House of Parliament;[5] and, according to rumors, a substantial amount of money. In return for this, the families would be declared reconciled, and Noorullah would stop pursuing the case. In the two following appeals—in the secondary court and at the Supreme Court—to the surprise of human rights advocates and supporters who had involved themselves in the case, Noorullah was no longer present in court. The punishments were said to be reduced, and there were rumors that the son of MP Payenda went in and out of prison at his convenience. In Sarepul, Sayed Noorullah described himself as having been defeated: "We were fighting against injustice, and we lost."[6]

The case in Sarepul was known all over the country. For some, the way that the family had spoken about the rape on national television was nothing less than shocking. Making such a violation public and openly appealing to the authorities for justice was a humiliating admission of weakness. Not only had the family been unable to prevent such an act—but also, in order to redress it, they evidently had no recourse other than to make public what should have remained private and to ask the government to act on their behalf. Yet in the media and in the accounts of the many human rights organizations and politicians who supported Sayed Noorullah, Bashira's uncle, the way the family had chosen to make the rape public was described as a momentous development: "The girl is thirteen years old and she has been raped, and yet by Afghan standards she is one of the luckier ones. Her family has recognized her trauma and is trying to get her some sort of justice; in many families, she might be viewed as an object of shame and thrown out. The fact that her family members have chosen to stand by her, and that they even spoke out on Afghan national television last month, is an important change in how Afghans view the abuse of women" (Kargar 2008).

However, closer attention to the language used by Sayed Noorullah shows that the case was not framed exclusively as an offense against Bashira, who had suffered the rape, but also—if, indeed, not primarily—as an offense against Noorullah himself. For instance, when later recounting to me how he had been offered money to withdraw his complaint, he indignantly said: "We are Afghans. And in our custom, taking money in such cases is like selling your *namus*" (honor, those things belonging to a man which should be inviolable). The government and the president were denounced as associates to usurpers of people's honor. They had allied with warlords and oppressors and, as a result, they were selling the *namus* of ordinary people. Noorullah recounted, with some embarrassment, how he had in anger hurled a great insult at the president even when called in for a personal audience, a meeting that had taken place following his denunciation of the country's leaders on national television. After this rather strongly worded speech on television ("Mr. Karzai, . . . if you don't have *gheirat,* then may God's curse be upon you and your whole clan, whoever you are"), the president's office had demanded that Noorullah be immediately brought in to speak to Hamid Karzai. There, the uncle continued to use strong language. The Taliban government might have been brutal and unpopular, he had said, but they were not *be-namus* (without honor). They had not been selling people's honor.[7]

Another indicator that Bashira's rape was acted upon mainly as infringement on family honor was the fact that Noorullah had agreed to receive a *baad* from the family of the rapist, a young girl whom he married to his son. This he did even though he was well aware of the consternation with which giving and receiving *baad* was viewed among his backers in human rights circles. The brokers of the reconciliation between Noorullah and Payenda's family were senior government officials and political leaders who also would have been conscious that *baad* was frowned upon in official circles. They had, according to Noorullah, suggested that there should be no mention of the *baad* in the document that stipulated the settlement between the families and made a host of leading politicians who had signed the document the guarantors of the uncle's life in return for his future silence about the rape. Instead, the document merely contained a vague statement to the effect that the families had agreed to strengthen their relations. The *baad* nonetheless took place, although, as will be shown later in the chapter, the identity of the girl who was given in *baad* meant that it fell short of expectations.

REPORTING RAPE WITH UNCERTAIN AGENDAS

The rapes in Sarepul that took place around 2008 were among the first in a series of sexual violations that generated intense public attention in Afghanistan. One thing that all these cases had in common was that, although they featured victims who appeared in public, these appearances were under circumstances arranged—and sometimes even manipulated—by others. In general, instances in which women reported rape on their own initiative were extremely rare. One exception could be when women discovered that they were pregnant as a result of the rape, and the impossibility of life as the mother of a child of unknown paternity took precedence over the risks entailed in approaching the authorities with a rape charge. Lawyers also reported that they were able to gain acquittals for women arrested for *zina* or "attempted *zina*" when they were able to prove that the women had been raped or kidnapped (Boggio-Cosadia 2014). In these instances, the women were typically far away from their home areas when arrested, and authorities there made little attempt to indict anyone for the rape.

In most cases when a rape was reported or prosecuted, the families were strongly behind going the authorities. Yet sometimes the reasons for this support were very different from how it first appeared, as many of the cases in the specialized prosecution unit in Kabul (see chapter 3) suggested. Families might use rape charges as leverage to get the standard bride-price or a *baad* and then withdraw the complaint once such a settlement had been achieved. In some scenarios, women had eloped or engaged in sexual relations out of free will, but without family sanction. Their relatives pressed rape charges in order to retrieve them, to obtain adequate compensation, or to repair their reputation.

Some cases showed with particular clarity how the intensity through which families or their supporters pursued rape claims did not center on the needs of the victims themselves. The public appearances of the women who had been raped could be unsettling, suggesting that they were pawns in other people's agendas. I received an early indication of this myself when I was researching the Sarepul rape cases in 2010. Having set up a meeting with the judge who had presided over one of the cases from the province, I received an unusually warm welcome. Some time into the conversation it became clear why. In came a young girl, looking around twelve, who was introduced to me as the judge's niece. The judge told me that his niece had been raped, but that the government had failed to arrest the perpetrators. Now, he wanted to help the girl by broadcasting her story on television. A television crew was expected at any moment. He suggested that I, as an "international expert on rape," should take part in the broadcast and offer some general comments on rape as a phenomenon. While waiting for the cameras to be set up, he said that I should interview the niece and "feel free to ask her any of [my] questions." Somewhat perplexed, I asked the girl if she wanted to sit with me in another room. I hesitantly asked her about what had happened to her, and she started to tell me a story of how she had been kidnapped from her home province in central Afghanistan and brought to Helmand, where a married man had kept her locked in a room and raped her several times. Soon she started to cry, and I decided to end the interview, feeling unsure about the setting and the girl's real ability to consent to being interviewed. As I prepared to leave, extracting myself from appearing on television, the girl was being placed before the television cameras.

I lost track of what happened to the girl or her legal case. When I called the judge again later, he was reluctant to speak, probably disappointed by my failure to involve myself in the case. But my memory of the girl lingered—the image of her in the room, unaccompanied but for the judge who claimed to be her uncle, being made to speak on camera to the group of male reporters and office staff, blinking as the sharp television lights hit her face. It seemed a strong hint that the new "openness" around rape in Afghanistan did not necessarily take into account the needs of the victims themselves.

The case of Lal Bibi, referred to in the introduction of this book, suggested likewise. Lal Bibi, an eighteen-year-old nomad woman from the province of Kunduz, came forward in Afghan and international media recounting how, in May 2012, she had been seized by armed men as revenge for her cousin's elopement with a woman of one of the kidnappers' family. Five days later, after suffering multiple sexual assaults, she was returned to her family. A large group of people from her extended family subsequently went to the provincial government to complain. The incident was quickly picked up by the media. Lal Bibi was shown crying and anxious, with her family declaring to journalists that unless justice was done, they would have no option but to kill her. Women activists in Kabul threw their support behind the woman and her family, and a few months later, an open trial in the capital sentenced four men to sixteen years in prison for the kidnapping and abuse of Lal Bibi.

Like the Sarepul cases discussed above, the fact that Lal Bibi and her family came forward to report the case and spoke publically about the crime was regarded as a sign of progress. Yet the way the young girl was shown on television, obviously distressed, raised questions about whether such openness about the discussion of rape represented a wholly positive development for the women involved. In the trial, Lal Bibi was subjected to further trauma, as one of the accused attempted to use her appearance as an argument for his innocence: "Unveil her and see her face and tell me if she deserves to get married with anyone," he stated in court (Sukhanyar and Rubin 2012). The case was also made part of the political campaign to end government support for informal militias, with the episode quickly presented as yet another case of abuse visited upon the Afghan people by the controversial Afghan Local Police (ALP). Established by the U.S. military, the ALP program involved establishing local police units, trained by U.S. Special Forces, who would serve as a first line of defense against Taliban insurgents. The program had been under heavy criticism since its inception, with opponents arguing that it was a short-term measure adding to the country's problems with armed, semiformal groups. A few days after the kidnapping became known, President Karzai, who had been ambiguous about his support of the ALP all along—if not outright opposed to them—personally intervened in the controversy by announcing that the entire ALP unit of the accused rapist would be disarmed.

STRONGER STATES OR CAPTURED STATES?

In Lal Bibi's case, and many others, it was activist and popular mobilization, rather than the regular workings of the justice system, that ensured that the perpetrators were punished. Analyzing how "weak" states deal with cases of rape, Roychowdhury (2016) suggests that they can be momentarily captured by both feminist and nonfeminist groups. She contrasts "strong" states such as the United States, where feminist movements against sexual violence might be co-opted by state officials using legal regulations as a mechanism for social control, with "weak" states (for example, India), which can be overwhelmed by popular groups—but in ways that may or may not entail progress from a feminist point of view. Roychowdhury's notion of the law being occasionally overpowered by popular politics in weak states is an accurate description of the dynamics played out in high-profile rape cases in Afghanistan. These moments of popular politics might have espoused a concern for gender justice to one degree or another, but what they had in common was that they did not represent the strengthening of the institutional power of the state. Rather, they were moments when the routine operation of law and legal institutions were set aside and were replaced by emergency measures or were taken over by local groups.

Perhaps the most spectacular example of this was the aftermath of the rapes in Paghman, a suburb of Kabul, referred to in the introduction of this chapter. In this case, relatives did not initiate any public calls for justice—indeed, they did not even report that the crimes had taken place. Instead, rumors began to circulate in social media and in the capital of a heinous incident in Paghman. I was in Kabul at the time, and I remember first hearing that six women had been taken from their car at gunpoint when an Afghan colleague told me about it as we were driving home from the city center. To both of us, the idea that something like this could take place only a half-hour drive from where we were defied belief. It brought to mind chilling stories of the civil war, when the capital collapsed into lawlessness.

By the time the rumors reached us, the incident was already a week old. On August 23, 2014, a group of family members had been stopped on their way back from a wedding party by armed men dressed as police officers, who had tied up the men and taken the women to a nearby orchard, where they had been stripped of their jewelry and raped repeatedly. The incident became known only when rumors spread from hospital where the women had been treated for their serious injuries. Growing public outrage that such an organized assault could take place on the highway right outside Kabul quickly led to the arrest of seven suspects. One week later, on the day of an announced demonstration in front of the Supreme Court—which activists said was guilty of arbitrarily releasing convicted rapists in the past—a two-hour trial took place. Five of the seven accused were sentenced to death, and the others to life imprisonment. The appeals proceeded at unusual speed. The five death sentences were confirmed both in the appeal court and in the Supreme Court and were signed by president Karzai on his last day in office, on September 24. The death sentences were carried out by hanging on October 8, during the first days of Ashraf Ghani's presidency.

The most vocal parts of civil society and the women's movement applauded the executions, seeing it as a sign that the government was taking a more resolute stand against rapists. But the diplomatic community in Kabul, as well as some local human rights advocates, protested that the trials had been far too swift. In addition, the government had been reluctant to disclose the details of the case, and in private, some people argued that this was because the assaults were part of personal vendetta between two feuding groups whose commanders had close ties to the government.[8]

The execution of rapists was unprecedented for post-2001 Afghanistan and was based on unclear legal foundations. Indeed, execution itself was relatively rare. Only thirty people had been executed during the thirteen years of Karzai's presidency. The death sentences in the Paghman case were not based on the 1976 Penal Code, but on an obscure provision of Afghanistan's communist-era 1987 Law on Crimes against Internal and External Security, which makes banditry punishable by death (HRW 2014).

There were several other unusual features of these trials. The victims appeared to identify the suspects from a line-up consisting of no men other than the seven suspects, and this event was broadcast on national television, with the faces of the women clearly visible. However transformative or taboo breaking this might seem, critics argued that the government had staged the event only to repair its tarnished image, with little regard for the consequences to the women themselves (Samandary 2014). Likewise, some of the other features of the trials were also irregular and appeared to be designed to placate the protesters rather than to closely follow the law. The rape charges in the primary court had been based on the Penal Code and were formulated as *zina*. When activists protested that the prosecution and the courts should have been using the EVAW law, which included rape as a distinct offense, the prosecutor in the appeal court simply replaced the indictments so that they were was based on the EVAW law, and the defendants were subsequently sentenced on this basis. But to introduce a new charge at the appeal level like this was contrary to Afghan law.[9] In any case, President Karzai had given little impression of judicial independence and due process. Instead, he signaled to the women activists that he was ready to see to it that their demands would be accommodated. On the evening of the first trial, he held a televised meeting with the activists and declared his wish to see the perpetrators executed: "I request the honorable chief justice to give them the death sentence" (HRW 2014).

All in all, the novel publicity of rape cases in this period appeared to involve few radical challenges to predominant gender ideologies. The kind of cases that entered the public domain and generated popular demands for government intervention were all articulated within "stable categories of gender" (Kapur 2014). The assaulted women were beyond questioning in terms of their virtue. They were either young teenagers or had been kidnapped at gunpoint in front of witnesses. In some cases, the crimes were articulated as matters of male honor and status rather than as violations primarily against the women themselves. Nonetheless, within these limited parameters, the publicity generated by the cases produced results—with perpetrators in some of them receiving lengthy prison sentences or even the death sentence. Yet it would be difficult to argue that these individual cases indicated a strengthening of the institutional ability of the state to protect women from rape. Rather, government intervention in these cases was the result of popular politics overpowering legal institutions in the way that Roychowdhury (2016) points out. It was ad hoc and contingent on public pressure and sometimes involved the circumvention of legal procedures.

Moreover, the force of popular mobilization could also be made to serve more directly political agendas. The fact that sexual transgressions were understood as matters that infringed on male status and authority potentially made them factors in ongoing political contests. This was particularly pronounced in the Sarepul case, in which the rape of Bashira became embroiled in a power struggle between competing factions in the province. It took me some time to detect these dynamics. When starting to gather material on the case, I was constantly mindful of the need to proceed with caution, and only after many months did I actually travel to Sarepul. Human rights activists who were familiar with the Sarepul case had told me it was extremely complicated, with the government trying to pull all kinds of strings to protect MP Payenda, father of one of the men who had raped Bashira, from being compromised. As I consulted with various people along the way, I gained the impression that Bashira's family, having been intimidated into silence by local power holders and the government, could be at great risk if they talked to outsiders about it. The unrelated case of the unexplained murder of Dilawar, the husband of Sarah, who had been raped by a government-allied commander in another northern province (see introduction), was still less than a year old. I did not want to arrive in Sarepul and, by meeting Bashira's family—or even just by asking around about the case—attract the attention of the local authorities and put the family in danger. It seemed that the only responsible thing to do was not to go to Sarepul until I could be sure that the family was prepared to meet and discuss the case, and even then, to travel discreetly and not stay too long.

Thus, after a series of reassuring introductions, I went, making the three-and-a-half-hour journey from Mazar-e Sharif in a local taxi with my then–research assistant, Jawad, and without contacting many people in the provincial capital beforehand. I was somewhat surprised that when we met Bashira's uncle, Sayed Noorullah, he appeared upbeat and even delighted by the opportunity to talk about the case, even though (upon his suggestion) we were meeting in the provincial council's office for all to see. We sat together for many hours in one of the rooms as he told us about the events that had followed the rape of his niece. He spoke about the constant threats and harassment by government officials that he had experienced following his decision to make a complaint about the rape. Not only was he targeted, but so were his relatives. In the end, it was fear of losing family members, Noorullah explained, that made him decide to give up pursuing the rape charge through government courts and instead agree to a reconciliation with the rapist's family. As part of this settlement, in addition to the *baad*, Noorullah received a guarantee that his life would be safe on the condition that he would never talk about the case again. However, Noorullah contended that despite the promise, he had wanted to talk to me. I was a researcher, and he felt that it was important that what had happened to his family should be documented. His fight against injustice and oppression should be recorded "so that future generations could learn from history."

But there were certain cracks in this narrative, and as time passed, they were becoming increasingly difficult to ignore. I wondered why, if the case was as sensitive as Noorullah claimed, and his position in the province so precarious, he had suggested to meet us at a government office, where his contact with a foreigner would no doubt be detected and raise suspicions that he was breaking his vow not to pursue the case. Noorullah's acceptance of the *baad* from Payenda's family also sat uneasily with his story of fighting injustice. Even if he felt too threatened to continue pursuing the case in government courts and wished to have a guarantee of his safety, what was the need for accepting the *baad,* something that discredited him among his liberal supporters in Kabul?[10] Could he not have settled for just the guarantee?

When I returned to Kabul, other fractures appeared. The judge who had presided over the rape case in the primary court in Kabul contradicted Noorullah's assertion that the sentence of Payenda's son had been decreased after an appeal. On the contrary, the twenty-year prison sentences for Payenda's son, his bodyguard, and their female abettor had been confirmed in the appeal court and again in the Supreme Court. Details of this had been published in an edition of the *Mizan Gazette,* a Supreme Court newsletter, of which I obtained a copy. If the government courts had applied the full force of the law, the local reconciliation and the *baad* made even less sense, as the justice Noorullah was calling for already appeared to have been served.

Eventually, through a series of conversations, an alternative version of the events following the rape of Bashira emerged. On important points, this version diverged from the way the case had become known to me through the media and the accounts of Noorullah and his backers. First, Bashira's family background was not quite as powerless and poor as had been implied. They hailed from a lineage claiming holy descent. Moreover, members of Bashira's family held important government positions in the province. It was partly through these positions that the family was able to gain access to the media and, doubtlessly, to mobilize some of their support among politicians and officials. Another dimension of the story, which had not featured in the national media coverage, in the calls for justice by human rights officials and activists, or in Noorullah's account was the ethnicized politics that quickly became part of the aftermath of the case.

In order to understand how Bashira's rape became enmeshed in Sarepul politics, it is necessary to relate some of the local history. Sarepul, like most parts of Afghanistan, has a recent history of frequently changing and contested control over territory, state institutions, and resources. Pashtun migrants had begun arriving in Sarepul in the late nineteenth century as part of a larger, government-supported Pashtun migration into northern Afghanistan. Backed by the central state, the mainly nomadic Pashtuns seized land and lucrative government posts, establishing themselves as a dominant minority group in much of the province, where groups of Hazaras, Uzbeks, Aymaqs, and Arabs were also living (Tapper 1991).

The advent of war altered the ethnic balance in the area. As armed resistance formed against the communist government that seized power in Kabul in 1978, mujahedin and pro-government militia groups emerged, and in the north, these often proved a vehicle for non-Pashtun groups to assert themselves. Arabs, who were previously a marginal group of pastoralists claiming descent from the Arab tribes that had been part of the original Islamic conquest, gained a new position in the province through this route. Four brothers, among them Haji Payenda, rose to prominence as members of a local self-defense unit mobilized by the Najibullah government. The brothers served under Abdul Rashid Dostum, the Uzbek military strongman who was to emerge as a key regional power broker in the decades that followed. With Dostum, the Uzbeks in the northern region also strengthened their position. Dostum initially worked with Najibullah but increasingly acted in defiance to the Pashtun-dominated central government as he established a regional network consisting of both pro-government militias and mujahedin commanders and finally spectacularly defected from the government in 1992 (Giustozzi 2009). In the mountainous south of Sarepul, mainly Hazara groups formed armed resistance factions against the communists, and in yet other districts, Tajik-dominated mujahedin emerged. These groups generally aligned with national-level mujahedin parties. In a pattern seen elsewhere in Afghanistan, local rivalries were fed by support from national party formations, which, in turn, led to a fragmentation of the local political landscape alongside party and ethnic lines. The importance of these fault lines lessened under the Taliban government, although many areas in Sarepul remained completely controlled by the mujahedin. With the overthrow of the Taliban government in 2001, the factions rooted in the mujahedin and militia groups of the pre-Taliban period again became dominant actors in Sarepul politics. Dostum's network became the Junbesh party, an important political actor in Sarepul and in Afghanistan as a whole. In sum, the upheavals of the decades of conflict had created a fluid situation where previously enduring political and ethnic hierarchies were constantly up for renegotiation. The post-2001 period saw the new elites of the jihad era—and their broader, mostly ethnically defined constituencies—vying for control over government posts, land, and influence.

It was this factional competition, some of my informants argued, that had been the driving force in the dynamics of the aftermath of Bashira's rape. In a bid to weaken Haji Payenda and, by extension, Arab domination, two key groups involved themselves in the case and threw their support behind Bashira's family. One of these groups was the local Uzbek power holders belonging to the Junbesh party. Sometime earlier, Payenda had dropped his allegiance with Junbesh, the

Uzbek-dominated party headed by Dostum, who, in turn, was supporting President Karzai. Instead, Payenda and a number of other Arabs had established their own political group, which eventually supported the opposition candidate, Dr. Abdullah, in the 2009 presidential election. The case against Payenda's son was also supported by Shia Hazara groups that wanted to strengthen their position in the province. Bashira was Hazara, and according one of my informants, the case became a way of unifying them: "When the case first came to the media, the Shia people got angry, and they united on how their honor had been insulted. They made it a big and very complicated case, in order to unite the Shias, make them one power."[11]

In these accounts, Bashira's young uncle, Noorullah, appeared less a self-driven campaigner for justice and more a figurehead for these discontented groups, having been handpicked as a suitable front-person when Bashira's father, who was in ill health, could not play that role. The pressure for Payenda to give a *baad* was not imposed from above as an attempt by powerful actors to make the case go away. Instead, the giving of *baad* had formed an integral demand of Noorullah's campaign all along, a demand that, if successful, would have placed Payenda on par with his adversaries. Giving a daughter in these circumstances would have signaled that Payenda was not above other groups in the province, that he was a social equal to Bashira's family; a daughter taken had to be compensated with a daughter given. On this matter, there was only a partial victory for Noorullah. The demand had been that Payenda give his own daughter, but he successfully refused this. Instead, a daughter of a poor man from Payenda's tribe, reportedly paid by Payenda, was given as a *baad* to Bashira's family. In the opinion of one of my informants, this showed how Payenda remained able to defy the obvious attempts to weaken him.[12]

Nonetheless, in versions that emphasize how the aftermath of Bashira's rape became a vehicle for local politics, it was Haji Payenda who appeared as the compromised party. Despite spending a considerable amount of money to influence the courts, he had been unable to prevent his son from feeling the full force of the law. Having been exposed as less than all-powerful in the province, he lost his parliamentary seat in the next election, in 2010, although this could also have been due to his alliance with the Jamiat party, which had a weak position in the province (Embassy of the United States Kabul 2009c). In the subsequent chapters of Sarepul politics, the groups that had supported Bashira's family came to dominate the local government. And in a further reversal of positions, episodes of rape and the kidnapping of women were now being used by factions linked to Haji Payenda and his brothers to mobilize public opinion against the Hazara-dominated provincial administration (Ruttig 2012). It seemed that public protestations against sexual infractions had become a standard part of the political repertoire in Sarepul. In a sense, protests were directed against the impunity afforded by government connections, impunity that was facilitated by access to government office and, in the next round of local politics, became the privilege of the new power holders.

If the unusual persistence of Bashira's family in pursuing the rape case in public could be explained, partly or fully, by the interest of local groups in using the case to challenge the political position of Payenda and his allies, this, in turn, serves as a reminder that "the state," as many scholars have reminded us, is a claim, a construct, not a thing or a fact. Bashira's uncle might have called for government action in a sense that suggested that there existed a unitary, independent Afghan state capable of autonomous action in one direction or the other. Likewise, other actors invoked similar images when calling for the state's responsibility to protect women against family abuses or, alternatively, to uphold kinship control over them. But these contending notions of state responsibility and justice are disputes over internal boundaries and personhood, the outcome of which has consequences for authority over domains and persons. They should not lead us to believe that there is such thing as a unitary, coherent state—"a person writ large" (T. Mitchell 1991: 83), a judge-like character insulated from society as a whole. As Mitchell argues, the appearance of the state as a discreet and relatively autonomous social institution is itself a reification that is constituted through everyday social practices. In reality, claims to statehood—as well as the gradual emergence of government apparatuses, armies, and bureaucracies—are always intertwined with struggles over resources and power.

This means that demands and counterdemands for state action, and claims to act on behalf of the state, must be situated in the local political economy—in other words, in conflicts between groups and classes over resources and influence. As the history of Sarepul clearly illustrates, access to government positions—and the associated ability to call upon bureaucratic and military enforcement mechanisms— have served as a tool for appropriation and accumulation. The primary fault line, then, is not necessarily between kinship (or families) and the government (i.e., between society and the state); it can also be between competing factions, whose success in controlling and accessing state power has waxed and waned.

From this perspective, it looks as if the Sarepul case—instead of being one man's thwarted campaign to secure a government reaction to the abuses visited upon his family—was locally understood, or at least seized upon, as an infraction against a larger collective by a rival group. The reaction to this violation had to assert the position of Payenda's rivals; it had to be a reaction that showed that Payenda and his group were not above, but of equal standing to, other groups, and that simultaneously could undermine his grip on power. The "state" here features as a vehicle for intergroup competition, a competition where authority over women serves as a marker of position and status. In other words, the renegotiation of power hierarchies in Sarepul—in which official positions constituted an important resource and which in the last decades had become increasingly open-ended as war offered novel ways for previously marginal groups to assert themselves—took place, in part, through public contestations over claims over women. Government courts and the media provided new arenas for such claims, which should be understood as assertions of position and status, expressed through the idiom of honor. But in these new arenas, the claims were framed somewhat differently. When Bashira's uncle appeared on national television, he did not ask President Karzai to arrange a *baad* from Payenda's family (such a demand could not have been expressed or granted openly), but he asked for the government to see to it that the rapists would feel the full force of the law. The rape was still spoken of as a violation of family honor, but demands of government action were framed in the language of justice and punishment.

It was this kind of language that led many outsiders and national actors to believe that something novel was happening—that people were now bravely speaking out against the violations visited upon their daughters by government allies, breaking a taboo in a desperate bid for some kind of reparation. Admittedly, the Bashira case and other episodes from Sarepul *were* novel in the way the victims' families were willing to openly mobilize national public opinion for their case. Still, the exceptional intensity with which public redress was sought must be understood as an extension of factional political conflict, played out, in part, in the public arenas of the media and the courts, rather than as an attempt by families to rearticulate government obligations to its (male) citizens.

CONCLUSIONS

The last decade has seen a significant amount of popular mobilization around rape cases in Afghanistan, and specifically around the state's obligation to hold perpetrators accountable. In this chapter, I have explored the broader significance of these developments, asking whether they have entailed transformations in gender relations or in governance in Afghanistan. Did they signal a new status for women in which violations of their bodily integrity were considered a public matter, and did this, in turn, suggest an extension of the domains of state power? Feminist literature offers plenty of warnings for those tempted to equate strong state action or public reactions on rape with gender justice, showing how sanctions against sexual violence can be integral to or appropriated by a host of other projects (Miller 2004; Halley et al. 2006; Bumiller 2008). Much of this literature has focused on so-called strong states, where legal interventions might be used as mechanisms of social control of marginalized groups or of women's private lives. In Afghanistan, where—as in other weak states—legal interventions are less institutionalized, assertive state action is typically the result of the mobilization of social groups around specific incidents. As a result, state interventions can be less predictable and may or may not support feminist agendas (Roychowdhury 2016).

As the cases in this chapter showed, intensified state regulation of gender violence and relations in Afghanistan did not necessarily lead to a more equal status for women. On the contrary, government regulation affirmed predominant gender ideologies by limiting itself to women well within the category of the unquestionably virtuous. Moreover, public discourse often validated family control over female bodies and specifically notions of honor, whereby male family members could claim a stake in women's sexuality.[13] Likewise, public discourse did not necessarily indicate a permanent increase in the government's interest or ability in regulating and policing matters of sexuality (i.e., as a stronger state expanding its domain and control of kinship power). The case from Sarepul shows that what could appear as a question of government obligations to uphold citizen's honor was perhaps better understood as a struggle for power between local groups. Appreciating this requires a shift in our perspective on the state itself; the government was not acted upon as a coherent structure, but as a vehicle of factional struggle. Through this lens, gender violence as a governance issue (i.e., a site of government action and intervention) was but one chapter in an ongoing struggle over power and resources.

I believe that the Sarepul case also illustrates the pitfalls of regarding the language of honor as somehow integral to a non-state logic of "kinship" society. According to the evolutionary perspectives often applied to Afghanistan (see introduction), honor *(namus)* is a "tribal" value, consonant with a pre-state social system based on kinship, egalitarianism, autonomy, and the strict seclusion of women. If such idioms make an appearance in state arenas, they are typically considered spillovers from the tribal system, where they properly belong, and it is assumed that they eventually will be eradicated by the modernizing touch of the state. The Sarepul case unsettles such binaries particularly well. It shows that honor, as a vocabulary of power and boundary marking, as a way of articulating violations and entitlements, can equally be employed in struggles *over* state power as employed in struggles *against* it. It is often those with a degree of influence and access to the state who can utilize official positions and public arenas to pursue gender violations—whether as a standalone issue or as a component of larger political projects—as was the case in Sarepul.

Conclusions

Protection at a Price?

On a beautiful Friday in April 2015, I was sitting in my garden in Kabul, relaxing and chatting with a friend. I cannot remember how it came up, but somehow the conversation turned to the murder of a woman named Farkhunda a month earlier. "You can see how it happened," my male Afghan friend said. "There is this anger, a feeling that many women are being provocative on purpose. First, it was that girl who went around not far from here without pants and scarf. And then the other one who was protesting—the one who had that metal dress showing off her body. And finally Farkhunda—that was reaction to all of it. Some people think certain women are just going too far." I remember feeling both perplexed and upset with my friend's argument. "But these were three completely different things," I protested. "It's unfair to put them together like that. That girl who went around with bare legs—the one who was filmed and put on the internet—clearly she was in distress; she did not do it to protest. Maybe she had run away from some situation at her house—what do we know? It wasn't the same as the girl who was protesting sexual harassment with that metal thing." This woman, a performance artist named Kubra Khademi had dressed up in self-designed body armor emphasizing her breasts and bottom, and braved a short walk through Kot-e Sangi, a busy suburb not far from Kabul University. She had been mobbed by male pedestrians and had gone into hiding after pictures and videos of her performance act had circulated in social media. "And Farkhunda," I continued. "That was something different again. She . . . well, doesn't it scare you, people being killed on the streets of Kabul just because someone shouts that they are infidels? It could happen to one of us, too." I wasn't very articulate that day, but I was trying to appeal to my friend's deep antipathy to religious fanaticism, trying to somehow induce him to show more solidarity, to see Farkhunda's murder as a danger to us all, not as some understandable or at least explainable reaction to women "going too far."

But, of course, there were stark gendered dimensions to what had happened to Farkhunda. To the mob that had killed her at Kabul's Shah-e Do Shamshira shrine, she represented everything that had to be opposed—a woman trespassing in public space, questioning male authority on religious issues, who then quickly turned into an infidel, burning the Quran, probably on the instruction of the Americans. I had been in Norway at the time of the murder, and I found myself on national television struggling to explain how it was possible that a woman could be lynched in the center of Kabul in front of a large group of people, with nobody—not even the police observing the crowd—intervening to stop it. I felt that the interviewer wanted me to paint a picture in which Afghan society was hopelessly primitive, captive to misogyny and backwardness beyond redemption—to confirm that Western efforts to modernize it and to save its women had been misguided from the start. In the few seconds available to me, it was difficult to communicate that while the radicalized politics of the last decades had made the murder possible, it was far from an ordinary occurrence somehow in line with traditional Afghan culture. To most Kabulis, the public murder of a woman by strangers was abhorrent and shocking.

What happened afterward was also remarkable, again suggesting that many Afghans had found the killing abhorrent. At Farkhunda's burial, a small group of women carried her coffin. It was a highly symbolic act in Afghanistan, where, as a rule, this is a task performed by men. At the time of her funeral, so soon after her death, it was still not clear exactly what had taken place at the shrine. The prevailing story was still that Farkhunda had burnt the Quran. Thus, the women who carried her coffin did so with considerable bravery, given the fact that they could easily fall prey to the same hateful and dangerous rhetoric and be painted as the accomplices of an infidel. By and large, they were not part of the more established women's rights networks that have featured prominently in this book—the groups that were running shelters, advocating for the EVAW law, and taking part in the many policy and advocacy events in Kabul. The women in those groups typically had a background in NGO work in Peshawar (Azarbaijani-Moghaddam 2006) or had held government positions during the communist era. Instead, the women who carried Farkhunda's coffin and took part in her burial were mostly of a younger generation, with various professional backgrounds and were not engaged in full-time women's rights work. They were also more radical. Many were self-declared feminists and appeared less intimidated by the prospect of being labeled by the mujahedin or the religious establishment. However, a few days later, thousands gathered for the largest demonstration seen in Kabul since the 1980s. At that point, it had been clearly established that Farkhunda had not burnt the Quran. She was, in fact, a deeply religious woman who had challenged the shrine keepers for what she considered an un-Islamic practice—profiting from selling *tawiz*—amulets containing pieces of holy scripture.

Although some of the perpetrators of the murder were quickly arrested, the legal case was complicated and remains inconclusive as I write this. It is not my intention to probe into the details of the case here. Rather, I bring it up as an illustration of two things. First, the murder of Farkhunda showed with terrifying clarity how potent the mix of gendered and religious denunciation could be. To her raging attackers, Farkhunda embodied all that was subversive, dangerous, and insulting in the post-2001 order—a woman asserting herself in public, attacking religion, instigated by foreigners. As my friend had detected, they felt justified in reining in a woman who had gone too far. Their reaction was given divine sanction by the now-routine framing of women who stepped out of line as religious detractors. But second, the aftermath of the killing hinted at something that has been largely absent in the processes covered in this book: a broad, popular mobilization confronting its adversaries head on. There had been small street demonstrations in Kabul on a few occasions, but nothing remotely close to the scale of what happened on March 24, 2015, when thousands of people marched to protest the killing of Farkhunda. It was as if the demonstrators' realization that their worst fears had become true prompted a determination to take a more direct and open stand against conservative forces. The large demonstration and—before that—the women carrying Farkhunda's coffin at her burial, represented a stark contrast to the more discreet, cautious, and often donor-dependent approaches featuring centrally in the processes discussed in this book.

My purpose in this book has been to explore the effects, limits, and politics of the focus on gender violence in post-2001 Afghanistan. My starting point was the fact that attempts to define and regulate acts of gender violence offer a window into shifting relations of gender, power, and governance. I set out to explore concrete processes and strategies through which definitions of gender violence have been articulated and renegotiated, and sovereign domains and jurisdictions claimed, affirmed, or disputed. The trajectory of the EVAW law has been central to my investigations. Derived in parts from the global VAW discourse, it defined violence against women in terms of violations of their bodily integrity (e.g., rape, forced marriage, and beating) as well as their civil rights (e.g., deprivation of inheritance and denial of access to education, work, and health care). As the EVAW law was reviewed in Parliament, there was a clear tendency toward reinstating some of the authority of fathers and husbands over their daughters and wives. For instance, fathers were exempted for punishment in cases of forced marriage, since it was argued that they were better placed to determine what was in their underage daughter's interest. But there were also attempts to ensure women their part of the deal; for instance, the nonpayment of wives' maintenance was inserted as a form of violence against women. Had the process in Parliament been completed and the

EVAW law ratified there, it is conceivable that the law would have defined gender violence in ways that partly constituted women as independent legal persons whose bodily integrity and sexual autonomy was inviolable and partly as gendered beings who, by virtue of being women, could call upon certain male obligations, such as maintenance. The latter would have amounted to a public regulation of patriarchy, curbing male and family excesses and guaranteeing women their part of the Afghan "patriarchal bargain" (Kandiyoti 1988). Instead, the law was kept as a decree and in the form that it was enacted as such. In other words, the compromises that a broader national settlement would have entailed were avoided through the ability to mobilize executive power, partly by international pressure.

Having explored battles unfolding on Afghanistan's legal terrain, I turned to two key parts of the institutional infrastructure that had been erected through similar dynamics as the EVAW law: the specialized prosecution units for crimes of violence against women and the women's shelters. The prosecution units were established through donor funds and initiatives. It was hoped that these units would provide a space where acts of gender violence could be pursued in insulation from the challenges affecting the overall justice system—a kind of ring-fenced site of intervention where reform could be fast-tracked. However, my analysis of the specialized unit in Kabul showed the limits of the kind of top-down change that the coalition behind the EVAW law was trying to bring about. As long as broader relations reinforcing women's dependence within the family remained intact, the unit was poised to do little more than to serve as a recourse for marital difficulties, as opposed to an institution enforcing the law. Yet even if this was not the kind of purpose the backers of the unit had envisaged, it still provided many women with a curtailed kind of empowerment. The shelters, on the other hand, were able to function as autonomous spaces, out of reach of the restraining power of conservative national actors. This enabled them to avoid the kind of concessions that a stronger national anchoring would have entailed, such as a more rigid screening of residents based on chastity. At the same time, the shelters were dependent on foreign funding and entangled in geopolitical tropes about saving Afghan women. In turn, their residents became reliant on the shelters for their survival, as they often had few prospects of being reintegrated back into broader society.

I started this research by posing the question of whether gender violence was becoming a governance or state matter in Afghanistan. Taking my cue from the literature on expanding state regulation over family and kinship, I wondered what such a shift would mean for gender relations and state power—a shift in which the state assumed a larger responsibility for intervening in acts of gender violence. However, as became evident fairly quickly, I could also have asked if gender violence in Afghanistan was becoming a *global* governance issue. The book has drawn upon insights of the literature on global governmentality and transnational gender activism to demonstrate how this has indeed been the case. The promotion and implementation of the EVAW law, the specialized prosecution units, and the institution of shelters came about through transnationally constituted assemblages and only to some extent were routed through the Afghan state. These efforts were certainly not driven by the centralizing impulses of an Afghan ruler seeking to expand the power of government by drawing women into the circle of government justice, wresting away the autonomy of their male relatives. In fact, President Karzai's strategy on violence against women was much more opportunistic and appeared primarily informed by his efforts to create and maintain personal alliances. As one activist suggested to me, unlike King Amanullah or the PDPA, "Karzai is not personally committed to women's rights, but he is committed to the international funding that comes with it."[1] Neither were there any signs that the Afghan president attempted to use government courts to achieve tighter state regulation of family and kinship in order to centralize power. As the Sarepul case shows, the government's response to issues such as rape was reactive and entangled in patrimonial politics. Whether by effect or intent, the EVAW law, the shelters, and, to some extent, the special prosecution units instead constructed a globalized zone of protection for Afghan women, dependent on external funds and political pressure.

My argument that the specific shape that formal sanctions of gender relations takes is not preordained by religion, culture, or other fixed societal attributes, but contingent on situated politics, resonates with academic literature on gender in the Middle East and beyond. Research on women and legal protection in the Middle East has documented the importance of the state's local power bases (Kandiyoti 1991; Molyneux 1995; Joseph 2000; Charrad 2001) for how women's rights are enshrined and enforced in government frameworks. This book has added another dimension to this literature by underlining the importance of zooming out beyond national borders when mapping the political constituencies shaping government policies. By pointing to the many and sometimes contradictory ways in which international pressure and funding shaped interventions into gender violence in Afghanistan, I have highlighted how transnational coalitions and political agendas can be as important for outcomes as national constituencies. An important part of this historicized perspective has been to unsettle the national state as the ultimate, self-contained unit of reference and guarantor of claims. As Kim-Puri notes, the theorization of the state in line with recent insights understanding it as a contingent set of institutions and relations (as opposed to a monolithic structure) has largely been absent in feminist sociology (Kim-Puri 2005: 144). Moreover, transnational feminist studies, while attending to the asymmetries and inequalities produced by the flows of global capital and geopolitics, have not explored in detail how the state has been reconfigured as a consequence of such flows.

The book has set up an analytical frame that sees state institutions as immersed in and partly expressive of transnational processes. It has done this by drawing upon the work of Sassen and others, demonstrating how the very notion of the

Afghan state, as a nationally contained, unitary, sovereign body makes little sense in the context of interventions into gender violence in Afghanistan. I have shown, for instance, how in the case of the EVAW law and in the push to end impunity for gender violence, certain state capabilities were reoriented toward more global projects (Sassen 2008). National institutions—courts, prosecutors, and the legislative bodies—became part of a globalized sovereign regime, in which Afghan women's security was made a global concern and ultimately guaranteed by external funds and pressure. In other words, the Afghan state was denationalized, in the sense of being reassembled as a vehicle for the operation of global sovereign claims.

However, if there was a global EVAW law assemblage working through national institutions, it should also be said that this assemblage was in no sense a totalizing, unidirectional force. National institutions did not simply seamlessly facilitate a global order. Rather, global templates intersected with local dynamics in ways that produced outcomes distinct to Afghanistan. The processes traced in chapter 2 show that rather than being two contradictory forces, personalized politics and external reform attempts often reinforced each other in particular ways. Executive power was strengthened as Western diplomats, looking for swift results, preferred to deal with the cabinet and the president rather than the unwieldy and capricious Parliament. But this strategy also enabled President Karzai to strengthen his personal power base through the granting of favors in an exchange of offerings and loyalty. He gifted the EVAW law to two of his constituencies—women activists and Western supporters. At the same time, he also bestowed on other of his constituencies a gift that, in some ways, cancelled out the EVAW law—the Shia law. Similarly, the emphasis placed on output and fundraising by the "NGO-ization" of women's activism also fed into personalized and patron-client politics, reflecting the link between development brokerage and patron-client systems pointed out by Olivier de Sardan (2005: 174). Overall, the force of the EVAW law assemblage was paradoxically both enabled and constrained by its dependence on the diplomatic and financial leverage of NATO countries. The short plenary debate about the law in Parliament in May 2013 served to underline the partial nature of its reach and its ambiguous status. And by 2015, it seemed possible that the entire law, so central to both local and donor-driven gender activism for almost a decade, could be turned into a historical footnote by the creation of comprehensive new penal code.

Nor was the EVAW law assemblage the only transnationally constituted sovereign claim in the field of gender violence. There was a significant difference between the more technocratic and international coalition that formed around the EVAW law and the more directly geopolitical agendas of NATO military victory being mobilized around the shelters. If, as Lisa Hajjar and others argue, struggles over women's rights are also struggles over authority, and if increased regulation of gender violence is also about expanding power, this book underlines the need to be open-minded about exactly what forms of authority and power are being expanded. We cannot meaningfully limit ourselves to predetermined templates (such as the state or global governance). Instead, we must map and dissect the actual constellations (or assemblages) that define and adjudicate gender violence in practice. The overall picture that emerges from subjecting the landscape of gender and violence in post-2001 Afghanistan to such a survey is one of fragmentation and partial-ness. And this is to say nothing of the shrinking control exercised over territory within Afghanistan's borders by either government officials or the international military—even within the contracting space that they operated in, there was no singular policy, institution, or sovereign power. The political and legal orders enforcing claims and counterclaims, the moral universes that gender relations were inserted into, and the bureaucratic machineries through which problems were delineated and remedied were multiple and evolving, appearing in historically specific configurations. Afghanistan in the first two decades of the new millennium revealed a thin but not inconsequential constellation of women's activists and progressive justice officials and diplomats, boosted by international funding and alliances. Sometimes entangled in orientalist tropes of saving Afghan women, its reach was compromised by its top-down mode of operation, but also by the dynamics of patronage politics and the war that was engulfing most of the country. The warring parties also launched their own attempts at rule through justice—the Taliban insurgents with their ostensibly pure sharia and (as I have discussed elsewhere in more detail) the foreign military with their experiments in tribal and traditional governance (Wimpelmann 2013). I problematized the notions of total, determinate logics further by showing how discourses of honor can function as a vocabulary of demands and assertions in struggles over access to state power. The cases discussed in chapter 5 and 6 demonstrated that gender ideologies where women were subsumed under family sovereignty operated across the social field and were not in any sense reducible to non-state, "tribal" structures or worlds.

From the perspective of feminist politics, the fragmentation characterizing the field of gender violence appeared both as an opportunity and a problem. It enabled forms of intervention that were somewhat autonomous from the conservative gender ideologies espoused by important power holders. But at the same time, these interventions were dependent on problematic, sometimes overtly imperial alliances. Moreover, in practice, they were constantly compromised by legal and social practices that castigated female autonomy, sexual and otherwise. The individual cases analyzed in part 3 of the book illustrated that what was often at stake in the contestations regarding the definitions of, interventions into, and protective measures against violence against women was the degree to which kin—in particular, male relatives and husbands—could claim legitimate interest in and authority over female sexuality. Runaway girls, safe houses for women, and government-mandated punishments for forced marriage or honor killings all potentially challenged or renegotiated notions and assertions that subordinated women to their families. Yet the totality of legal practices and the social relations underpinning them mostly went in the other direction. As chapter 4 showed, the legal apparatus operated with an extremely broad definition of female moral transgression. Not only was *zina*—sexual intercourse outside of or prior to marriage—a criminal act, but also, women's very presence outside of government or family surveillance was made into an offense, suggesting that what was at stake was the prospect of female autonomy per se. Similarly, the problematization of women's existence outside of the family unit had ramifications for the degree to which justice institutions were able (or inclined) to punish gender violence. Because women's prospects for survival outside of family settings were so limited, both justice officials and women themselves often preferred reconciliation with their abusers or their families rather than criminal sanctions. To some, this was an unproblematic and culturally appropriate solution—MOWA, for instance, in its 2014 report on the implementation of the EVAW law, had stated, "Mediation . . . has emerged as the most preferred and commonly used method of resolution of cases of violence against women because it respects the sanctity of 'family' as a unit and is in consonance with cultural traditions" (MOWA 2014: 12).

However, this conservative and ahistorical statement was, in fact, a symptom that the post-2001 focus on gender violence had left much of the structural relations that underpinned women's vulnerability to family violence unquestioned and intact. Kapur, analyzing the Indian women's movement, suggests that there is an inherent tension between attempts to delineate an indigenous, "culturally appropriate" feminism and pursuing equality between the sexes. She is worth quoting at some length.

> [Feminism in India] has been charged with being a product of "decadent Western capitalism" . . . based on a foreign culture of no relevance to women in the Third World. Therefore, feminists have adamantly denied allegations of being Western and have sought to establish a distinctively Indian feminism, based on the notion of an authentic Indian woman, one who is routinely a victim of oppression and violence. Any discussion of female choice, especially in sexual matters, has been muted. Sexual pleasure per se has been regarded by many within the women's movement as a foreign contaminant and something that distinguishes Indian women and culture from the "West." Thus the women's movement in India has remained simultaneously tied to a revolutionary and a nonrevolutionary sensibility. It continues to invest in an essentialist and conservative notion of Indian culture and womanhood while pursuing the revolutionary enterprise of achieving equality between men and women. This tension continues to inform feminists' engagements with the law, which have focused on securing formal equal rights with men without disrupting the dominant cultural, familial and sexual norms that define Indian womanhood. (Kapur 2012: 336)

While Kapur is far from the first scholar to point to the complicated relationship between postcolonial feminism and nationalism (Chatterjee 1993; Yuval

Davis 1997; Parker et al. 1992), she goes on to argue that the focus on the "authentic women" has enabled an alliance between third-world feminism and a certain strand of Western feminism. For this alliance, a joint focus on violence against women has been a natural common ground. This focus disrupts neither gender nor global hierarchies, instead it reinforces at all levels the notion of the women of the Global South affected by gender violence as a "victim-subject" in need of protectionist intervention. In post-2001 Afghanistan, the dynamics underpinning this protectionist logic were unusually pronounced. There was constant slippage between women's general ability to live, move, and support themselves outside of family settings and their morality and chastity. In turn, women's chastity—or mere non-deference—was routinely translated into questions of religious adherence, intertwined with notions of national resistance to Western impositions. Thus, all kinds of female defiance—escaping the family home, living in a shelter, setting up an independent household, attempting to marry a man of one's choice, arguing for women's civil rights, questioning male religious authority—could be constructed as defiance against Islam. This would cause a woman to enter a perilous terrain where charges of ultimate betrayal—being a nonbeliever—could be easily invoked.

Of course, religion, as elsewhere, did not appear in a "pure" form, and so there were competing ways of envisioning women's positions, interwoven with ideologies of conservative nationalism (in the articulation of the jihadis) or modernist enlightenment (in the articulation of Afghan feminists and liberal religious scholars). However, as witnessed, for instance, in the parliamentary debate over the EVAW law, the jihadi version tended to prevail. This was based on a number of contingent factors, among which were the former mujahedin's powers of intimidation, their ability to mobilize around the need for national and religious assertion in the midst of a political order underwritten by Western infidels, and their appeal to patriarchal sentiments. The broader backdrop was a constant tension between three key aspects of the post-2001 order: foreign military operations, the rehabilitation of the mujahedin, and external attempts to promote Afghan women's rights. In a setting where many power holders evidently owed much of their current positions to Western funds and armed support, taking a conservative position on women's rights became a valuable way of demonstrating one's nationalist and Islamic credentials.

In this landscape, there were few attempts to directly confront the gender ideologies that placed an absolute premium on female propriety. Discussions about forced marriage or the shelters emphasized women's right to choose their own husbands and to be free of family violence, but they did not attempt to dethrone the imperative of female chastity. Thus, the validity of a distinguishing line between "good" and "bad" women, between those deserving protection and those beyond the pale of respectability, was not fundamentally disrupted. Instead, the line was merely pushed back and forth. Perhaps, for Afghan women, who only a decade earlier had been banned from the public domain altogether, and for whom public presence was still extremely tenuous, this was far too risky a topic. Most already felt the need to carefully maintain a virtuous public persona. To enter into a debate that would put them in solidarity with non-chaste women would almost certainly taint them as "bad women" or outcasts. Neither did international actors challenge the distinction per se. Although U.N. staff and others were supportive of the efforts to distinguish *zina* from running away and from rape, they did not challenge the criminalization of *zina,* which could have been framed as interfering in religious issues. All things considered, the interest, whether genuine or strategic, that many Western governments held in promoting women's rights in Afghanistan constantly clashed with other objectives, such as stability and force protection and a general wish not to add to a local image of occupiers unduly interfering in religious and social life. Moreover, the dominant aid modality in Afghanistan—project delivery through private contractors and NGOs—tended to favor measurable outputs and individual achievements over broader and more political mobilization.

It was no wonder then that Western support to Afghan women's rights mainly took the form of narrow, targeted interventions rather than investment in more transformative change, reinforcing the overall "protect and rescue" approach that characterized efforts against gender violence in the decade and half following the 2001 invasion. The shelters were, in many ways, a prime example of this narrow approach. They were able to evade local binaries between chaste and unchaste women by partly exiting national regulatory mechanisms. But this reinforced their dependence on external backers, and shelter residents themselves were often unable to move out of the shelters, because of the strong social sanctions against women living on their own. In this sense, they were also left in a state of dependence—on the continued support of the shelters.

I would suggest that in many ways, Afghan women and feminists were facing the choice of two models of protection. Protection, as a number of feminist writers have pointed out is a hierarchical, often gendered concept, entailing a bargain of material and physical protection against loyalty, propriety, and subordination (Kandiyoti 1988; Kapur 2002; Young 2003; Miller 2004). Familial, national, and transnational bargains of protection in return for "propriety" should be placed in the same analytical frame; all entail demands for loyalty, dependence, and submission. The book has shown how protection, whether extended to Afghan women by male guardians, by government courts, or by the shelters, routinely came with demands to conform to certain normative ideals. Exactly what these ideals comprised was somewhat contentious—women could be deemed unworthy of protection (or deserving of violent punishment) for defying husbands' authority, for unauthorized public forays, or for being in the company of unrelated men, although sexual indiscretions were a fairly agreed-upon disqualifier. In other words, and as many Afghan feminists complained, women were asked to renounce their autonomy, sexually and otherwise, in return for protection. But there was also a price to be paid for the protection afforded by the laws and institutions that, in part, were realized through transnational actors. The price for the EVAW law was to bypass the parliamentary process and thus the opportunity for the politics of women's rights to be anchored in broader local constituencies. Instead, the law was quietly promoted through informal Kabul-based networks, reinforcing a political mode bearing more resemblance to court politics than any kind of broad-based women's movement. This made gains dependent on good relations with the presidential palace, which, in turn, differentiated between women politically affiliated with the executive and those closer to the opposition. And a tenuous local anchoring was not the only price to pay for transnationally derived protection. The NGOs running the shelters, and the transnational alliances they were part of, often mobilized orientalist tropes of saving Afghan women in a way that rendered them dependent on salvation by NATO. In this sense, renegotiating one hierarchy often meant getting entangled in another. The shelters, while out of familial and government supervision, became beholden to Western good will—and even military force.

Yet to what extent would it be realistic to expect Afghan women to negotiate a position independent from all of these sets of relations? One must be alert to the danger that the notion of "pure" or autonomous women's movements becomes an ideal that holds practical feminist gains hostage (Roy 2011). Understanding the definitions of and jurisdiction over gender violence as forged out of historicized struggles also brings into view the fact that possibilities mostly come attached with some accommodations and trade-offs. For instance, the alternative to keeping the EVAW law as a presidential decree was a modified version in Parliament—where it looked fated to become subject to problematic amendments, or where it could even have been rejected altogether. To many of the supporters of the EVAW law, the opportunity to have, for the first time in history, a law that directly addressed abuses against Afghan women was too important to let pass, even if the way it was obtained was far from perfect. Many of them saw no prospects or time to engage in broader mobilization and coalition building. Although the victory of getting the EVAW law decreed seemed to bring with it some kind of external dependence, as many Afghan feminist pointed out, the price of gaining the "protection" of one's family or husband could also be very high. And so could submitting to the demands of government and their conservative constituencies, as the attempts to establish a screening regime of the shelters testified to.

Perhaps the uncomfortable truth is that we must abandon the ideal of total autonomy; all guarantees have to be negotiated with someone. Afghanistan during the first decade and a half after the 2001 invasion is a particular stark reminder of this. Carefully laying out the nature and background of such compromises, which is what this book has attempted to do, is therefore not the same as condemning those who make them. It must also be kept in mind that the terms of these kind of bargains are never set in stone. It is too early to say what will be the long-term legacy of the struggles over gender violence in Afghanistan during the last fifteen years. Maybe, as many women rights advocates hope, the infrastructure erected with international support will gradually consolidate and expand, slowly washing away the significance of the compromises and external dependence that brought it into being.

INTRODUCTION

1. In Afghanistan, where government registers often do not exist and war has caused displacement, it may be possible for someone to falsely deny an actually existing family relationship, for instance, to a sister or a sister-in-law.

2. In most Afghan communities, bride-price *(walwar)* has long been an integral part of weddings, with large sums and assets being transferred to the bride's family (primarily her father) from the groom and his family. Bride-price is widely spoken of as a social ill that impoverishes young men and because corrupt fathers marry their daughters to old or otherwise unsuitable husbands, yet it has proven difficult to curtail.

3. The term *mujahed* (plural, *mujahedin*) means "one engaged in jihad," but *mujahedin* usually refers to the resistance fighters who fought the pro-Soviet government of Afghanistan during the Cold War. After the Taliban was removed from power in 2001, many former mujahedin commanders (some of whom had been partners to the American-led invasion) gained important positions in government, the security apparatus, and Parliament. See chapter 1 for more details on their post-2001 rehabilitation to power.

4. Interview with a human rights official, Mazar-e Sharif, March 2010.

5. Schueller (2011) points out that critiques of colonial rescue binaries also comes from "within," from Western accounts that do not problematize the U.S.-led invasion but nonetheless seek to rehabilitate Afghan women's agency. Statements such as "Afghan women can save themselves, and I need to be saved too" (7) invite an individualized crosscultural solidarity without attending to different positions inhabited by Afghan and Western women.

6. In his 1996 book *Heroes of the Age,* David Edwards introduces his hypothesis that Afghanistan's troubles over the last decade in the last instance can be explained by "certain deep-seated moral contradictions that press against each other like tectonic plates at geological fault lines below the surface of events" (3). Honor, Islam, and the rule of the state are

to Edwards distinct moral orders that are in many respects "incompatible with one another" (4). However in his 2002 sequel, Edwards appears open to a revision of this hypothesis observing that by the mid-twentieth century, "old divisions" were breaking down and divisions (e.g., between tribe and state) were becoming blurred, opening up possibilities for new hybrid orders. (Edwards 2002: 102–3).

7. Kamali's (1985) discussion of family law is a partial exception, although this detailed discussion on Afghan family law, constitutions, and the judiciary is a conventional legal study that does not explicitly consider how law is productive of gender and power.

8. This is particularly the case with rape and sexual violence. But see work on Ottoman Egypt (Sonbol 1997; Kozma 2004) and Pakistan (Quraishi 2000; Zia 1994; Lau 2007). "Honor killings" as a state sanctioning of relatives' claim over female family members have received somewhat more attention.

9. Given this dearth of earlier scholarly work, this book contains a rather extensive discussion on the evolvement of the Afghan legal system (see chapter 1).

CHAPTER 1. INTRUSIONS, INVASIONS, AND INTERVENTIONS

1. Field notes, Kabul, July 23, 2009.

2. In Muslim countries, the basis of law has been the will of God, as revealed in the Quran and in the exemplary sayings and actions of the Prophet (the Sunnah). *Sharia* is defined as "The rules given by God to His servants" (Peters 2003: 82) and covers both what is considered the field of law in the West and other areas of life, such as prayer and fasting. *Fiqh,* on the other hand, refers to the methodology of ascertaining legal conclusions from divine sources (the Quran and the Sunnah). Thus "if sharia is God's law, fiqh is the scholarly discourse aimed at formulating the prescriptions of the sharia on the basis of the revealed texts and using various hermeneutic devices." (Peters 2003: 84) There are five major such established *fiqh* schools; Hanafi, Maliki, Shafi'i, and Hanbali (all Sunni) and Jafari (Shia). *Fiqh* texts are not law codes, but scholarly discussions where different perspectives are juxtaposed. Such texts do not contain unequivocal or authoritative provisions. Instead, issuing legal rulings have historically been at the discretion of religiously trained scholars, by virtue of their knowledge of *fiqh* as a scholarly discourse. However, contemporary Muslim states (with the exception of Saudi Arabia) have codified laws in most domains, depriving the ulema of their legal monopoly in the process.

3. Nawid points out that "although British sources refer consistently to Amanullah's apathy towards religious groups, other sources indicate that he cultivated excellent personal relations with eminent religious leaders in Kabul long before ascending the throne" (Nawid 1999: 57).

4. For an overview of Amanullah's *nizam-namas,* see Polluda 1973: 66–91.

5. The category *hadd* (plural, *hudood*) includes crimes for which there are immutable punishments (punishments believed to have been set by God: amputation, stoning, or lashing); *qisas* includes crimes for which relatives or victims were allowed retaliation; *diat* refers to crimes that can be settled by compensation or "blood money"; and *tazir* applies to crimes for which punishments were discretionary (determined by a judge) and for purposes of prevention and deterrence.

6. Even if *hadd* crimes are crimes for which punishments are regarded as immutable, scholars and Islamic judges have nonetheless understood the evidential requirements and exact definitions of and punishments for these crimes differently. Crimes normally categorized as *hadd* include *zina* (adultery), *sariq* (theft), *harida* (violent theft), *qazf* (false accusation of *zina*), *ridda* (apostasy), and *shurb kamr* (consumption of alcohol) (Peters 2005: 53).

7. Eastern tribes, who were facing the abolishment of existing privileges in conscription and taxation, were the other main group behind this rebellion, called the 1924 Khost rebellion (Polluda 1973).

8. This Constitution was a relatively liberal document, but "in reality the King had more powers than any other head of a constitutional monarchy could dream of enjoying" (Saikal 2004: 146). Article 15 of the Constitution stated, "The King is not accountable to anyone and shall be respected by all."

9. Interview with female judge at the Supreme Court, Kabul, March 2015. According to this judge, there were around thirty female judges in Kabul at the time. They were generally placed in the family courts and were not considered for promotion.

10. Like in many other Muslim countries, the Civil Code actually drew upon Maliki *fiqh* on the issue of divorce, since this school were more detailed in this question (Kamali 1985).

11. *Hudood* is the plural form of *hadd*, *qassas* is an alternate spelling of *qisas*. On *hadd*, see note 5 in this chapter, for *hadd, tazir, qisas, and diat,* see note 4.

12. For a more detailed discussion about the content of these two codes and the gender relations they sanctioned, see chapter 2.

13. Interview with a former PDPA official, Kabul, February 2015.

14. Interview with a former female judge, Kabul, March 2015.

15. Interview with a female prosecutor, Herat, May 2015.

16. Cited in Nawid 2007.

17. The Sharia Ordinances on Veiling *(Fatawa-ye shara'i –ye mawrad-e hijab),* issued by the Afghan Supreme Court, 1994.

18. Nancy Dupree reports that these restrictions were first enforced in a haphazard manner, varying from region to region and dependent on personalities, the degree of accommodation with aid agencies, and the level of administrative control (Dupree 1998). Restrictions became progressively harsher, particularly in the cities. Dupree also suggests that the written rules and regulations were mostly directed toward the U.N. aid groups and NGOs. "The general populace is informed of regulations over *Radio Shariat*" (156, n. 41).

19. Interview with a religious leader, Herat, March 2015.

20. According to a recent compilation of public executions during the Taliban period, there were at least seven executions, most of them by stoning, for adultery. The majority of these executions were of women (Strick 2015). The actual number, however, is probably somewhat higher. In addition, lashing (for premarital sex) was a frequent occurrence, as was amputation for theft.

21. Interview with a former female judge, Kabul, February 2015.

22. Although nationwide consultations were organized, the tight time schedule and the fact that the draft of the Constitution was not made available in advance meant that this exercise appeared mostly as symbolic window dressing (Suhrke 2011). The United States,

Interim President Karzai, and a bloc of military commanders dominated the subsequent Constitutional Jirga assembled in the capital to review and approve the document.

23. Article 130 reads, "The courts in the cases under their consideration shall apply the provisions of this Constitution and other laws. Whenever no provision exits in the Constitution or the laws for a case under consideration, the court shall follow the provisions of the Hanafi jurisprudence and within the provisions set forth in this Constitution render a decision that secures justice in the best possible way."

24. For instance, Hartmann reports that Assadullah Sarwari, intelligence chief under the communist government, was sentenced to death with reference to this article, although the sentence was later changed to eighteen years in prison. His trial is the only case of prosecution for war crimes in Afghanistan to date. (Hartmann 2011: 187).

25. Article 83 states that from each province, two of the elected members to the Lower House shall be females. Article 84 states that one-third of members of the Upper House will be presidential appointments, and half of them must be women.

26. However, the Supreme Court was the institution authorized to interpret the Constitution.

27. Royce Wiles, *Finding Aid for Afghanistan Legislation and Translations,* Afghanistan Research and Evaluation Unit (AREU) (unpublished overview).

28. A *stage* course is post-degree training program leading to a qualification to serve as a judge, prosecutor, or lawyer. A French term, its usage in Afghanistan reflects similarities with the French legal system—both countries have civil law systems.

29. A 2008 presidential decree further strengthened the Supreme Court, authorizing it to increase or decrease punishments. Prior to this, the Supreme Court had only been only allowed to check cases for legal accuracy. These sessions were also attended by the representatives from the Attorney General's Office, but neither the accused nor defense lawyers were allowed to attend.

30. For example, Abdul Rahman, indicted under article 130 for apostasy, was eventually declared mentally ill and taken to Italy. Sayed Pervez Kambash, found guilty under article 130 for blasphemy, was first given the death penalty, which was later reduced to the maximum prison sentence. He was pardoned by the president and repatriated to Norway. Two people charged with blasphemy were sentenced to twenty years in prison under article 130. See Hartmann 2011.

31. Personal communication with IDLO staff, March 2015.

32. One of the mujahedin parties receiving Western and Pakistani support during the 1980s.

33. Interview with USAID Rule of Law official, Kabul, July 2010.

CHAPTER 2. "GOOD WOMEN HAVE NO NEED FOR THIS LAW"

1. An earlier version of the first part of this chapter was published in *Women's Studies International Forum* 51 (2015): 101–9.

2. UNAMA Human Rights, *Concerns on Shi'a Personal Status Law,* August 18, 2009. On file with author.

3. Ali Reza Rohani, presentation at seminar on the EVAW law, Kateb University, Kabul, December 16, 2009; interview with Huma Alizoi, judge, juvenile court, Kabul, February 8, 2010.

4. Dari is a gender-neutral language; it does not distinguish between gender in personal pronouns. The article could equally be translated: "A person, defending her honor, who sees her spouse." However, the article was understood to refer to men only. A woman who killed her adulterous husband or a male relative claiming defense of honor would make little sense, since male relatives' sexual behavior did not reflect on women in this way. Moreover, as one of my informants stated, to kill a man caught in adulterous behavior on the spot was perilous, because men had to right to enter into polygamous marriages, and one could not know if the man had not recently married the woman he had been found with. Interview with Qazi Ahmed Nazir Hanafi, Kabul, January 2010.

5. This title in the original is *Zina, lawat va hatke namus*. The term *lawat*, here translated as "sodomy," is often translated as "pederasty" or "'active' sodomy," but also sometimes as "homosexuality." My research does not cover the theme of how homosexual practices are regulated by the Afghan government—a field that would benefit from future research. Some prosecutors suggested to me that they would pursue cases of *lawat* only if one person was a minor and that they would consider only the older party liable for prosecution.

6. Neither the *hadd* punishments for *zina* (stoning or lashing) nor the evidentiary conditions (normally held to be four witnesses to the act of penetration or a voluntary confession) required to apply such punishments was spelt out in the code. It should also be added that in theory, premarital and extramarital sex were only classified as *zina* when these evidentiary conditions were fulfilled. However, in everyday speak, many Afghans refer to all extramarital sex as *zina*, and the Penal Code also refers to adultery as *zina* also when the evidence to punish it as a *hadd* crime is not in existence.

7. The Penal Code contains six "Principal Punishments": (1) execution; (2) continued imprisonment (16–18 years); (3) long-term imprisonment (5–15 years); (4) medium-term imprisonment (1–5 years); (5) short-term imprisonment (24 hours–1 year); and (6) the payment of a fine.

8. *Taqnin* literally means "making a code" (*qanun*).

9. However, the MOWA's offices in the provinces; the Department of Women's Affairs (DOWA) sometimes played a role in helping women who were in conflict with their families or had other problems. The effectiveness of DOWA in such situations was generally determined by personalities and the local security situation (see chapters 5 and 6).

10. Interview with an Afghan staff member at international women's rights organization, Kabul, August 2009.

11. According to the Afghan Constitution, only the government (including ministers) or the Parliament could submit laws to the *Taqnin*.

12. Interview with Qadria Yazanpardast, Kabul, October 2009.

13. Interview with a female MP, Kabul, March 2012.

14. Interviews with UNODC staff members, Kabul, September 2009.

15. Interview with Qazi Nazir Ahmed Hanafi, Kabul, January 2010.

16. Interviews with Western diplomats, Kabul, December 2009.

17. The name of the legislation commission in Parliament is *Taqnin*, but to distinguish it from the *Taqnin* in the Ministry of Justice, this book calls it the *legislation commission*.

18. Interview with an Afghan women's rights activist, Kabul, June 2015.

19. In a meeting at Kabul University arranged in April 2010 to disseminate the EVAW law, several students at the faculty of sharia reportedly expressed the opinion that rape *(tajavoz-e jinsi)*, unlike *zina,* was not known to Islamic societies. Instead, rape was "brought" to Afghanistan by "foreigners" and to accept the difference between rape and *zina* would be to open up for changing the basic provisions of Islam. Interview with an international staff member at IDLO, Kabul, May 2010.

20. Article 426 merely states that if *hadd* conditions are not fulfilled, perpetrators should be punished according to this chapter [of the Penal Code]. Article 427 (1) then states that "a person who commits adultery *(zina)* or pederasty [sodomy] *(lawat)* shall be sentenced to long-term imprisonment" (i.e., no less than five years and no more than fifteen).

21. Article 86 of the Civil Code reads, "Polygamy can take place after the following conditions are fulfilled: 1. When there is no fear of injustice between the wives. 2. When the person has financial sufficiency to sustain the wives. That is, when he can provide food, clothes, suitable house, and medical treatment. 3. When there is legal expediency, that is when the first wife is childless or when she suffers from diseases which are hard to be treated." Whereas conditions 1 and 2 are also standard conditions in Islamic *fiqh,* condition 3 is more restrictive than what is found in classic *fiqh.*

22. Despite my best efforts, I have not succeed in obtaining the first MOWA draft, which truncates the analysis in this section somewhat.

23. Draft of the Law on Prevention of Violence against Women. Drafted by the Afghan Women's Network, the Afghan Independent Human Rights Commission, Rights and Democracy, Humanitarian Assistance for the Women and Children of Afghanistan Ministry of Women's Affairs. On file with author (Dari).

24. The accusation that a woman had not been a virgin was a fairly common occurance in Afghanistan, often grounded in the mistaken belief that a virgin bride will always bleed on her wedding night. Such accusations could result in a new bride being sent home in shame to her parents and could expose her to serious sanctions by her kin or in-laws. The *hadd* punishment for slander *(qazf)* is lashing. See chapter 1 for an explanation.

25. Interview with the head of the legal department at MOWA, Kabul, March 2010.

26. Review of the EVAW law by UNODC et al., April 2009. On file with author.

27. One senior U.N. official later complained to me, "This language must have been put there by somebody who has never worked in a court. How do you prove 'forced' prostitution? Do pimps use guns? No. It should be facilitation (of prostitution). And how do you prove 'forced suicide'?" Interview with UNAMA official, Kabul, June 2015.

28. Explanatory Note on Proposed Amendments to Draft EVAW Law. UNODC and UNAMA, October 1, 2009. On file with author.

29. Review of EVAW law by UNODC et al., April 2009. On file with author.

30. Sayed Yusuf Halim, who was appointed the chief justice in Afghanistan in July 2015.

31. Interview with Sayed Yusuf Halim, Kabul, January 2010.

32. Interview with an Afghan staff member at international women's rights organization, Kabul, August 2009.

33. Technical Advisory Group meeting, September 29, 2009. Meeting notes on file with author.

34. I attended four of the seven sessions in the Joint Commission where the EVAW law was debated, whereas my research assistant also attended the last session. I also conducted interviews with the key participants in the debate as well as parliamentary staff. My analysis of the parliamentary process is based on the Dari transcripts of the proceedings by my assistant, the television footage of the plenary debate in 2013, as well as press reports, interviews, and the written amendments submitted by various commissions.

35. Interview with a female MP from Kabul, Kabul, October 2010.

36. At the center of this group were (apart from Qazi Nazir Ahmed Hanafi): Haji Niyaz Mohammad Amiry, Commission for Telecommunication; engineer Mohammad Asim, Commission for Martyrs and Disabled Persons; and Ataullah Ludin, Commission for Justice and Legal Affairs.

37. Amendments to Law on Elimination of Violence against Women. Legislation *(Taqnin)* Commission of Parliament. Undated document. On file with author.

38. Second Joint Commission meeting on the EVAW law, November 3, 2009.

39. Amendments to Law on Elimination of Violence against Women. Legislation *(Taqnin)* Commission of Parliament. Undated document, page 2. On file with author.

40. Second Joint Commission meeting on the EVAW law, November 3, 2009.

41. Amendments to Law on Elimination of Violence against Women. Legislation *(Taqnin)* Commission of Parliament.

42. Fifth Joint Commission meeting on the EVAW law, November 15, 2009.

43. Amendments to Law on Elimination of Violence against Women. Legislation *(Taqnin)* Commission of Parliament. Undated.

44. Joint Session's Amendment Concerning Law on Elimination of Violence against Women (undated). On file with author.

45. Seventh Joint Commission meeting on the EVAW law, November 19, 2009.

46. Seventh Joint Commission meeting on the EVAW law, November 19, 2009.

47. As one of the other conservatives MPs later stated, "MOWA was offending a fellow *mujahed,* and we are not going to the debate anymore." Interview with Qazi Hanafi, Kabul, January 2010.

48. Personal communication, Fawzia Koofi, November 2013. I was out of the country and did not attend these sessions. The Parliament does not produce transcripts of meetings in the joint mission.

49. *Mahram* originally means "unmarriagable kin," with whom intercourse would be considered incestuous. In current usage, it also refers to a male escort without whom a woman cannot travel or leave the house, such as her husband or a close relative. The Taliban government enforced this on a universal basis, meaning that no Afghan woman was permitted outside without a *mahram*. Many Afghan families still uphold the practice of *mahram* in this sense, especially when their female members travel some distance.

50. Amendments to Law on Elimination of Violence against Women. Legislation *(Taqnin)* Commission of Parliament. 05.06.1390 (August 27, 2011), page 5. On file with author.

51. Jafari *fiqh* is Shia; Hanafi *fiqh* is Sunni. Second Joint Commission meeting on the EVAW law, November 3, 2009.

52. This quote and the following were transcribed and translated by the author from a television broadcast of the plenary debate in Parliament on May 18, 2013.

53. Sixth Joint Commission meeting on the EVAW law, November 17, 2009.

54. Fifth Joint Commission meeting on the EVAW law, November 15, 2009.

55. Personal communication with an Afghan staff member at international NGO, November 2009.

56. Personal communication with a law student, Kabul, December 2009.

57. Sixth Joint Commission meeting on the EVAW law, November 17, 2009.

58. Interview with a shelter manager, Herat, January 2010.

59. Interview with an Afghan staff member at international NGO, November 2009. In chapters 4 and 5, I explore in greater detail how "leaving the house" constituted a testing ground for clashing gender orders.

60. Interview with Qadria Yazanpardast, Kabul, October 2009.

61. I was given a taste of the intensity of this competition when, in the middle of one of the meetings in the Joint Commission, I was asked to come outside by one of the female MPs, whom I had interviewed a few weeks earlier. She told me that she needed to inform me about the personal life of some of the other women in the room. It was their illicit affairs with married men, she said, that caused them to push for polygamy to be made more difficult by the EVAW law. This would lead their lovers to divorce their first wives instead of taking them as co-wives. The circulation of these kinds of rumors about the personal lives of female politicians was common.

62. Personal communication, former UNODC staff, March 2012.

63. See embassy cables: Embassy of the United States Kabul, 2009a; Embassy of the United States Kabul 2009b.

64. See chapter 1 for a description of the mujahedin and the rise of Islamism in Afghanistan.

65. Some years later, the public killing of a woman named Farkhunda, who had been accused of burning a copy of the Quran, was understood by many Afghans as a horrifying sign of the hostility against women who "went too far" and could be labeled immoral women, infidels, and Western agents. I write more about this case in the conclusion of this book.

66. Personal communication with a women's rights activist, September 2009.

67. Some civil society activists thought the speaker, who was not a particularly influential MP, had agreed to this because he wished to remain on good terms with Western embassies. Interview with a women's rights activist, Kabul, June 2015. See also Larson 2016.

68. Interviews with a senior U.N. official, June 2015, and an Afghan lawyer, Kabul, April 2015.

69. Interview with a senior U.N. official, Kabul, June 2015

70. Interview with a senior U.N. official, Kabul, June 2015.

71. The U.S. government alone allocated around US$700 million to women's rights activities in Afghanistan in the period 2001–2014 (SIGAR 2014).

72. Personal communication, IDLO staff member, February 2015.

73. Phone interviews with judges in the primary court of Kabul, March 2010.

74. Government of Afghanistan's Hard Deliverables no. 7 [out of 17 in total]: "MOWA, MOI [Ministry of Interior] and the AGO [attorney general's office] coordinate to produce

a detailed report on the application of the EVAW law in each province. The report should include: the number of VAW [violence against women] cases brought to the police, disposition of each case (whether prosecuted or not) and the outcome of the prosecuted cases. The data collected should be made public and serve as a baseline for future analyses of EVAW law implementation."

75. The Afghan year of 1391 (March 2012–March 2013).

76. A smaller number of cases were "solved" by the courts by granting a divorce or referring the victim to a shelter.

CHAPTER 3. BROKERS OF JUSTICE

1. In provinces that did not have a special unit, cases were processed by the normal prosecution.

2. There was, however, some methodological unclarity about the number of cases registered with the prosecution, meaning that the actual rate of prosecution and conviction could be lower. See Shahabi and Wimpelmann, 2015.

3. Badahkshan, Baghlan, Bamiyan, Herat, Kabul, Kandahar, Khost, and Nangarhar.

4. For details on the methodology and data collection for this chapter, see the section "Research Trajectories" in the introduction.

5. The Penal Code (1976) does not list the acts considered felonies, but article 24 states, "Felony is a crime whose doer is sentenced to death or continued imprisonment or long imprisonment." The EVAW law (2009) implies that rape, forced prostitution, recording and publishing the identity of the victim, burning or using chemical substances, forced self-immolation, and forced suicide are crimes that must be investigated independently of a petition.

6. Rural prosecutors were more likely to require physical marks as a minimum requirement for registering a complaint, although there were few signs of consistency on this question.

7. Both forced and consensual anal intercourse *(lawat)* are crimes under Afghan law, even when involving a man and woman married to each other.

8. According to Afghan family law (in the 1977 Civil Code), women can ask for divorce to be granted by the courts under certain conditions, such as harm inflicted by the husband, impotence, or long-term abandonment. A divorce granted by the court on these grounds is called *tafreeq*, and the woman retains the right to her *mahr* (dowry), which should have been paid upon marriage (though, in practice, it is often paid only in the case of divorce). She also keeps her *mahr* if her husband unilaterally divorces her (such a divorce is called *talaaq*). In both scenarios, she is also due alimony for a transition period of three months (this transition period is called *iddat*). However, if she does not have valid grounds for divorce, she can obtain it only if her husband consents, and in that case, he can then ask for financial compensation, such as requiring her to give up her *mahr* (either by returning it, if it had been paid upon marriage, or by forfeiting it, if the payment had been deferred). Such a "consensual" divorce is called *khula*.

9. The EVAW Law (article 23) provides for imprisonment for no more than three months for beating (not resulting in injury or disability), whereas the equivalent article in the Penal

Code (article 409) provides for imprisonment not exceeding six months, although article 409 is somewhat unclear about whether beating that doesn't result in long-term injury is punishable at all.

10. The prosecutors frequently used government-issued business licenses as a form of bail—either the license of the suspect/defendant or that of an acquaintance. If the conditions of bail or the conditions in the guarantee were breached, the prosecutors could see to it that the license was revoked.

11. Article 250 states that the court can extend this custody for up to two years, and article 251 states that the court can grant custody to another person (other than the custody holder) if it is to the benefit of the child.

12. See note 6 above.

13. The instruction about the misuse of a cell phone probably meant that the wife should refrain from conversations with men she was not related to over the phone.

14. In India, conviction rates under section 498 of the Penal Code, which deals with domestic violence, are reported to be 2 percent or less. It is thought that a main reason for this is that a woman effectively loses her access to her matrimonial home by filing a complaint (Basu 2006).

CHAPTER 4. WITH A LITTLE HELP FROM THE WAR ON TERROR

1. Huma Sultani, former staff at the Afghan Independent Human Rights Commission, Kankash, Tolo Television, February 19, 2011.

2. Qazi Ahmed Nazir Hanafi, MP, Kankash, Tolo Television, February 19, 2011.

3. Interview with head of juvenile detention center, Herat, January 2010.

4. The government would generally not release disaggregated data on women incarcerated for "running away" but, instead, lumped together female prisoners charged with or convicted for all "moral crimes": running away, *zina*, and "attempted *zina*." This number stayed fairly stable throughout the Karzai period (2001–2014) ranging from four hundred to seven hundred nationwide (HRW 2012).

5. Personal communication, U.N. official, Herat, January 2010.

6. Articles 426–29 of the 1976 Penal Code.

7. Personal communication with staff at UNAMA, IDLO, and Afghan legal aid organizations, 2010–11.

8. Approval 572, dated August 24, 2010, of High Council of Supreme Court. English translation by UNODC, Kabul. On file with author.

9. Qazi Ahmed Nazir Hanafi, MP, Kankash, Tolo Television, February 19, 2011.

10. Interview with Soraya Parlika, Kabul, March 2015.

11. Interview with Mary Akrami, Kabul, March 2015.

12. In Kabul, there were four shelters, run by Women for Afghan Women (WAW), Humanitarian Assistance for Women and Children (HAWCA), and Afghan Women's Skills Development Center (AWSDC). In addition, there was one shelter each in several other cities: Herat (run by Voice of Women), Mazar-e Sharif (Cooperation Center for Afghanistan [CCA]), Bamiyan (Shuhada organization), Jalalabad (UNIFEM), and Charikar (also UNIFEM). The number of shelters proliferated significantly between 2010 and 2015.

13. Interview with shelter manager, Jalalabad, February 2010.

14. Interview with MOWA staff, Jalalabad, February 2010.

15. Interview with shelter manager and NGO staff, Kabul, April 2010 and May 2011.

16. Personal communication with former shelter manager and staff at an international legal development organization, February 2011 and March 2015.

17. Aryn Baker, "Afghan Women and the Return of the Taliban," *Time*, August 9, 2010.

18. Personal communication with former shelter manager, February 2011.

19. Afghan Women, Security and United States Strategy, WAW press release, December 1, 2009.

20. Jamiat-e Islami (Society of Islam) was one of the mujahedin parties during the jihad years and was registered as a political party after 2001. It was led by Burhanuddin Rabbani until his assassination in September 2011.

21. Interview with Nasto Naderi, Kabul, May 2011.

22. Interview with Nasto Naderi.

23. Interview with women's right activist, Kabul, May 2011.

24. Interview with Nasto Naderi.

25. After the fall of the communist government in 1992, Afghanistan was for the first time declared an Islamic republic by the victorious mujahedin, although the new government soon collapsed into infighting. The 2004 Constitution also named Afghanistan an Islamic republic.

26. Interview with Nasto Naderi.

27. This group had also reviewed the EVAW law (see chapter 2).

28. Interviews with Afghan human rights official, Kabul, May 2011; Afghan human rights activist, Kabul, May 2011; Afghan staff member of Women for Afghan Women, Kabul, May 2011.

29. Draft Regulation on Women's Protection Centers. On file with author.

30. Interview with the head of the legal department, MOWA, Kabul, May 2010.

31. Interview with an Afghan human rights official, Kabul, May 2010.

32. "Afghan Government Seeking to Take Control of Women's Shelters" *Canadian Women for Women in Afghanistan,* February 1, 2011, www.cw4wafghan.ca/news/2011/02/01/afghan-government-seeking-take-control-womens-shelters.

33. A version of the regulations with all of the concerns of shelters incorporated was developed by the CLRWG, dated February 9, 2011. On file with author.

34. Entitled "Afghan Proposal Would Clamp Down on Women's Shelters," an article about the regulations appeared in the *New York Times* on February 10, 2011.

35. Interview with Western diplomat, Kabul, May 2011.

36. Interviews with Afghan human rights official Kabul, May 2011; Afghan human rights activist, Kabul, May 2011; and Afghan staff member of Women for Afghan Women, Kabul, May 2011.

37. Well-known women activists who had established shelters included Mary Akrami, director of the Afghan Women Skills Development Center (AWSDC); Orzala Ashraf Nemat, previous director of Humanitarian Assistance for Women and Children of Afghanistan (HAWCA); Suraya Pakzad, director of Voice of Women Organization; and Manizha Naderi, national director of Women for Afghan Women (WAW).

38. The letter of the Afghan Women's Network can be seen here: www.aiwr.org/files/The_Gatekeepers_of_Women.pdf. The letters of the U.S. senators and the statement of the assistant secretary of state are discussed here: U. Moore, "Afghan Shelter Crackdown Sparks International Advocacy," U.N. Dispatch, February 19, 2011, www.undispatch.com/afghan-shelter-crackdown-sparks-international-advocacy.

39. Interviews with Afghan human rights official, Kabul, May 2011; Afghan human rights activist, Kabul, May 2011; and Afghan staff member of Women for Afghan Women, Kabul, May 2011.

40. Interview with Afghan human rights official, Kabul, May 2011.

41. Interview with U.S. diplomat, Kabul, May 2011.

42. A version of the regulations with all of the concerns of shelters incorporated was developed by the CLRWG, dated February 9, 2011. But when the international press broke the story on February 10, they referred to the regulations in their original form, and fronts subsequently hardened, with MOWA also reverting to the original version in its press conference on February 15.

CHAPTER 5. RUNAWAY WOMEN

1. The material in this chapter is based on around one hundred interviews in Afghanistan with family members, government officials, religious and community leaders, shelter personnel, human rights workers, lawyers, and journalists, mostly in the period from 2010 to 2011. Some details have been changed or omitted for confidentiality purposes. I have referred to specific interviews in the notes only when I have directly cited someone.

2. *Jirga* is a Pashto word referring to a local gathering for the purpose of decision making or dispute settlement (Wardak 2004). In its ideal form, a *jirga* is conducted by a group of respected male elders who collectively reach decisions—and is an embodiment of the egalitarian and autonomous ideology of Pashtun tribal society (Wimpelmann 2013).

3. Interview with a judge, Central Afghanistan, April 2010.

4. It has become quite common for the *nikah* ceremony to take place at this point—at the time of the formal engagement—so that, from the perspective of Islamic law, the couple is already married. But until the wedding feast has taken place and the bride has moved to her husband's house, they are spoken of as only engaged, and they cannot socially be considered a married couple.

5. Interview with juvenile prosecutor, central Afghanistan, June 2010.

6. Interview with prison attorney, central Afghanistan, June 2010.

7. Article 17 of the EVAW law concerns rape: "If a person commits rape with an adult woman, the offender shall be sentenced to continued imprisonment in accordance with the provision of Article (426) of the Penal Code, and if it results in the death of victim, the perpetrator shall be sentenced to death penalty."

8. This was a rather complicated procedure, requiring the signature of the deputy minister of justice and the head of the National Prison Directorate. The process was made more complicated since I was not a journalist but a researcher, for which no category existed. Eventually the authorities issued me the permit without a press card.

9. A U.N. employee whom I spoke with said that the last time he had tried to get the lawyer to take a stronger interest in the case, the lawyer claimed to have lost the file (Kabul, June 2010). I was asked to mention this to the head of the Afghan bar association, which I did.

10. Interview with the head of the provincial council, central Afghanistan, June 2010.

11. Interview with Nafisa's fiancé's brother, central Afghanistan, June 2010.

12. Interview with local *jirga* expert 1, central Afghanistan, June 2010.

13. Interview with local *jirga* expert 2, central Afghanistan, June 2010.

14. Interview with female member of the provincial council, central Afghanistan, June 2010.

15. Interview with former head of DOWA, central Afghanistan, June 2010.

16. Interview with staff at AIHRC, Kabul, June 2010.

17. Due to staff shortage, the primary and appeal courts were presided over by the same judge.

18. Interview with Fereshta's mother, Radio Azadi March 19, 2010.

19. As I started to piece together the event a few weeks later, I was offered a chance to buy the video, filmed by someone in the crowd, for a few hundred dollars. I declined. Some months later, the video appeared in the media and was posted on YouTube.

20. Edwards (2002) recounts a story from the 1980s of a young woman who denounces her husband as he goes to complete his military services with the communist government, in an area where all other young men are supporting the jihad against the Soviet-backed regime. She convinces her male cousin to escape with her, but they are caught by *Hizb-e Islami,* one of the mujahedin parties, and she is sentenced to death by stoning by a religious judge, recently returned from Saudi Arabia, even though the local community widely endorsed her elopement. To the narrator in Edwards' book, this imposition symbolized the rising power of mullahs in Afghan society. Previously dependent on tribal leaders, they were now asserting their power more independently.

21. Siddiqa, like Fereshta, had been engaged to her cousin, so (unlike in Nafisa's case) there was no question of answering to an external family. It was Siddiqa's family, not her fiancé, who played the leading act in the aftermath of her escape.

22. Interview with relative of Qayam, Kunduz, August 2010.

23. Personal communication with researcher based in Kunduz, May 2011.

24. As work on a new, comprehensive penal code began in 2012, the then minister of justice Habibullah Ghalib took the initiative to codify *hadd* punishments for *zina,* theft, alcohol consumption, and so on, and the task of codification was given to the Afghan Bar Association. Information about the existence of this draft was leaked to the press two years later and caused strong international reactions. At the time of writing (2015), it was not clear whether a codification of *hadd* punishments would be included in the full draft of the penal code. Some Afghans argued for it on the basis that such a codification would actually spell out that the conditions for imposing such physical punishments could never be fulfilled in practice. Others argued that the Afghan Constitution of 2004 deemed such punishments illegal.

25. Radio Azadi, March 19, 2010.

26. Mohammad Omar Omarzada, legal scholar, speaking on Radio Azadi, March 19, 2010.

27. Interview with head of AIHRC, Herat, January 2010.

28. According to mostly anecdotal reports, large networks for trafficking and selling of women and children for prostitution exist in Afghanistan, both for domestic markets and abroad.

29. Decree Number 104, dated May 17, 1419 H.Q. [Islamic lunar year] of the Islamic Emirate of Afghanistan regarding women's rights in society.

30. Medica Mondiale, in a review of the cases that their lawyers have worked on, found a similar pattern. Judges and prosecutors would convict women of premarital or extramarital intercourse regardless of the abusive circumstances that women had found themselves in (Boggio-Cosadia 2014).

31. Interview with AIHRC official, Kunduz, August 2010.

32. Interview with juvenile attorney, central Afghanistan, June 2010.

33. In 2012 three single women who had rented a room with a family in a relatively liberal part of Kabul (Kart-e Se) were attacked by a mob when attempting to move to another location. One of the women was killed, and the others went into hiding. Police and others accused them of being prostitutes, since they could not see how else they could make a living on their own (Graham-Harrison 2012).

CHAPTER 6. UPHOLDING CITIZEN HONOR?

1. In the Afghan year of 1391 (March 2012–March 2013), statistics compiled by the Ministry of Women's Affairs in twenty-five of Afghanistan's thirty-four provinces found 188 cases of reported rape or sexual violence (against women). This would suggest around 0.5 rapes reported per 100,000 population (MOWA 2014).

2. Although he was, in fact, the girl's uncle, he often referred to himself as her father, since Bashira's actual father was ill and could not represent her.

3. In an unrelated event, President Karzai had dismissed the attorney general, Abdul Jabar Sabet, on July 17, 2008.

4. Tolo Television, July 19, 2008.

5. Sighbatullah Mujadiddi was a former mujahedin fighter and a personal friend of President Karzai. He held a number of high-level official positions during the post-2001 period.

6. Interview with Sayed Noorullah, Sarepul, March 2010.

7. This face-to-face denunciation of the president as basically a man without morality, a purveyor of honor, must have taken him back, but to the relief of Bashira's uncle, the president reacted calmly and expressed his sympathy for his plight.

8. Author's personal communication in Kabul, September 2014.

9. Author's interview with U.N. legal official, June 2015.

10. Noorullah lightheartedly recalled how Sima Samar, the head of the AIHRC, had declared that she would never talk to him again should she come to hear that the uncle would pursue a *baad*.

11. Interview with Afghan human rights official, Mazar-e Sharif, April 2010.

12. Interview with Afghan human rights official, Mazar-e Sharif, April 2010.

13. Kogacioglu (2004) makes a similar argument for Turkey, where she points out that the legal and institutional accommodation of "honor killings" makes questionable these same institutions' presentation of them as acts of tradition.

CONCLUSIONS

1. Interview with a male women's rights activist, Kabul, March 2012.

REFERENCES

Abi-Habib, M. 2010. "TV Host Targets Afghan Women's Shelters." *Wall Street Journal,* August 3.

Abu-Lughod, L. 1998. *Remaking Women: Feminism and Modernity in the Middle East.* Princeton, NJ: Princeton University Press.

———. 2002. "Do Muslim Women Really Need Saving? Anthropological Reflections on Cultural Relativism and Its Others." *American Anthropologist* 104: 783–90.

———. 2010. "The Active Social Life of 'Muslim Women's Rights': A Plea for Ethnography, Not Polemic, with Cases from Egypt and Palestine." *Journal of Middle East Women's Studies* 6: 1–45.

Agnes, F., and S. V. Ghosh, eds. 2012. *Negotiating Spaces. Legal Domains, Gender Concerns, and Community Constructs,* New Delhi: Oxford University Press.

Ahmadi, S. 2016. "2015 Performance of the Wolesi Jirga: Low Attendance, Nominal Oversight." *Afghanistan Analysts.* www.afghanistan-analysts.org/2015-performance-of-the-wolesi-jirga-low-attendance-nominal-oversight.

Ahmed, F. 2015. "Istanbul and Kabul in Courtly Contact: The Question of Exchange between the Ottoman Empire and Afghanistan in the Late Nineteenth Century." *Journal of Ottoman Studies* 45: 265–96.

Ahmed-Ghosh, H. 2003. "A History of Women in Afghanistan: Lessons Learnt for the Future or Yesterdays and Tomorrow: Women in Afghanistan." *Journal of International Women's Studies* 4 (3): 1–4.

Arbabzadah, N. 2011. "In Search of a Real but Invisible Afghan Feminist Icon: CSW Research Scholar Returns to Kabul to Explore the Legacy of Queen Soraya Tarzi." *CSW Update Newsletter.* UCLA Center for the Study of Women.

Arghandiwal, M., and I. Aziz. 2013. "Afghan Parliament Fails to Pass Divisive Women's Law." *Reuters,* May 18.

Ayotte, K. J., and M. E. Husain. 2005. "Securing Afghan Women: Neocolonialism, Epistemic Violence, and the Rhetoric of the Veil." *NWSA Journal* 17: 112–33.

Azarbaijani-Moghaddam, S. 2006. "Gender in Afghanistan." *Publication Series on Promoting Democracy under Conditions of State Fragility. Issue 1: Afghanistan.* Berlin: Heinrich Böll Foundation.

Barfield, T. 2010. *Afghanistan: A Cultural and Political History.* Princeton, NJ: Princeton University Press.

Baron, B. 2006. "Women, Honour, and the State: Evidence from Egypt." *Middle Eastern Studies* 42: 1–20.

Barr, H. 2016. "Dispatches: A Law Ignored and Another Horror in Afghanistan." *Human Rights Watch,* January 20. www.hrw.org/news/2016/01/20/dispatches-law-ignored-and-another-horror-afghanistan.

Basu, S. 2006. "Playing Off Courts: The Negotiation of Divorce and Violence in Plural Legal Settings in Kolkata." *The Journal of Legal Pluralism and Unofficial Law* 38: 41–75.

———. 2011. "Judges of Normality: Mediating Marriage in the Family Courts of Kolkata." *Signs* 37: 469–92.

———. 2015. *The Trouble with Marriage. Feminists Confront Law and Violence in India.* Oakland: University of California Press.

BBC. 2007. "Afghan Warlords in Amnesty Rally." *BBC,* February 23.

Bertelsen, B. E. 2009. "Multiple Sovereignties and Summary Justice in Mozambique: A Critique of Some Legal Anthropological Terms." *Social Analysis* 53: 123–47.

Billaud, J. 2015. *Kabul Carnival. Gender Politics in Postwar Afghanistan,* Philadelphia: University of Pennsylvania Press.

Boggio-Cosadia, F. 2014. "Elimination of Violence against Women in Medica Legal Aid Practice Second Report." Kabul: Medica Afghanistan.

Boone, J. 2009. "'Worse Than the Taliban': New Law Rolls Back Rights for Afghan Women." *Guardian,* March 31.

Bumiller, K. 2008. *In an Abusive State. How Neoliberalism Appropriated Feminist Movements against Sexual Violence.* Durham, NC: Duke University Press.

Burawoy, M. 2000. *Global Ethnography: Forces, Connections, and Imaginations in a Postmodern World.* Berkeley: University of California Press.

Butler, M. 2009. "Canadian Women and the (Re)production of Women in Afghanistan." *Cambridge Review of International Affairs* 22: 217–34.

Charrad, M. M. 2001. *States and Women's Rights: The Making of Postcolonial Tunisia, Algeria and Morocco,* Berkeley: University of California Press.

Chatterjee, P. 1993. *The Nation and Its Fragments,* Princeton, NJ: Princeton University Press.

Chaudhary, T. W., O. A. Nemat, and A. Suhrke. 2011. "Promoting Women's Rights in Afghanistan: The Ambiguous Footprint of the West." In *A Liberal Peace? The Problems and Practices of Peacebuilding,* edited by S. Campbell, D. Chandler, and M. Sabaratnam, 106–20. London: Zed Books.

Chesterman, S. 2004. "Bush, the United Nations and Nation-Building." *Survival* 46: 101–16.

Coburn, N. 2011. *Bazaar Politics. Power and Pottery in an Afghan Market Town.* Stanford, CA: Stanford University Press.

Cole, J. R. I. 2008. "The Taliban, Women and the Hegelian Private Sphere." In *The Taliban and the Crisis of Afghanistan,* edited by R. D. Crews and A. Tarzi, 118–54. Cambridge, MA: Harvard University Press.

Comaroff, J., and J. L. Comaroff. 2006. "Law and Disorder in the Postcolony: An Introduction." In *Law and Disorder in the Postcolony,* edited by J. Comaroff and J. L. Comaroff, 1–56. Chicago: University of Chicago Press.

Comaroff, J. L., and J. Comaroff. 2009. "Reflections on the Anthropology of Law, Governance and Sovereignty." In *Rules of Law and Laws of Ruling,* edited by F. Von Benda-Beckmann, K. Von Benda-Beckmann, and J. Eckert, 31–60. Abingdon, England: Ashgate.

Coomaraswamy, R. 2000. "Report of the Special Rapporteur on Violence against Women, Its Causes and Consequences. Mission to Pakistan and Afghanistan, (1–13 September 1999)." United Nations.

Cuno, K. M. 2009. "Disobedient Wives and Neglectful Husbands: Marital Relations and the First Phase of Family Law Reform in Egypt." In *Family, Gender and Law in a Globalizing Middle East and South Asia,* edited by K. M. Cuno and M. Desai, 3–18. Syracuse, NY: Syracuse University Press.

De Lauri, A. 2015. "Between Law and Customs: Normative Interconnections in Kabul's Tribunals." *Diogenes* 60: 45–57.

Dorronsoro, G. 2005. *Revolution Unending. Afghanistan: 1979 to the Present.* London: Hurst.

———. 2012. "The Transformation of the Afghanistan-Pakistan Border." In *Under the Drones: Modern Lives in the Afghanistan-Pakistan Borderlands,* edited by S. Bashir and R. D. Crews, 30–44. Cambridge, MA: Harvard University Press.

Dupree, N. H. 1984. "Revolutionary Rhetoric and Afghan Women." In *Revolutions and Rebellions in Afghanistan: Anthropological Perspectives,* edited by N. M. Shahrani and R. L. Canfield, 306–40. Berkeley: University of California, Institute of International Studies.

———. 1998. "Afghan Women under the Taliban." In *Fundamentalism Reborn? Afghanistan and the Taliban,* edited by W. Maley, 145–66. New York: New York University Press.

Edwards, D. B. 1996. *Heroes of the Age: Moral Fault Lines on the Afghan Frontier.* Berkeley: University of California Press.

———. 2002. *Before Taliban: Genealogies of the Afghan Jihad.* Berkeley: University of California Press.

Emadi, H. 2002. *Repression, Resistance and Women in Afghanistan.* Westport, CT: Praeger.

Embassy of the United States Kabul. 2009a. "Elimination of Violence Against Women Law: MOJ Draft Complete; Cable." May 6.

———. 2009b. "Justice Minister Danesh, Slow Movement on Shia Law Amendments, Faster on Eliminating Violence against Women Draft Bill." May 27.

———. 2009c. "With Deep Pockets, Governor Atta Leads Charge For Abdullah. Cable 09KABUL1838."

Etling, B. 2004. "Legal Authorities in the Afghan Legal System (1964–1979)." Cambridge, MA: Harvard Law School, Islamic Legal Studies Program.

Farmer, B. 2011. "Reforms of Afghan Women's Shelters Criticised." *Irish Times,* February 9.

Forsberg, C. 2010. *Politics and Power in Kandahar.* Washington DC: Institute for the Study of War.

Gall, C., and S. Rahimi. 2009. "Karzai Vows to Review Family Law." *New York Times,* April 4.

Ghani, A. 1983. "Disputes in a Court of Sharia, Kunar Valley, Afghanistan 1885–1890." *International Journal of Middle East Studies* 15: 353–67.

Giustozzi, A. 2008. *Koran, Kalashnikov and Laptop: The Neo-Taliban Insurgency in Afghanistan.* London: Columbia University Press.

———. 2009. *Empires of Mud. Wars and Warlords in Afghanistan.* London: Hurst and Company.

Gluckman, M. 1965. *Politics, Law and Ritual in Tribal Society.* Oxford: Blackwell.

Graham-Harrison, E. 2012. "Kabul Attack on Female Actors Leaves Survivors Facing More 'Punishment.'" *Guardian,* September 6.

Green, N. 2008. "Tribe, Diaspora, and Sainthood in Afghan History." *Journal of Asian Studies* 67: 171–211.

Gregorian, V. 1969. *The Emergence of Modern Afghanistan: Politics of Reform and Modernization, 1880–1946.* Stanford, CA: Stanford University Press.

Hagmann, T., and D. Péclard. 2010. "Negotiating Statehood: Dynamics of Power and Domination in Africa." *Development and Change* 41: 539–62.

Hajjar, L. 2004. "Religion, State Power and Domestic Violence in Muslim Societies: A Framework for Comparative Analysis." *Law and Social Inquiry* 29: 1–38.

Halley, J., P. Kotiswaran, H. Shamir, and C. Thomas. 2006. "From the International to the Local in Feminist Legal Responses to Rape, Prostitution/Sex Work, and Sex Trafficking: Four Studies in Contemporary Governance Feminism." *Harvard Journal of Law and Gender* 29: 335–424.

Handelman, D. 2005. "The Extended Case: Interactional Foundations and Prospective Dimensions." In *The Manchester School: Practice and Ethnographic Praxis in Anthropology,* edited by T. M. S. Evens and D. Handelman, 94–117. New York: Berghahn Books.

Hansen, T. B., and F. Stepputat. 2006. "Sovereignty Revisited." *Annual Review of Anthropology* 35 (1): 295–315.

Hartmann, M. E. 2011. "Casualties of Myopia." In Mason 2011a, 172–204.

Hartmann, M. E., and A. Klonowiecka-Milart. 2011. "Lost in Translation: Legal Transplants without Consensus-Based Adaption." In Mason 2011a, 266–98.

Heathershaw, J. 2011. "Tajikistan amidst Globalization: State Failure or State Transformation?" *Central Asian Survey* 30: 147–68.

Heathershaw, J., and J. Lambach. 2008. "Introduction: Post-Conflict Spaces and Approaches to Statebuilding." *Journal of Intervention and Statebuilding* 2: 269–89.

HRW. 2001. "Afghanistan: Crisis of Impunity: The Role of Pakistan, Russia, and Iran in Fueling the Civil War in Afghanistan." Human Rights Watch, July.

———. 2012. "'I Had to Run Away': The Imprisonment of Women and Girls for 'Moral Crimes' in Afghanistan." Human Rights Watch, 4 March.

———. 2014. "Afghanistan: Gang Rape Trial Badly Flawed: Due Process Violations, Political Interference Undermine Justice." Human Rights Watch, September 8.

Humayoon, H. 2010. "The Re-Election of Hamid Karzai." *Afghanistan Report 4.* Washington DC: Institute for the Study of War.

Humphrey, C. 2004. "Sovereignty." In *A Companion to the Anthropology of Politics,* edited by D. Nugent and J. Vincent, 418–36. Oxford: Blackwell.

Ibrahami, N. 2009. "Divide and Rule: State Penetration in Hazarajat (Afghanistan) from the Monarchy to the Taliban." Crisis States Working Papers Series No. 2. Crisis States Research Centre.

IDLO. 2014. "Women's Professional Participation in Afghanistan's Justice Sector: Challenges and Opportunities." Rome: International Law Development Organization.

Jad, I. 2004. "The NGO-isation of Arab Women's Movements." *IDS Bulletin* 35: 34–42.

———. 2007. "NGOs: Between Buzzwords and Social Movements." *Development in Practice* 17: 622–29.

Joseph, S., ed. 2000. *Gender and Citizenship in the Middle East.* Syracuse, NY: Syracuse University Press.

Kamali, M. H. 1985. *Law in Afghanistan: A Study of the Constitutions, Matrimonial Law and the Judiciary.* Leiden: Brill.

Kandiyoti, D. 1988. "Bargaining with Patriarchy." *Gender and Society* 2: 274–90.

———, ed. 1991. *Women, Islam and the State.* Basingstoke, England: Macmillan.

———. 1996. *Gendering the Middle East: Emerging Perspectives.* London: I. B. Tauris.

———. 2007. "Old Dilemmas or New Challenges? The Politics of Gender and Reconstruction in Afghanistan." *Development and Change* 38: 169–99.

———. 2009. "The Lures and Perils of Gender Activism in Afghanistan." The Anthony Hyman Memorial Lecture, School of Oriental and African Studies, University of London.

Kapur, R. 2002. "The Tragedy of Victimization Rhetoric: Resurrecting the Native Subject in International/Postcolonial Feminist Legal Politics." *Harvard Human Rights Law Journal* 15: 1–38.

———. 2012. "Hecklers to Power? The Waning of Liberal Rights and Challenges to Feminism in India." In *South Asian Feminisms,* edited by A. Loomba and R. A. Lukose, 333–56. Durham, NC: Duke University Press.

———. 2014. "Gender, Sovereignty and the Rise of a Sexual Security Regime in International Law and Postcolonial India." *Melbourne Journal of International Law* 14: 1–29.

Kargar, Z. 2008. "Facing Up to Rape in Afghanistan." *Washington Post,* September 11.

Kātib, F. M. A. I. S. D. M. A. M. 2013. *The History of Afghanistan: Fayz Muhammad Katib Hazarah's Siraj al-Tawarikh.* Translated by R. D. McChesney and M. M. Khorrami. Boston: Brill.

Keddie, N. R., and B. Baron, eds. 1991. *Women in Middle Eastern History. Shifting Boundaries in Sex and Gender.* New Haven, CT: Yale University Press.

Khan, M. M. S. M., ed. 1980. *The Life of Abdur Rahman, Amir of Afghanistan.* Vol. 2. Karachi: Oxford University Press.

Khan, S. 2003. "'Zina' and the Moral Regulation of Pakistani Women." *Feminist Review* 75: 75–100.

———. 2006. *Zina, Transnational Feminism, and the Moral Regulation of Pakistani Women.* Vancouver: University of British Columbia Press.

Kim-Puri, H. J. 2005. "Conceptualizing Gender-Sexuality-State-Nation: An Introduction." *Gender and Society* 19: 137–59.

Kogacioglu, D. 2004. "The Tradition Effect: Framing Honor Crimes in Turkey." *Differences* 15: 118–51.

Kozma, L. 2004. "Negotiating Virginity: Narratives of Defloration from Late Nineteenth-Century Egypt." *Comparative Studies of South Asia, Africa and the Middle East* 24: 57–69.

Kuovo, S. 2011. "Taking Women Seriously? Conflict, State-Building and Gender in Afghanistan." In *Feminist Perspectives in Contemporary International Law: Between Resistance and Compliance?* edited by S. Kuovo and Z. Pearson, 159–76. Oñati International Series in Law and Society 41. Oxford: Hart.

Larson, A. 2009. "Afghanistan's New Democratic Parties: A Means to Organise Democratisation?" *Briefing Paper Series*. Kabul: Afghanistan Research and Evaluation Unit.

———. 2016. "Women and Power: Mobilising around Afghanistan's Elimination of Violence Against Women Law." London: Overseas Development Institute.

Lau, M. 2003. "Islamic Law and the Afghan Legal System." In *Yearbook of Islamic and Middle Eastern Law 2001–2002*, edited by E. Cotran, 27–44. The Hague: Kluwer International.

———. 2007. "Twenty-Five Years of Hudood Ordinances: A Review." *Washington and Lee Law Review* 64: 1292–314.

Lund, C. 2006. "Twilight Institutions: Public Authority and Local Politics in Africa." *Development and Change* 37: 685–705.

Majrooh, P. A. 1989. "Afghan Women between Marxism and Islamic Fundamentalism." *Society for Central Asian Studies* 8: 87–98.

Malikyar, H. 1997. "Development of Family Law in Afghanistan: The Roles of the Hanafi Madhab, Customary Practices, and Power Politics." *Central Asian Survey* 16: 389–99.

Marcus, G. 1995. "Ethnography in/of the World System: The Emergence of Multi-Sited Ethnography." *Annual Review of Anthropology* 24: 95–117.

Mason, W., ed. 2011a. *The Rule of Law in Afghanistan: Missing in Inaction*. Cambridge: Cambridge University Press.

———. 2011b. Introduction to Mason 2011a, 1–12.

Meriwether, M. C., and J. E. Tucker, eds. 1999. *Social History of Gender in the Modern Muslim Middle East*. Boulder, CO: Westview Press.

Merry, S. E. 2006. *Human Rights and Gender Violence: Translating International Law into Local Justice*. Chicago: University of Chicago Press.

———. 2009. *Gender Violence: A Cultural Perspective*. Malden, MA: Wiley-Blackwell.

Miller, A. M. 2004. "Sexuality, Violence against Women, and Human Rights: Women Make Demands and Ladies Get Protection." *Health and Human Rights* 7: 16–47.

Mir-Hosseini, Z. 2010. "Criminalizing Sexuality: Zina Laws as Violence against Women in Muslim Contexts. *Violence Is Not Our Culture: The Global Campaign to Stop Killing and Stoning Women in the Name of Culture*. www.violenceisnotourculture.org/content/criminalizing-sexuality-zina-laws-violence-against-women-muslim-contexts.

Mir-Hosseini, Z., and V. Hamzić. 2010. *Control and Sexuality: The Revival of Zina Laws in Muslim Contexts*. London: Women Living under Muslim Law.

Mitchell, J. C. 1956. *The Kalela Dance*. Manchester, England: Manchester University Press.

Mitchell, T. 1999. "Society, Economy, and the State Effect." In *State/Culture: State-Formation after the Cultural Turn*, edited by G. Steinmetz, 76–97. Ithaca, NY: Cornell University Press.

Molyneux, M. 1995. "Women's Rights and Political Contingency: The Case of Yemen, 1990–1994." *Middle East Journal* 49: 418–31.

Moschtaghi, R. 2006. "Organisation and Jurisdiction of the Newly Established Afghan Courts- The Compliance of the Formal System of Justice with the Bonn Agreement." In *Max Planck Yearbook of United Nations Law,* edited by R. Wolfrum, A. Von Bogdandy, and C. E. Philipp, vol. 10, 531–90. Leiden: Brill.

MOWA. 2014. "First Report on the Implementation of the Elimination of Violence against Women (EVAW) Law in Afghanistan." Kabul: Islamic Republic of Afghanistan, Ministry of Women's Affairs.

Nawid, S. K. 1999. *Religious Response to Social Change in Afghanistan, 1919–29: King Aman-Allah and the Afghan Ulama.* Costa Mesa, CA: Mazda.

———. 2007. "Afghan Women under Marxism." In *From Patriarchy to Empowerment: Women's Participation, Movements, and Rights in the Middle East, North Africa, and South Asia,* edited by V. M. Moghadam, 58–72. Syracuse, NY: Syracuse University Press.

Noelle-Karimi, C. 2002. "History Lessons." *Women's Review of Books* 19: 1–3.

Nordland, R. 2010. "Portrait of Pain Ignites Debate over Afghan War." *New York Times,* August 4.

Oates, L. 2009. "A Closer Look. The Policy and Law-Making Process behind the Shiite Personal Status Law." Kabul: Afghan Research and Evaluation Unit.

O'Hanlon, M. E., and H. Sherjan. 2010. *Toughing It Out in Afghanistan.* Washington DC: Brookings Institution Press.

Olesen, A. 1995. *Islam and Politics in Afghanistan.* Richmond, Surrey, England: Curzon Press.

Olivier de Sardan, J.-P. 2005. *Anthropology and Development: Understanding Contemporary Social Change.* Translated by Antoinette Tidjani Alou. London: Zed Books.

Parker, A., M. Russo, D. Sommer, and P. Yaeger, eds. 1992. *Nationalisms and Sexualities.* New York: Routledge.

Peters, R. 2003. "From Jurists' Law to Statue Law or What Happens When the Shari'a is Codified." In *Shaping the Current Islamic Reformation,* edited by B. A. Roberson, 81–94. London: Frank Cass.

———. 2005. *Crime and Punishment in Islamic Law: Theory and Practice from the Sixteenth to the Twenty-First Century.* Cambridge: Cambridge University Press.

Pohly, M. 2002. "Perceptions of State and Organization of the Northern Alliance." In *Afghanistan: A Country without a State?* edited by C. Noelle-Karimi, C. Schetter, and R. Schlagintweit, 179–89. Frankfurt am Main: IKO, Verlag Interkulturelle Kommunikation.

Polluda, L. B. 1973. *Reform and Rebellion in Afghanistan, 1919–29: King Amanullah's Failure to Modernize a Tribal Society.* Ithaca, NY: Cornell University Press.

Quraishi, A. 2000. "Her Honour: An Islamic Critique of the Rape Laws of Pakistan from a Woman-Sensitive Perspective." In *Windows of Faith: Muslim Women Scholar-Activists in North America,* edited by G. Webb, 102–35. Syracuse, NY: Syracuse University Press.

Reynolds, A. 2006. "The Curious Case of Afghanistan." *Journal of Democracy* 17:104–17.

Roy, S. 2011. "Politics, Passion and Professionalization in Contemporary Indian Feminism." *Sociology* 45: 587–602.

Roychowdhury, P. 2015. "Victims to Saviors: Governmentality and the Regendering of Citizenship in India." *Gender and Society* 29: 792–816.

———. 2016. "Rape and the Seduction of Popular Politics." *Gender and Society* 30: 80–94.

Rubin, A. J. 2011. "Afghan Proposal Would Clamp Down on Women's Shelters." *New York Times,* February 10.

———. 2012. "Afghan Rape Case Turns Focus on Local Police." *New York Times,* June 27.

———. 2015. "A Thin Line of Defense against 'Honor Killings.'" *New York Times,* March 2.

Rubin, B. R. 2004. "Crafting a Constitution for Afghanistan." *Journal of Democracy* 15: 5–19.

Ruttig, T. 2006. "Islamists, Leftists—and a Void in the Center. Afghanistan's Political Parties and Where They Come From (1902–2006)." *Konrad Adenauer Stiftung,* November 27.

———. 2012. "Protests and Factional Conflict in Sarepul." *Afghanistan Analysts Network.* www.afghanistan-analysts.org/protests-and-factional-conflict-in-sarepul.

Saghal, G. 2006. "Legislating Utopia? Violence against Women: Identities and Interventions." In *The Situated Politics of Belonging,* edited by N. Yuval-Davis, K. Kannabiran, and U. Vieten, 205–24. London: Sage.

Saikal, A. 2004. *Modern Afghanistan: A History of Struggle and Survival.* London: I. B. Tauris.

Samandary, W. 2014. "Shame and Impunity: Is Violence against Women Becoming More Brutal? *Afghanistan Analysts Network.* www.afghanistan-analysts.org/shame-and-impunity-is-domestic-violence-becoming-more-brutal.

Sassen, S. 2008. "Neither Global Nor National: Novel Assemblages of Territory, Authority and Rights." *Ethics and Global Politics* 1:61–79.

———. 2011. "Much of the Global Is Still Dressed in the Clothes of the National—Saskia Sassen." Interview by Luis Martín. *Truman,* April 26. http://trumanfactor.com/2011/saskia-sassen-interview-2225.html.

Schneider, E. 1991. "The Violence of Privacy." *Connecticut Law Review* 23:973–99.

Schueller, M. J. 2011. "Cross-Cultural Identification, Neoliberal Feminism, and Afghan Women." *Genders* 53.

Sethna, R. 2013. "Afghan Women's Rights under Threat." *Guardian,* June 20.

Shahabi, M. J., and T. Wimpelmann. 2015. "Prosecuting of Acts of Violence against Women in Afghanistan: A Closer Look at the Data." Kabul: Research Institute for Women, Peace and Security / Chr. Michelsen Institute.

Shahabi, M. J., T. Wimpelmann, and F. Elyassi. 2016. "The Specialized Units for Prosecution of Violence Against Women in Afghanistan: Shortcuts or Detours to Empowerment?" Kabul: Research Institute for Women, Peace and Security / Chr. Michelsen Institute.

Sharan, T., and J. Heathershaw. 2011. "Identity Politics and Statebuilding in Post-Bonn Afghanistan: The 2009 Presidential Election." *Ethnopolitics* 10: 297–319.

Shahrani, M. N. 1986. "State Building and Social Fragmentation in Afghanistan: A Historical Perspective." In *The State, Religion, and Ethnic Politics. Afghanistan, Iran and Pakistan,* edited by A. Banuazizi and M. Weiner, 23–74. Syracuse, NY: Syracuse University Press.

Shehada, N. 2009. "House of Obedience: Social Norms, Individual Agency, and Historical Contingency." *Journal of Middle East Women's Studies* 5: 24–49.

Siddiqi, D. M. 2011. "Transnational Feminism and Local Realities: The Imperiled Muslim Woman and the Production of (In)Justice." *Journal of Women of the Middle East and the Islamic World* 9: 76–96.

SIGAR. 2014. "Afghan Women: Comprehensive Assessments Needed to Determine and Measure DOD, State, and USAID Progress." SIGAR 15–24 Audit Report, December 2014. Special Inspector General for Afghanistan Reconstruction (SIGAR).

Sonbol, A. 1997. "Rape and Law in Ottoman and Modern Egypt." In *Women in the Ottoman Empire*, edited by M. C. Zilfi, 214–32. Leiden: Brill.

———. 1998. "Ta'a and Modern Legal Reform: A Rereading." *Islam and Christian–Muslim Relations* 9: 285–94.

———. 2003. "Women in Shari'ah Courts: A Historical and Methodological Discussion." *Fordham International Law Journal* 27.

Stabile, C. A. A. D. K. 2005. "Unveiling Imperialism: Media, Gender, and the War on Afghanistan." *Media, Culture and Society* 27: 765–82.

Strick, A. 2015. "Taliban Public Punishments, 1996–2001." *Alex Strick* (blog). www.alexstrick.com/blog/2015/9/taliban-public-punishments-19962001.

Suhrke, A. 2011. *When More Is Less: The International Project in Afghanistan*. London: Hurst; New York: Columbia.

Sukhanyar, J., and A. J. Rubin. 2012. "Four Members of Afghan Police Are Found Guilty in Rape." *New York Times*, November 7.

Tapper, N. 1991. *Bartered Brides: Politics, Gender, and Marriage in an Afghan Tribal Society*. Cambridge: Cambridge University Press.

Tarzi, A. 2003. *The Judicial State: Evolution and Centralization of the Courts in Afghanistan*. PhD diss., New York University.

Tondini, M. 2009. *State Building and Justice Reform Post-Conflict Reconstruction in Afghanistan*. London: Routledge.

Tucker, J. E. 2008. *Women, Family, and Gender in Islamic Law*. Cambridge: Cambridge University Press.

UN Commission on Human Rights. 1998. "Situation of Human Rights in Afghanistan," March 12, E/CN.4/1998/71.

UNAMA. 2012. "Still a Long Way to Go: Implementation of the Elimination of Violence against Women Law in Afghanistan." Kabul, Afghanistan: United Nations Assistance Mission to Afghanistan, December.

UNAMA/OHCHR. 2015. "Justice through the Eyes of Afghan Women: Cases of Violence against Women Addressed through Mediation and Court Adjudication." Kabul: United Nations Assistance Mission to Afghanistan / United Nations Office of the High Commissioner for Human Rights.

UNDP. 2013. "A Promise Is a Promise—Time to Take Action on Ending Violence against Women and Girls."

USIP. 2010. "Informal Dispute Resolution in Afghanistan." *USIP Special report*. United States Institute of Peace.

Vatuk, S. 2013. "The 'Women's Courts' in India: An Alternative Dispute Resolution Body for Women in Distress." *The Journal of Legal Pluralism and Unofficial Law* 45: 76–103.

Velsen, J. V. 1964. *The Politics of Kinship: A Study in Social Manipulation among the Lakeside Tonga of Nyasaland*. Manchester, England: Manchester University Press, for Rhodes-Livingston Institute.

Wardak, A. 2004. "Building a Post-War Justice System in Afghanistan." *Crime Law and Social Change* 41: 319–41.

Weinbaum, M. G. 1980. "Legal Elites in Afghan Society." *International Journal of Middle East Studies* 12: 39–57.

Wimpelmann, T. 2013. "Nexuses of Knowledge and Power in Afghanistan: The Rise and Fall of the Informal Justice Assemblage." *Central Asian Survey* 32: 406–22.

Yassari, N., and M. H. Saboory. 2010. "Sharia and National Law in Afghanistan." In *Sharia Incorporated: A Comparative Overview of the Legal Systems of Twelve Muslim Countries in Past and Present,* edited by J. M. Otto, 273–318. Amsterdam: Leiden University Press.

Young, I. M. 2003. "The Logic of Masculinist Protection: Reflections on the Current Security State." *Signs* 29: 1–25.

Yuval-Davis, N. 1997. *Gender and Nation.* London: Sage.

Zia, A. S. 1994. *Sex Crime in the Islamic Context: Rape, Class and Gender in Pakistan.* Lahore, Pakistan: ASR.

Zuhur, S. 2005. *Gender, Sexuality and the Criminal Laws in the Middle East and North Africa. A Comparative Study.* Istanbul: Women for Women's Human Rights (WWHR) — New Ways.

Zulfacar, M. 2006. "The Pendulum of Gender Politics in Afghanistan." *Central Asian Survey* 25: 27–59.

INDEX

abandonment, 99–100
Abd al Shakur, Qazi, 29–30
Abdullah, Abdullah, 43, 49 164
Abdul Rahman Khan, Amir of Afghanistan,
    30–31, 50, 79, 149
abortion, 6
Abu-Lughod, L., 12
adultery, 2, 35–37; abandonment and, 100;
    criminalization of, 16; EVAW law and,
    51, 61, 67; honor killings and, 67; PDPA
    and, 37; Penal Code and, 35–36, 53, 61; rape
    vs. 36, 51, 53, 61; runaway woman and, 113,
    115, 128; shelters and, 116, 117, 122; stoning
    and, 29, 141–47; VAW unit and, 103–4. See
    also *zina*
Advocates Law, 46
Afghan Bar Association, 46, 193n24
Afghan Independent Human Rights
    Commission (AIHRC), 9, 44, 55, 115, 117,
    121–23, 134–35, 139–40, 143–44, 149, 151,
    194n10
Afghanistan: civil war (1992–95), 44; communist
    period (1978–92), 18, 22, 28, 36–38, 43; coup
    (1973), 34–35; coup (1978, 8th of Saur), 36,
    74, 76; as Islamic republic, 38–40, 42, 121,
    191n25; monarchy (pre-1973), 31–35; national
    unity government (2014–16), 49; Republic
    of (1973–78), 34–35; revolutionary council
    (1978), 36; U.S.-led invasion (2001), 40–41,
    81, 118–20

Afghan Local Police (ALP), 158
Afghan Ministry of Interior, 120
Afghan Ministry of Justice, 27, 45, 46, 54–55, 57,
    63, 71, 74, 77, 79, 122, 135
Afghan Ministry of Women's Affairs (MOWA),
    20, 54, 71, 185n9, 187n47, 194n1; EVAW law
    and, 54–55, 58, 62–63, 67, 71, 73, 79; EVAW
    law report (2014), 78, 88–89, 176; NGOs
    and, 54–55, 72, 124; shelters and, 115–17, 119,
    122–24, 128, 192n42
Afghan Parliament, 2, 4, 9, 13, 15, 18, 20, 22, 28,
    34, 36, 42–46, 49; Constitution and, 34,
    36; EVAW law and, 2, 9, 13, 15, 20, 22, 28,
    53, 57–59, 64–76, 79–81, 149, 171–72, 174,
    177, 179; Ghani and, 49; jihadis and, 75–76;
    Karzai and, 46; legislative process, 44–45, 73;
    political ambiguity and, 74–76; Quran and,
    4; rape cases and, 154, 164; Shia law and, 28,
    56–57; Western diplomats and, 174; women
    in, 42, 184n24. *See also* Joint Commission;
    Legislation Commission
Afghan Supreme Court, 17, 34, 36, 38–39, 45–47,
    49, 183n17, 184nn26,28; established, 34;
    Constitution and, 36, 45; decree on women
    leaving home, 38; decree on women's
    education, 39; directive on runaway
    woman, 113, 115, 126, 128, 137, 147; EVAW
    law and, 55, 63; Nafisa and, 135; rape cases
    and, 155, 159, 162; religious council and, 45;
    shelters and, 122

Afghan Women's Network (AWN), 55, 77, 124, 191n38, 192n38
Afghan Women's Skills Development Center (AWSDC), 190n12, 191n37
Afzali, Amina, 118
Ahmed-Ghosh, H., 11
Aisha, Bibi, 118–21
Ajmal, Mohammad, 132–33, 136
Akrami, Mary, 114, 191n37
Al-Azhar University (Egypt), 33
Al Qaida, 41
Amanullah, King of Afghanistan, 31–33, 35, 50, 79, 146, 173, 182n3
Amin, 133–34, 136–37, 143, 151
Amiry, Haji Niyaz Mohammad, 187n36
Amnesty from War Crimes Prosecution (2007), 44
Anglo-Afghan War, Third (1919), 31
Arabic language, 68
Arabs, 163–64
Arbabzadah, N., 32
Aryana Television, 154
Asim, Mohammad, 187n36
assemblages, 3, 8–9, 11, 79–81, 173–75
Ataturk, Mustafa Kemal, 31
Attorney General's Office (AGO), 34, 39, 45–46, 77, 184n29. See also Special Units on Violence Against Women
Aymaqs, 163
Azimi, Abdul Salam, 46

baad (marriage as compensation), 1–2, 133, 137, 149–50, 154, 156, 161–62, 164, 166, 194n10; EVAW law and, 62; Penal Code and, 36, 53; Taliban and, 39; VAW units and, 102
Bamiyan, 190n12
Bangladesh, 104
bargaining position of women, 98, 105–7, 151
Bashira, 153–56, 161–66, 194n2
Basu, S., 94
beating, 2, 5, 52, 88; conviction rate, 88; divorce and, 98; EVAW law and, 58, 61, 65, 68, 79, 189n–90n9; guarantees and, 94–98, 106; financial compensation and, 98; Quran and, 58; VAW unit and, 86, 88–99
Bibi, Lal, 1–3, 157–58
Billaud, Julie, 11, 19
Bonn agreement (2001), 41, 43–44, 54
bribes, 90, 134
bride-price, 8, 30, 87, 106, 133, 156, 181n2
Britain, 30–31

Burawoy, M., 13
burka (chadari), 39

cabinet, 34
CEDAW (Convention on the Elimination on All Forms of Discrimination against Women), 60, 78
cell phones, 133, 136, 190n13
chadari (burka), 39
Charikar, 190n12
chastity, 91, 109, 114, 122, 126, 177–78. See also propriety; virginity
child custody, 96–98, 102, 106, 190n11
child marriage. See underage marriage
Chr. Michelsen Institute, 18
Civil Code (1977), 35, 37, 183n10, 189n8; abandonment and, 99; EVAW law and, 62, 64, 66, 69; family law section, 35; forced marriage and, 149; polygamy and, 66; Shia law and, 14–15, 27
civilian casualties, 47–48
civilising mission, 118
civil rights of women, 171, 177
civil society, 54–55, 59, 62–63, 70–73, 159
Cold War, 43, 181n3
Cole, J., 39
colonial rescue binaries, 181n5
Comaroff, J., 4–5
Comaroff, J.L., 4–5
communist era, 36–38, 43, 114, 124, 163, 170, 181n3, 184n24, 193n20
conservative MPs: EVAW law and, 64–71, 75, 80–81, 187n47; shelters and, 114, 116–17, 124
conservative nationalism, 177
Constitution: (1923), 31; (1924), 32; (1931), 33; (1964), 33–35; (1977), 36; (1980), 36; (1987), 38
Constitution (2004), 15, 27–28, 33, 42–45, 183–84nn8,22, 185n11, 191n25, 193n24; articles (3), 42, 68–69; (7), 42, 69; (12), 69; (22), 42, 69; (54), 69; (58), 42; (79), 57; (83), 184n25; (130), 42, 113, 140, 184nn23,30; (131), 42, 55; court structure and, 45; female representation quotas and, 42; presidential powers and, 43; Shia law and, 15, 27–28
Constitutional Loya Jirga (2003), 44, 184n22
Cooperation Center for Afghanistan (CCA), 190n12
corruption, 17, 41, 47, 49, 124
courts, 8, 13, 17, 30, 143; primary, 33–34; provincial, 34; rape and, 155, 159–60, 162;

sharia vs. statutory, 33–34; Taliban and, 39–40; VAW unit and, 88

Criminal Code: (1924–25), 31–32; (1976), 35. *See also* Penal Code

Criminal Law Reform Working Group (CLRWG), 57, 122–25, 191n33, 192n42

cronyism, 46

cursing of a woman, 6, 61, 61, 63

Danesh, Sarwar, 74

Daoud, Mohammad, 34–36

Dari dialect, 4, 19, 185n4

decree number 7, 36–37

Department of Women's Affairs (DOWA), 138–40, 143–44, 185n9

diat crimes, 182n5

Dilawar, 14, 161

Din, Qamar al-, 29–30

divorce, 183n10; abandonment and, 100; Civil Code and, 35; dowry and, 86, 93, 100, 189n8; kidnapping and, 103; PDPA family courts and, 37; VAW unit and, 86–87, 92–93, 97–98, 100, 102–3, 106

donors. *See* international aid

Dostum, Abdul Rashid, 163–64

dowry *(mahr)*, 36–37, 86, 93, 100, 189n8

drugs, 62, 117

Dupree, Nancy, 183n18

Edwards, David, 11, 143, 181–82n6, 193n20

Egypt, 33, 111, 182n8

Eikenberry, Karl, 120

elections, parliamentary: (1965, 1969), 34; (2005), 43; (2010), 59, 164

elections, presidential: (2004), 43; (2009), 43, 164; (2014), 49

electoral system, 74

Elimination of Violence against Women (EVAW) law, 1–3, 6, 9, 14–15, 18, 20, 22, 27–28, 44–45, 49, 51–71, 152, 160, 170–72; acts defined under, 6, 60–61; articles (17), 66, 135, 192n7; (23), 61, 189n9; (29), 61; (43), 56, 64; (63), 62; assemblages and, 52, 79–81, 172–74; *baad* and, 149; Civil Code and, 15, 27, 28; complex political and gendered landscapes and, 107; Constitution and, 69; crimes independent of petition and, 189n5; donors and, 18, 77–78; enforcement and implementation of, 2, 93, 151; fragmentary law making and, 44–45; gender orders and domains of governance and, 78–79; Ghani and, 76–81; impact of,

78–80; Joint Commission and, 15, 187n34, 188n61; Karzai and, 49; legal regimes and, 2–3, 20, 79; MOWA report on, 78, 176, 189n74; Nafisa and, 135; Parliament and, 2, 15, 22, 59, 62–71, 75–76, 171–72, 174, 177, 179; Penal Code and, 63–64, 77; political ambiguity and lobbying on, 71–78; as presidential decree, 2, 51–53, 57–59, 72–76, 172, 179; prosecution and conviction rates and, 106; sharia and, 9; shelters and, 127; Shia law and, 15, 27–28, 52, 55–57, 74, 79; text of, 60–62; top-down thinking and, 64; trade-offs and, 20; training and, 78; VAW units and, 85–107; Western community and, 28, 78, 80; women's rights activists and, 72–73; *See also* beating; forced marriage; rape; underage marriage; *and other specific acts*

elopement, 87, 115, 133, 136–37, 142, 156

Elyassi, Farangis, 18

"escape from house" *(farar az manzel)*, 109–14, 131. *See also* runaway woman

ethnic politics, 162–63

EVAW Commission, 54

executions, 183n20. *See also* stoning

executive power, 174, 179

extended case method, 13

Fahim, Marshal, 122

family: control of women by, 5, 23, 79, 110, 126, 132, 143–48, 150, 152, 167; EVAW law and, 52, 61, 70, 79; false charges by, 106; government regulation of, 30–31; guarantees by, 140–41; honor and, 87, 136, 152; public domain vs., 7–8; rape and, 24, 106, 152–53, 156–58; shelters and, 23, 115, 121, 126; VAW units and, 87, 90, 99, 103–4; women's survival outside, 117, 176–77

family courts, 35, 37, 149

family law, 182n7; child custody and, 96–97; Islamic law and, 145–46; incarceration of women and, 109; kinship structures, 8; Shia law and, 55

Farkhunda, 169–71, 188n65

female autonomy, 151, 175–80

female prosecutors, 87

female representation quotas, 42–43

female sexuality,, 24 110, 126, 132, 142–47, 150, 152, 175

feminism, 4–5, 11, 20–21, 27, 170; "culturally appropriate," 176–77; political praxis and, 20–21; protection model and, 178–79; rape and, 166; state and, 158, 173

Fereshta, 118, 132, 139–41, 143–44, 148–49, 151, 193n21
fiancé, marriage to someone else, 101–2
fiqh. *See* Islamic jurisprudence; *and specific types*
forced marriage, 1–2, 6, 36, 90; banned, 36; EVAW law and, 51, 59, 62, 65–66, 68; family courts and, 149; Fereshta and, 139–41, 143, 148–49; Islam and, 150; Nafisa and, 132–39, 142, 148; Penal Code and, 36, 53; punishment for, 171, 175; Siddiqa and, 142, 148
foreign influence, 54; EVAW law and, 70–71, 79; shelters and, 115, 172. *See also* global power structures; international aid; transnational alliances; West; *and specific countries and organizations*
forensic evidence, 90, 92, 97
French legal model, 33, 184n28

gender order (ideologies), 3, 4, 99, 104–5, 112, 126, 131, 160, 167, 175, 177; women as legal minors and, 109–10
Ghalib, Habibullah, 193n24
Ghani, Ashraf, 30, 49, 76–77, 93, 159
Ghazanfar, Dr. Husn Banu, 116–17
Giustozzi, A., 47
global power structures, 6–9, 11, 54, 79, 81, 172–74. *See also* assemblages; transnational alliances
guarantee agreements, 94–97, 106
gynecological examinations, 92, 115

hadd punishments, 31–32, 35–36, 53, 146, 182n5, 183n6,11, 185n6, 193n24
Hajjar, 7, Lisa, 174
Halim, Sayed Yusuf, 186n30
Hamzić, V., 145–46
Hanafi, Qazi Nazir Ahmed, 58–59, 64–65, 68, 76, 114, 116
Hanafi *fiqh*, 31–35, 37, 42, 68, 113, 182n2
Hanbali *fiqh*, 182n2
harassment, 61, 63
Hartmann, M.E., 73, 184n24
Hazarajat, 30
Hazaras, 31, 43, 163, 164
Herat Province, 16, 17, 40, 78, 110, 115, 149, 190n12
Heroes of the Age (Edwards), 181n6
Hizb-e Islami, 47, 193n20
homosexuality, 185n5
honor (*namus*), 11, 24, 90, 145, 150–52, 155–56, 160, 166–67, 175, 181n6. *See also* shame

honor killings, 6, 145, 175, 182n8, 185n4, 195n13; EVAW law and, 66–67; Penal Code and, 53
"house of obedience" (*bayt al-ta'a*), 111
Hudood Ordinances (Pakistan), 146
Humanitarian Assistance for the Women and Children of Afghanistan (HAWCA), 55, 190n12, 191n37
human rights, 5, 14, 28, 41–42, 69. *See also* women's rights
human rights workers, 154–56, 161
Humphrey, C., 5
husband: abandonment by, 99–100; beatings and guarantees by, 94–96, 106; beatings and reprimands to, 89–94; Egyptian personal law and, 111; EVAW law debates and, 65; runaway woman and, 109, 113; sexual access and, 58

Ibrahimi, Abdul Raof, 59, 76
immolation and acid attacks, 61, 89
India, 104, 158, 176, 190n14
inheritance, 51, 62, 70
insurgency: (1979–88), 36; (2009–11), 48
international aid (donors), 2, 9, 12, 72, 124, 175; chastity and, 178; conditionalities and, 78; EVAW law and, 52, 54, 56, 60, 71, 77–81; justice sector and, 45–47; Karzai and, 47, 49; lawmaking by decree and, 73; MOWA and, 54; shelters and, 109, 113–14, 117, 120, 123–25, 127–28; Shia law and, 51; Supreme Court and, 45–46; VAW units and, 23, 87–88, 106, 172
International Bar Association, 46
International Development Law Organization (IDLO), 81, 87–88, 113, 186n19
international law, 5
International Security Assistance Force (ISAF), 41, 47–48
International Women's Day, 71
Iran, 114–15
Islam, 6, 12, 31, 38; Constitution and (1923), 31; (1987), 38; EVAW law and, 59, 70–71, 75; female defiance and, 177; runaway women and, 111–12; 150
Islamic jurisprudence (*fiqh*), 9, 11, 27, 28, 30, 111, 113, 145–47, 150, 182n2, 186n21; Constitution and (2004), 42; criminal law and, 31–32, 146; EVAW law and, 62–63, 65. *See also* sharia law; *and specific types*

Jad, I., 72
Jafari *fiqh*, 182n2
Jalalabad, 115, 190n12

Jamiat-al Ulema, 33
Jamiat-e Islami party, 120, 164
jihadis, 43, 52, 58, 75, 121, 177
jirga, 133, 136–37, 192n2
Joint Commission, 15, 57–59, 64–66, 68, 149,
    187n34, 188n61
Joya, Malalai, 44
judges, 17, 28, 33, 77–78, 113, 157; female, 28, 46,
    54, 183n9
Junbesh party, 163–64
justice system, 18, 24, 30–31, 37, 42, 45–49

Kabul, 18, 23, 47–48, 85–107, 114
Kabul Bank scandal, 48
Kabul Times, 37
Kabul University, 33–34, 55, 186n19
Kamali, M., 182n7
Kambash, Sayet Pervez, 184n30
Kapur, R., 6–7, 176–77
Karzai, Hamid, 27–28, 37, 41, 43, 45–49, 119,
    184n22, 194nn3,5,7; EVAW law and, 51–52,
    56–57, 68–69, 74, 77, 79–80, 173–74; MOWA
    and, 54; patronage and, 47; Penal code and,
    77; rape cases and, 66, 154–56, 158–60, 164,
    166; runaway women and, 110, 112; shelters
    and, 124–25, 127; Shia law and, 14, 51–52,
    56–57, 68–69, 80, 174; Supreme Court and,
    45–46; VAW units and, 93; West and, 80
Khademi, Kubra, 169
Khan, S., 146
Khawasi, Abdul Satar, 68
Khost rebellion, 183n7
kidnapping, 92, 102–4, 106, 156
Kim-Puri, H., 173
kinship groups, 7–8, 79, 109, 112, 132, 147, 150, 152,
    167, 175
Klonowiecka-Milart, A., 73
Kogacioglu, D., 195n13
Koofi, Fawzia, 57, 59–60, 68, 71–72, 76
Kunduz Province, 141, 143–44, 146–47, 150, 157

labor, forced, 62
Larson, A., 74–75
lashing, 35, 36, 40, 53, 146, 147, 183n20, 185n6,
    186n24
Law on Crimes against Internal and External
    Security (1987), 160
legal aid organizations, 15, 46
legal education, 33
legal system, 14–15, 42, 150, 184n28;
    fragmentation of, 27–29, 44–45; history of,

29–38, 50; kinship and gender vs., 106–7;
    lawmaking by decree and, 73
Legislation Commission, 64–66, 68, 75–75,
    185n17
Levirate (marrying widow to brother-in-law),
    30, 39
Loya Jirga (1924), 32
Ludin, Ataullah, 187n36

madrassas, 33
mahram (legal intimate), 113, 187n49
maintenance payments, 66, 111, 171
Maliki *fiqh*, 182n2, 183n10
Malikyar, H., 112
Manchester school, 13
marriage: choice in, 70, 177; cursing or
    preventing, 65; engagement play and, 133;
    exchange relationship in, 111; families and,
    150; kings and, 30–31; parents and, 2, 51; rape
    in, 62; selling woman for, 62; sexual relations
    and, 51; unequal rights in, 99, 107. *See also*
    forced marriage; *nikah* ceremony; polygamy;
    underage marriage
Marxism, 38
Mazar-e Sharif, 190n12
media, 13, 114, 116, 119–25, 154–55, 157–58, 160
Medica Mondiale, 194n30
Merry, S.E., 5
Middle East, gender relations in, 11–12, 173
militias, 163
Mir-Hosseini, Z., 111, 145, 146
Mitchell, T., 165
Mizan Gazette, 162
mobile ethnography, 13
mobility of women, 109, 112–14, 121
moral crimes, 80, 110, 122, 128, 152, 176, 177
"moral systems," 11
Mosheni, Asif, 55, 57
Mujadiddi, Sighbatullah, 154, 194n5
mujahedin, 9, 22, 43–44, 64–65, 75, 121, 163, 177,
    181n3, 193n20; government by (1992–96),
    36–38, 112
murder, 52, 88, 89, 131, 148. *See also* honor
    killings; *and individual victims*
My Homeland (TV show), 120, 121

Naderi, Manizha, 120, 191n37
Naderi, Nasto, 120–21, 124–25
Nadery, Nader, 123
Nadir Shah, King of Afghanistan, 32–33
Nafisa, 132–39, 143–44, 149–51

Najibullah, Dr., 38, 163
National Prison Directorate, 192n8
Nawid, S.K., 182n3
Nemat, Orzala Ashraf, 15, 191n37
New York Times, 120, 125
nikah ceremony (wedding), 91, 103, 115, 133, 136, 139, 192n4
nizam-namas (regulations of King Amanullah), 31, 146
nongovernmental organizations (NGOs), 28, 46, 54–55, 72, 80, 170, 174, 178, 183n18; shelters and, 23, 109, 114, 117, 121–28, 179
non-Muslim minorities, 31–32
Noorin Television, 120
Noorullah, Sayed, 153–56, 161–62, 164–65, 194nn2,7,10
North Atlantic Treaty Organization (NATO), 12–13, 18–19, 28–29, 44–49, 74, 118–20, 174, 179
Northern Alliance, 41
Norway, 78

Obama, Barack, 19, 48
obedience, defining, 111
Olesen, A., 30
Omar, Mullah, 40
open-ended, practice-oriented perspective, 11
Ordinance Concerning Women's Rights and Duties (1996), 39
Orientalist tropes, 175, 179
Ottoman Empire, 30, 182n8

Paghman rape cases, 153, 159–60
Pakistan, 38, 43, 115, 146–47, 182n8
Pakzad, Suraya, 191n37
Panjshir Valley, 41
Parwan Province, 139, 143–44, 148
Pashtuns, 31, 41, 43, 112, 132–39, 162–63, 192n2
"patriarchal bargain," 79, 99, 172
patronage, 47, 74, 80, 174, 175
Payenda, Haji, 153–56, 161–66
peace-building, 8, 41, 173
Penal Code (1976), 35, 39, 52–54, 160, 185nn6,7, 189n5; articles (24), 189n5; (86), 186n21; (398), 53, 62, 67; (409), 190n9; (426), 53, 186n20, 192n7; (427), 428, 53, 186n20; (429), 53; (517), 53; *baad* and, 149; EVAW law and, 61, 63–64, 67, 69; Nafisa and, 135; new draft of, 193n24
People's Democratic Party of Afghanistan (PDPA), 36, 37, 50, 112, 173
Peshawar, 170

police, 115, 128, 143–44
polygamy, 15, 31, 35, 37, 185n4, 186n21, 188n61; abandonment and, 100; Civil Code and, 35; EVAW law and, 58–59, 62, 65–66, 68, 79; PDPA and, 37
power: broader fields of, 7–9; studying, through "Afghan woman," 10–12. *See also* global power structures
pregnancy, 6, 156
private/public domains, 2, 4, 7–8
Prohibition of Means, 113
propriety, 109
prostitution: forced, 62, 63, 186n27, 194n28; runaway woman and, 113; shelters and, 116, 120
provincial councils, 42
public space, women as trespassers in, 110, 112–13, 170, 178

Qanooni, Yunus, 59, 72, 154
Qayam, Abdul, 141–42, 144–47
Quli, Mulla, 145, 151
Quran, 4, 58, 65–66, 68, 170, 182n2

Rabbani, Burhanuddin, 38, 112
Rahman, Abdul, 184n30
rape, 1–3, 7–8, 24, 36, 40, 89, 152–67, 186n19; adultery vs., 36, 51, 53, 61–62, 178; ambiguous agendas and, 3, 156–57; Bashira and ethnic politics and, 163–65; as crime vs. woman or family, 2, 24, 157; death sentences and, 159–60; EVAW law and, 51, 61–63, 66; by government officials, 154; gynecological examination and, 92; Lal Bibi and, 157–58; marital 62; media and, 160; Nafisa and, 134, 137–38; Paghman cases and, 153, 159–60; penalty for, 192n7; pregnancy and, 156; prevalence of, 194n1; public discourse and, 157, 167; runaway women and, 131; statutory, 61; Taliban and, 40; VAW unit and, 88–89, 92, 102–4, 106; women's initiative in claims of, 156
Rasouli, Anisa, 49
reconciliation agreements, 95, 104, 121, 140–41, 145, 156, 161–62, 176
rescue, discourses of, 118–20, 181n5
Research Institute for Women, Peace, and Security, 18
"résumé law reform," 73
Roychowdhury, P., 158, 160
runaway woman, 16–17, 37–38, 40, 108–16, 128, 131–51, 175; arrest of, 37–38, 110, 112–13, 115,

147, 150–51, 190n4; beatings and, 91; defiance vs. Islam and, 177; Fereshta and, 139–41; Nafisa as, 132–39; shelters and, 24, 108–9, 115; stoning in Kunduz and, 141–42; Supreme Court and, 113–14, 128; Taliban and, 40; as transgressor, 16–17, 108–16, 132; *zina* and, 178
rural provinces, 90, 106

Sabet, Abdul Jabar, 194n3
Safi woman, stoning of, 143
Samar, Sima, 194n10
Saqeb, Sabrina, 59, 72
Sarah, rape case and, 14, 161
Sardan, Olivier de, 174
Sarepul Province rape cases, 153, 155–57, 161–67, 173
Sarwari, Assadullah, 184n24
Sassen, Saskia, 8–9, 79, 173–74
Saudi Arabia, 39, 43, 182n2, 193n20
Sayyaf, Abdul Rasool, 44–45, 75
Schueller, M.J., 181n5
secular law, 27, 31, 33
sex trafficking, 6
sexual availability, 114
sexual harassment, 6
sexual violence vs. men, 7, 63
Shafi'i *fiqh*, 182n2
Shahabi, Mohammad Jawad, 15–16, 18
Shah-e Do Shamshira shrine, 170–71
shame, 132–39, 152, 155. *See also* honor
sharia, 9, 27, 32–33, 39–40, 42; Constitution and (1931), 33; (2004), 42; Criminal Code and (1924–25), 32; defined, 182n2; EVAW law and, 62–63, 65, 68–70; runaway woman and, 140; stoning and, 146; Taliban and, 39, 40, 175; statutory law vs., 33, 42
Sharia Ordinances on Veiling, 183n17
shelters, 3–5, 9, 16–17, 108–28, 170, 172, 191n37; admission to, 115–17, 119, 122–23, 125–26; controversies over, 4, 9, 19–20, 22–23, 68, 108–9, 117–23; established, 108, 114; EVAW law and, 70; hymen examinations and, 115; Islam and, 177; nationalization attempt and, 109, 116–17, 122–28, 191n38; number and locations of, 127–28, 138, 190n12; provincial, 114–15; runaway woman cases and, 108–16, 131, 139–40; sovereignty and, 4, 17, 23, 109, 173–75; transnational networks and, 5, 17, 19–20, 23, 109, 127, 174–75, 178–79
Shia Hazaras, 30–31, 164
Shia Muslims, 31, 68

Shia Personal Status Law (Shia law, 2009), 14–15, 27–28, 42, 51–52, 55–57, 74, 79–80, 125, 174, 182n2
Shinwari, Fazal Hadi, 45–46
Shuhada organization, 190n
Shura-ye Nazar (supervisory council), 41
Siddiqa, 132, 141–47, 149–51, 193n21
Siddiqi, Dina, 150
Single Non-Transferable Vote (SNTV), 74
Siraj al Tawarikh (Torch of Histories), 29
slavery, 31
sodomy, 53, 92, 189n7
Sonbol, A., 111
Soraya, Queen of Afghanistan, 32
South Asia, 12
sovereignty, 3–5, 8–9, 52, 116–17, 126
Soviet Union, 36–38, 43
Special Prosecution Units for Crimes of Violence against Women (VAW units), 18, 22–23, 85–107, 172; abandonment and, 99–100; bargaining and, 98–99, 104–7; beatings and, 89–98; bribes and, 90; case filings and convictions, 85–91, 93, 105–6; cases closed prior to trial, 86–87, 90; child custody and, 96; courts and, 86, 88–89; divorce and, 86–87; donors and, 87; global governance and, 173; guarantees by husband and, 86–87, 94–97; murders and, 88–89; rape and, 88–89, 102–4; 156; rural provinces and, 89–90
state-building, 27, 28–29, 41–42, 48–49
statelessness, 29
state power: family and, 8, 150–51; Kunduz stoning and, 147; lack of single authority and, 52; opposing visions of, 127; strong vs. weak, 158–66; transnational processes and, 8, 173–74; tribe vs., 10–11; VAW and, 8, 172–73
state welfare model, 124, 127
stoning, 131, 137, 141–47, 150, 183n20, 193n20
Sufi networks, 33
suicide, forced, 62, 63, 90, 186n27
suicide bombers, 85
Sunnah, 182n2
Sunni Islam, 31, 55, 68, 182n2

Tajiks, 41, 43
Taliban, 16, 50, 75, 110, 149, 151, 163, 181n3; overthrow of 2001, 2, 12, 41, 109; public executions and, 183n20; rape and, 155–56, 158; rule by (1996–2001), 18, 22, 28, 37–41, 112; runaway woman and, 37, 112; sharia and, 175; shelters and, 4, 118–20, 123, 125–27; stoning and, 141–43, 145–47; women not permitted outside by, 187n49

Tamanaha, 47
Taqnin (legislation) department, 54–55, 58, 62–64, 66–67, 185nn8,11,17
Taraki, 37
tazir punishments, 32, 36, 53, 182n5
Time magazine, 118
To The Gatekeepers of Women's Honor (AWN open letter), 124
transnational alliances, 3, 5, 11, 13, 22, 41, 50, 81, 109, 118–19, 124–25, 127, 172–75, 179. *See also* global power structures; international aid; West; *and specific organizations*
tribal power, 8, 10–11, 29, 32–33, 39, 175
Turkey, 31, 195n13

ulema council, 30–33, 63, 122, 142
underage marriage, 6, 8, 15, 30–31, 35–36; Civil Code and, 35; EVAW law and, 51, 58–59, 62, 65, 68–69, 149; rights of fathers and, 58, 65–66, 79; Shia law and, 51, 57
United Nations, 5, 9, 41–42, 114, 178, 183n18; Charter, 42; Declaration on Human Rights, 42, 69; EVAW law and, 54, 77, 81, 93; human rights section, 14, 28, 88, 134, 135
United Nations Assistance Mission in Afghanistan (UNAMA), 63
United Nations Development Fund for Women (UNIFEM, *later* UNWOMEN), 54, 55, 62, 63, 114, 128, 190n12
United Nations Office on Drugs and Crime (UNODC), 57, 63
United States, 43, 49, 118, 128, 158, 188n71
United States Agency for International Development (USAID), 48
U.S. Defense Department, 48
U.S. embassy, 73, 74, 120
U.S.-led military forces, 19, 75, 109, 158, 181n3; invasion of 2001, 40–41, 81, 118–20; surge of 2009–10, 48–49, 120
U.S. Special Forces, 158
U.S. State Department, 125
Uruzgan Province, 118
Uzbeks, 43, 163–64

Vatuk, 105
VAW units. *See* Special Prosecution Units for Crimes of Violence against Women
veiling, 38, 39, 112
verbal abuse, 61, 63
Verveer, 74

vice and virtue police, 39
violence, definitions of, 4, 131
violence against women (VAW), 3; analytical entry points and, 3–7; comparative perspectives on, 11–12; compromises and, 179–80; definitions and contexts of, 3–7, 11, 150; extended case method and, 13; effects of focus on, 171–72; fields of power and, 7–9; fragmentation and, 175; governance and, 14, 87, 172–73; private/public domains and, 3, 7–8; research trajectories on, 12–18; third-world and Western feminism and, 177
virginity, 112, 115, 122, 186n24
Voice of Women Organization, 190n12, 191n37

Wahabis, 45
war crimes, 44, 184n24
West, 2, 6, 8–9, 19, 75, 93, 174, 177–79; EVAW law, 28–29, 59, 80–81; shelters and, 117, 125, 127, 179; VAW units and, 93
widowhood violations, 6
Women for Afghan Women (WAW), 116, 118–20, 123, 124, 127, 139–40, 190n12, 191n37
Women's Affairs Commission of Parliament (WACP), 55, 57–59, 64, 71–72
"women's courts," 104
women's education, 32–33, 35–40, 51, 62, 70
women's emancipation, decrees of 1978 on, 36
women's labor participation, 35–37, 39, 51, 62
women's rights, 7, 30–40, 120; Constitution and, 42; "culturally appropriate" feminism and, 176; discourses of salvation and, 118; external promotion of, 22, 177; Ghani and, 49; Islamic law and, 28; Islamist rule and, 38–40; Karzai and, 49; Soviet period and, 35–38; state-building vs. tribal law and, 29; struggles over authority and, 174; WAW and, 119; women as independent holders and, 51
women's rights activists, 2, 5, 9, 20–21, 27, 51–52, 54, 56, 58, 63–64, 71–77, 80, 93, 113, 117, 125, 170, 175
women's right to vote, 35
World Bank, 17

Yazanpardast, Qadria, 55, 71
Yemen, 111

Zahir Shan, King of Afghanistan, 33–35
Zia ul-Haq, 146

zina (extramarital or premarital sex), 110, 183n6; criminalization of, 176, 178; false accusations of, 62; incarceration and, 110, 112–13, 194n30; Penal Code and, 36, 53, 61; punishments for, 146, 185n6; rape and, 152, 156, 160, 178, 186n19; runaway women and, 151, 178; shelters and, 115; stoning and, 144–47; VAW units and, 104; *See also* adultery

Zina Ordinance (Pakistan), 146–47

Zulu chiefs, 13